COVER
Detail from 1882 Planisphere Celeste
by Claude-Joseph Drioux and Charles Leroy

ISSUE 2 / SUMMER 2023

wayfaremagazine.org

FaithMatters

ISSUE 2 (SUMMER 2023)
WAYFARE MAGAZINE IS PUBLISHED BY THE FAITH MATTERS FOUNDATION.
FOR INQUIRIES, PLEASE CONTACT WAYFARE@FAITHMATTERS.ORG.

Rose Datoc Dall

ESSAYS

POEMS

HYMN

STORY

REVIEW

EXHIBITS

INTERVIEW

CELESTIAL NAVIGATION

ZACHARY DAVIS

WHEN EUROPEAN EXPLORERS first chanced upon the islands of Polynesia in the sixteenth-century, they were confronted with a puzzle. These mariners from Spain, Holland, and England had themselves only recently developed the ability to cross the oceans and reach these remote islands. Yet on island after island in this unfathomably vast stretch of sea they found people already living there—people who lacked large ships, compasses, sextants, or any of the other devices vital to European oceanic expansion. How had the inhabitants first reached these remote islands when they appeared to lack the seafaring technology necessary for such voyages?

A belief took hold among Westerners that the South Pacific was randomly populated by sailors blown off course by storms. But Polynesians themselves believed otherwise. In Hawaii in 1973, anthropologist Ben Finney, artist Herb Kawainui Kāne, and sailor Charles Tommy Holmes organized the Polynesian Voyaging Society to help prove the alternative theory that the native Oceanic peoples had reached their island homes via purposeful trips, not aimless drifting. The Society's first project was to reconstruct a traditional Polynesian double-hulled voyaging canoe and make the 2,500-mile journey from Hawaii to Tahiti using indigenous techniques and knowledge.

Since no examples of actual ancient voyaging canoes were available as models, the design was based on eighteenth-century drawings of canoes made by artists and draftsmen employed by the British Naval Captain James Cook and other early explorers of the Pacific. After two years of construction, the Society had a sixty-two-foot, double-hulled canoe ready to sail with a crew of twelve.

At first the group couldn't agree on a name for the vessel. Then Herb Kāne had a vision. "One exceptionally clear night, I dreamed of stars. My attention was attracted to Arcturus, which we call Hokule'a, 'star of gladness.' It appeared to grow larger and brighter, so brilliant that I awoke." The canoe now had its name: Hokule'a.

André Thevet

Stars often communicate important messages. You could even say they are a language of God. "Let there be lights in the vault of the sky to separate the day from the night, and let them serve as signs." In ancient times, learning to read these divine signs was difficult, reserved for wisest or holiest. Sometimes, God taught such knowledge face to face. Abraham was taught the names and properties of the stars. Moses received a direct vision of "the heavens, they are many, and they cannot be numbered unto man; but they are numbered unto me."

But even without a private divine tutorial, those sensitive to spiritual things could perceive God's messages written in the sky. The magi from the east (very possibly Zoroastrian astrologers)

Edward Burne-Jones

observed a new star and understood its meaning. "They set out; and there, ahead of them, went the star that they had seen at its rising, until it stopped over the place where the child was. When they saw that the star had stopped, they were overwhelmed with joy."

Stars testify of Christ in other ways too. The Prophet Joseph Smith revealed that Christ is "the light of the stars, and the power thereof by which they were made." Perhaps that is why at Jesus's death the stars fell dark. At the Second Coming it is prophesied that likewise "the stars shall refuse their shining." The Apostle Peter compared Christ to a "light shining in a dark place . . . a day star that rises in your hearts." And as he tells us himself in Revelation, "I, Jesus, am the Bright and Morning Star."

Celestial navigation is the art and science of finding your way by the sun, moon, stars, and planets. The Polynesian Voyaging Society was convinced their ancestors had mastered this art to explore and settle the South Pacific. Unfortunately, they couldn't prove it. Knowledge of traditional wayfaring had essentially disappeared among Polynesian cultures after contact with Europeans. Not one person on Hawaii possessed the skills to sail Hokule'a. So the Society began a search across Polynesia to discover if anyone on the other islands still possessed knowledge of traditional navigation.

The quest took them to the tiny Micronesian island of Satawal, a solitary coral atoll about one mile long, with a population of about five hundred people. The Satawal community was the last to practice precolonial maritime wayfinding, a sacred knowledge passed from elder to apprentice. But there was a problem. The six master navigators that remained refused to reveal their ways to outsiders. All the navigators, that is, except for one. Mau Piailug, the youngest of them, had come to fear that knowledge of traditional navigation would die in his own culture, just as it had in Hawaii. His efforts to train the next generation of Satawalese had largely failed; they were more interested in Western education and culture. So despite the taboo against teaching outsiders, and despite barely knowing any English, Mau Piailug agreed to navigate the Hokule'a and teach his knowledge to a member of the crew, Nainoa Thompson, a direct descendant of Kamehameha I, the first ruler of the Kingdom of Hawaii. "In myself," Thompson revealed later, "there was a deep desire to learn navigation, to learn who I am by knowing where I come from."

There was a reason the young people in Satawal had resisted Piailug's lessons. Becoming a master Polynesian navigator involved learning an impossibly complex set of skills. First, you had to learn to read the night sky. Unlike planets, stars hold fixed celestial positions year-round, changing only their rising time with the seasons. Each star has a specific declination granting a bearing for navigation as the star rises or sets. Polynesian voyagers would set course by a star near the horizon, switching to a new one once the first rose too high. They would memorize a specific sequence of stars for each route. They knew the sky the way we know the melody of a favorite song or the face of a beloved.

But because clouds can obscure the sky, Polynesian navigators also learned to wayfind with an astonishing array of other inputs, such as the color, temperature, and salinity of seawater; floating plant debris; sightings of land-based seabirds flying out to fish; cloud type, color, and movement; wind direction, speed, and temperature; the direction and nature of ocean swells and waves; and the estimation of the speed, current set, and leeway of the sailing craft.

To become adept at this required many years of training, and even then not everyone reached the point of being a *palu,* or fully initiated navigator. Those who did were seen as equal or superior to the village chief. Mau Piailug was a *palu* and thus capable of executing the great navigational task entrusted to him, and teaching the art to others.

On May 1, 1976, to the sounding of ceremonial conch shells, Hokule'a left Honolua Bay, Hawaii, on her maiden voyage to Tahiti. Thirty-three

John Webber

days later, Hokule'a arrived in Papeete, Tahiti, to a jubilant crowd of more than seventeen thousand—over half of the island—who had come to welcome their brothers to shore and witness the rebirth of an ancient art. It was the first time in eight hundred years that Polynesian sailors navigated between the two islands by canoe, guided primarily by the stars.

Since then, the Hokule'a has undertaken voyages to other islands in Polynesia, including Samoa, Tonga, and New Zealand, and has even successfully circumnavigated the globe. And before his death in 2010, Mau Piailug trained and initiated dozens of navigators into *palus*, ensuring the survival of his sacred art.

Unfortunately, for most of us, the stars are fading from view. The first electric streetlight was invented by Pavel Yablochkov and installed in the Galeries du Louvre in Paris in 1876 (thus earning it the nickname City of Lights). Since then, electric lights have rapidly expanded across the globe, crowding out the lights of heaven. More than 80 percent of the world's population, and 99 percent of Americans and Europeans, live under a haze of grayish glow that obscures our view of the stars. In our Promethean quest to control nature, we risk becoming blind to it.

Some pockets of starsight remain, though they must be sought out. When I was fifteen, I attended a weeklong scout camp in the Pine Valley Mountains of Southern Utah. One day, after a delirious, joyful afternoon of pine-cone warfare with a rival troop, a friend and I took our sleeping bags and trekked out away from the camp to sleep out in the open. We came to a clearing and watched the sun descend and the vast millions of stars emerge in clusters across the sky. Suddenly, a light streaked across the canopy, and then another. A meteor shower. We watched for what seemed like hours, in silent wonder, pulled upward into the bosom of eternity.

The stars still have messages to convey. We are ever swirling beneath a vast canvas of divine creativity and love. As we become more sensitive and skilled wayfarers, we not only seek out the guiding light of the stars, but stop to witness their wondrous dance.

The writing and art that follow express some of the witnessing and wayfinding practices of our faith. Some explore birds and bodies, solitude and communion. Others navigate grief and loss, fear and forgiveness, memory and attention. Our hope is that, like Dante, you will find that your "desire and will were moved—like a wheel revolving uniformly—by the Love that moves the sun and the other stars." ✸

THE SACRAMENT OF ATTENTION

The Kingdom of God and the Cost of Love

MICHAEL AUSTIN

"Attention is the rarest and purest form of generosity."
— Simone Weil, Letter to Joë Bousquet, 13 April 1942

FOR GOOD REASONS, OUR LANguage often frames attention as an economic commodity. We *pay* attention to things we value. If we talk to someone for too long, they might think we are *monopolizing* their attention. And if someone doesn't give enough attention to something, or does not have enough attention to give, they might be diagnosed with an attention *deficit* disorder. We can devote ourselves to entertainment and pleasure while others—usually those who provide the entertainment and pleasure—sell our attention to the highest bidder. Quantities of attention can be divided into clicks, impressions, and page views, and converted directly into cash. In 2021, companies worldwide spent almost 600 billion dollars competing for your attention on the internet.

We often use time as a measure of attention, but there is only a weak correlation between the two things. We can devote enormous amounts of time to projects that receive very little of our attention, and we can devote all of our attention to something for a very brief time. This is also true for people. Being with somebody for an hour is much easier than paying attention to somebody for an hour. The former requires only physical (or virtual) proximity, and we do it every day. The latter happens only rarely. It requires us to donate all our emotional, spiritual, and intellectual energy to being with another person. I can recall only a few occasions in my life when I spent time with somebody and felt that they focused their entire attention on knowing and understanding me. Each time was a gift beyond measure.

How we allocate our attention defines us even more than our purchases do. People have different amounts of money, so the things we buy don't reflect values in the same way for everyone. The same purchase might represent a tremendous sacrifice for one person and a mere afterthought to another. But we all have the same widow's mite of attention to distribute among the many things competing for it: family, friends, education, health, careers, church, politics, great books, lousy books, clickbait headlines, and viral posts about ridiculous people doing ridiculous things for no particular reason. Our limited attention budget forces us to make choices, and those choices both reveal our values and create our characters. We can say that we value an almost infinite number of people

James Rees

The most basic and universal human needs include the need to be seen and understood, the need to be taken seriously, the need to be appreciated, and the need to be paid attention to.

and things, and we might even believe it. But we can only dedicate our attention to a few of them—and those few things determine who we become.

Like every resource, our attention can be bought, sold, or given away. And it can be consecrated to the Kingdom of God. This is the main point of one of the most challenging and rewarding pieces of writing I have ever read: Simone Weil's "Reflections on the Right Use of School Studies with a View to the Love of God," from her collection *Waiting for God.* Superficially, the essay is about the spiritual importance of secular education. But really, it is about prayer. "Prayer consists of attention," she tells us in the first sentence. "It is the orientation of all the attention of which the soul is capable toward God."[1] For Weil, the primary value of any kind of education is that it develops our ability to focus our attention on something for a substantial amount of time. It doesn't matter what we study, she argues, or even if we end up learning it. Algebra, French, history, music, biology, and economics all require us to develop the capacity to pay sustained attention to a single thing. And we need to develop that capacity as fully as possible to have a meaningful relationship with God.

In making this argument, Weil frames Christian prayer as a kind of Old Testament sacrifice. When people's wealth took the form of crops and livestock, offering an animal to God required one to part with a significant economic asset. To place a bull or flawless lamb on the altar of God, one had to make a difficult choice about a scarce resource. One had to choose God over something else in a meaningful way. In a culture whose most valuable resource is attention, concentrating wholly on God requires precisely the same kind of sacrifice. Where your attention is, there will your heart be also.

According to Jesus, the first great commandment is, "Thou shalt love the Lord thy God with all thy heart, and with all thy soul, and with all thy mind" (Matthew 22:37). This, too, has much to do with attention. Taken together, the heart, soul, and mind—representing the emotional, spiritual, and intellectual components of our consciousness—mean about the same thing that Weil means by attention. When we love God in all these ways, we reciprocate God's love for us, for God's attention is infinite and perfect. This is also the way God, through the second great commandment, instructs us to love each other, as Weil explains:

> Not only does the love of God have attention for its substance; the love of our neighbor, which we know to be the same love, is made of this same substance. Those who are unhappy have no need for anything in this world but people capable of giving them their attention. The capacity to give one's attention to a sufferer is a very rare and difficult thing; it is almost a miracle; it is a miracle. Nearly all those who think they have this capacity do not possess it. Warmth of heart, impulsiveness, pity are not enough.[2]

To me, these are the most challenging words in the essay, and possibly the most challenging words in the world. They call us to take service and charity further than even the New Testament does. Weil says that loving other people requires us to give them our full attention. This includes noticing and ministering to physical needs like food and shelter, but that is just a small part. The most basic and universal human needs include the need to be seen and understood, the need to be taken seriously, the need to be appreciated, and the need to be paid attention to. "The love of our neighbor in all its fullness simply means being able to say . . . 'What are you going through?'" Weil suggests at the end of her great essay, "Only [those] capable of attention can do this."[3]

When I read Weil, I am reminded of another concept from a very different field of study that concerns the ways that we demonstrate attention. I refer to the concept of "costly signaling," which scientists use to explain why organisms sometimes do things that seem directly contrary to their evolutionary interests.[4] Consider the strange stotting behavior of the Thomson's gazelle. When facing a predator, some gazelles will start stotting, or jumping up and down to call attention to themselves. Interpreted by popular science writer Jared Diamond, the stotting gazelle wants to send a message that goes something like, "I am a superior, fast gazelle! You'll never succeed in catching me, so don't waste your time and energy on trying."[5] However, since any gazelle can claim to be superior and fast, a hungry cheetah will be more inclined to believe this message if it is associated with a cost—in this case, the increased risk of attracting a predator's attention.

Humans pay attention to the costs of signals too. Think of the last time you received a handwritten thank-you note compared to the last time you got a mass-distributed thank-you email.

James Rees

Even if they contained the exact same words, you likely felt more gratitude from the handwritten note because you knew that it took money to purchase the card and time to write and mail it. Or think of the way that offering "thoughts and prayers" after a tragedy has become an ironic cliché—a shorthand way to say "not doing anything at all." Thoughts and prayers are not bad things to do; they are easy things to say. They promise sustained attention without incurring any costs or requiring any choices. Humans and other organisms have been genetically programmed to be skeptical about such messages. They are just too easy to fake.

The Kingdom of God can only be built on honest, and therefore costly, communication between people who love each other and pay attention to each other's needs. This sounds easier than it is, though, because we often have a hard time telling the difference between paying attention to other people's needs and paying attention to ourselves by interacting with other people's needs. We need to feel wanted, needed, and respected. We want people to see our help as valuable and our efforts as sincere. We want people to be grateful for what we give them. And all too often we just want to eliminate the nagging feelings of guilt and shame that come when we fail to live up to our proclaimed values. Meeting these needs can look a lot like loving our neighbors, but we are not quite building Zion when we turn other people into containers for our own attention to ourselves.

This, I think, is the most important lesson that we learn from the Book of Job. When Job's comforters sat with him for seven days and seven nights without saying a word, they gave their full attention to their suffering friend. This is a master class in mourning with those who mourn, which has nothing to do with fixing a problem and everything to do with just paying attention to somebody else's needs. But as soon as they start talking, they ruin everything. They stop mourning with one who mourns and start trying to explain Job's pain. And it becomes increasingly clear that they are not focusing on Job's needs at all. They are trying to comfort themselves. By simply existing, Job has upended their understanding of God and morality, which says that God rewards those who do good things and punishes those who do bad things. In their minds, Job ceases to become a friend to be mourned with and becomes instead a theological problem to solve.

Focusing attention on other people to the exclusion of our own needs is decidedly unnatural. It defeats the logic of natural selection, which is driven by organisms pursuing their own interests or the interests of their genes. This is why Jesus must resort so often to paradox when trying to describe the Kingdom of God: "Whoever loses their life shall save it" (Mark 8:35), "If any desire to be first, the same shall be last" (Mark 8:35), and "Blessed are the meek, for they shall inherit the earth" (Matt. 5:5). These things don't make sense in our world. The urgent message of Jesus's earthly ministry was that the Kingdom of God cannot exist without them.

We err, I think, when we see the great commandments as prescriptive statements, as though loving God and our neighbors were the purchase price of eternal salvation. The great commandments are not injunctions on how to qualify for heaven after we die, but instructions for how to *build* heaven while we are still on earth. The Kingdom of God is, by definition, a society in which everybody focuses their attention on God and each other—rather than on their own needs and desires. The overwhelming message of the New Testament is that we can have this society anytime we want it, but we cannot have it cheaply, because the only way to create it is to give up everything else. This has everything to do with how we allocate our attention. ✸

1. Simone Weil, *Waiting for God,* trans. Emma Craufurd (New York: Harper & Row, 1951), 105.
2. Weil, *Waiting for God,* 114.
3. Weil, *Waiting for God,* 115.
4. For an overview, see William A. Searcy and Stephen Nowicki, *The Evolution of Animal Communication: Reliability and Deception in Signaling Systems* (Princeton: Princeton University Press, 2005).
5. Jared M. Diamond, *The Third Chimpanzee: The Evolution and Future of the Human Animal* (New York: HarperCollins, 2006), 196.

ETERNAL LIVES, EMBODIED

Tasting a Fullness of Joy

RACHAEL JOHNSON

THE MORE I EXCAVATE THE HISTORICAL and theological significance Mormonism grants the physical body, the more insistently the question presses on me: what if being embodied is a task, and not simply a state we inhabit?

To the scandal of deists, secularists, Protestants, and Catholics, Joseph Smith claimed that the body was not something to be abstracted, exploited, or transcended; to Latter-day Saints, embodiment was, as one observer scoffed, "a necessary step in their progress towards perfection and divinity."[1] Joseph Smith's claims about the embodiment of God and the thoroughly material nature of existence were widely recognized by contemporary observers as striking theological innovations. Embodiment enabled our progress and empowerment, Smith claimed—but it also, principally, promised our joy. "The great principle of happiness consists in having a body,"[2] he exulted: a physical body with enduring particularities, enmeshed in salvific interdependent relationships, and capable of infinite generativity.

I didn't always grasp this "great principle." In fact, it took years of immersing myself in the study of baroque Catholicism, with its embodied extravagances, to recognize the early Mormon romance with materialism. A compelling tale can be told about the latter's complex theological and historical legacy, but there's a personal one as well: it's a tale of conversion, in a sense, from my own conflicted relationship with the body to an awakening to embodiment as a fundamentally spiritual task.

When I understand embodiment as a task rather than a state, I affix intentionality to its givenness. I recognize that some forms of embodiment are conducive to life, and others lead to death, both physical and spiritual. In the natural embodiment of childhood, the disembodiment of adolescence, an over-bodied season of mental illness, pregnancy, and childbirth, and an ongoing re-embodiment mediated by relationships, I have come to feel the resonance of Joseph Smith's material sensibilities and to sense the divine tutorial in our embodiment. When I consciously live in embodied presence, I am more alive to the luminous beauty and the generative frictions of being a particular physical body in a shared material universe.

Emily Fox King

BIRTH

My earliest memories are saturated with sensation: enjoying the warm sunshine on my bare legs as a summer breeze rustles the folds of my pale blue dress; the golden hour settling like amber honey on the trees above the creaking swing set; the jewel-like colors shining out of a gumball machine gifted at my birthday. Remembering these childhood moments is an act of re-membering; the sensory qualities of these experiences reassemble themselves effortlessly, imbuing my nose, my ears, my eyes, my skin, with a dim but tangible vitality.

A unity of sensation and consciousness, emotion and thought, the world around me and myself, pervaded those first years. I didn't stand apart from these physical experiences as a detached observer; I was woven into them, born into what Merleau-Ponty calls a "primordial communion." Amidst the typical ordeals of childhood—the sibling skirmishes, the nerves that accompanied moving or starting a new school year—a sense of belonging created a steady background for the freshness of new encounters.

The child's body eludes what Charles Taylor calls the disenchantment and excarnation of modernity.[3] I was spellbound by a spider's web and the hue of a cerulean crayon; I was porous to the sun's warm beams as my breath fell into cadence with the sighing swings; I hugged, laughed, and climbed trees unselfconsciously at home in my body and at home in creation, "whole...from the foundation of the world."[4]

DEATH

Somewhere in adolescence, that natural embodiedness seemed to split apart like a husk and fruit, into a body and mind. This sensation was partly developmental: the slowly emerging prefrontal cortex and its more sophisticated cognitive functions kick into high gear during adolescence. It was also sociological: adolescence in late '90s middle-class America was a late-capitalist bourgeois exercise of self-representation. Teens stitched together a self from commodities owned and brands worn, producing a body with sufficient social and sexual capital to compete for status and belonging. This required the self to be abstracted and objectified—like the week before starting sixth grade when my friends and I, sitting on the floor with notebooks and pencils in hand, considered alternative clothes, interests, and social groups as if we were rearranging the elements of a mise-en-scène.

But there were limits to the imagined possibilities: I couldn't afford the right clothes or things, and my body remained childlike while other girls' grew curves. My product—my body—floundered in the middle school marketplace. But another option presented itself. At the lunch table in seventh grade, I cocked my head with interest as the girls nearby pushed away trays of food and discussed their new diets to be "thin." Here was a strategy with better odds: it required being less, rather than more; it depended on willpower rather than desirability. Willpower I had in spades; honed by a religious and familial upbringing that prized self-discipline—the full-day fasting, the daily scripture study and prayer, the crack-of-dawn seminary classes, the academic rigor—the cards, at last, were stacked in *my* favor.

So pound by pound, calorie by calorie, and mile after mile, I began to whittle my flesh down with an all-consuming focus. But this bid for belonging bent inward; my regimen soon cannibalized most of my interests and relationships into instruments of discipline or distractions to be avoided. On daily runs, I was blind to the trails' leafy canopies and earthy smells, too busy calculating my mileage, pace, and caloric burn. I viewed peers not as friends, but as metrics of comparison, a corporate Frankenstein of body parts I needed to best. Once, giving in to a wistful curiosity, I ventured out to a party, but I couldn't take my attention off the sights and smells of the food. It was too taxing, so I left. I eventually spent school lunch periods in deserted bathrooms and found excuses to avoid family dinners. By the time I was seventeen, I was still amenorrheic, subsisting on scant net calories, and achingly isolated.

Anorexia has been called a "psychosemantic fallacy"—a disease in which "the concept of

Emily Fox King

the whole person is so confused, so dialectically divided, that 'I' can at the same time be choosing to live, as the self, and choosing to die, as the body."[5] But the underlying delusion of the anorexic is that the body ceases being part of the "I"—it is an alien element, a bulbous disease.

Joseph Smith asserted that the body and spirit comprise the soul of man: "the elements are eternal, and spirit and element, inseparably connected, receive a fulness of joy; and when separated, man cannot receive a fulness of joy."[6] More starkly still, Joseph claimed "that which is without body or parts is nothing."[7] We are used to thinking of these ideas in lofty metaphysical terms, perhaps, but the slow severing of my body and spirit gave me a foretaste of the physical and emotional price of this separation. Though there were undoubtedly moments of happiness and connection amidst this struggle, I find it difficult to conjure vivid memories from this period of my life. While I can re-create with sensory clarity fleeting memories that happened much earlier in my childhood, my adolescent years are wrapped in wintry frost. I pry at them with numb fingers, grieving the half-dead years.

RESURRECTION

The grip of anorexia gradually loosened through the compassionate wisdom of a college roommate, then the earnest self-forgetfulness of mission service, and eventually a happy, if untested, marriage. But its mark remained. The years of disassociating myself from my body's primal signals of hunger and fatigue left my body-self dulled; meanwhile, a grueling doctoral program fed my mind-self steroids. Initially planning on studying themes of bodily transcendence and sexless souls in seventeenth- and eighteenth-century Enlightenment feminism, I found myself drawn instead to medieval mysticism and baroque Catholicism; their utter immersion in bodily matter both repulsed and fascinated me. I studied philosophies of the body, even as my own prepared a coup.

The mental and emotional pressures of graduate school and a fraying marriage began to split the seams of the body-self I had so long tried to compress and control. Panic attacks and dissociations broke my illusion of mental sovereignty and bodily discipline. In those stretches of time when my mind looped or dissolved into static, I was conscious only of a wild desperation to breathe, of an urge to beat my body-self back into working order like hammering the sides of a faulty vending machine. It was a bodily takeover that left me with tear-stained cheeks, bruises and headaches, and air-hungry lungs.

Like any good millennial, but with the reservations of a bootstrap-style upbringing, I took myself to therapy. I was chagrined when my therapist gently insisted on trying things like locating feelings "in my body." It was like trying to find a pulse in a stone. I didn't know how to be both a mind and a body. I could only lurch from one to another: ensconced in my head and my books, or crushed by unexpected tsunamis of sensation. My therapist wanted me to own these sensations, befriend them even, to align with my "true self" (a proposition that bewildered me); instead, I was inclined to see therapy as hostage negotiation training, finding ways to convince my amygdala to lower its weapons and hand over my brain.

> **The twelfth-century mystic Bernard of Clairvaux, who was quite taken with the metaphor of suckling, clearly never had mastitis.**

I eventually learned that my body was not merely a threat to be managed or a wild force to be placated; it was also a source of life-giving power, of astonishing complexity and intelligence. I discovered this not in the therapist's chair, but in carrying my first child. Pregnancy was a different bodily takeover, one as gradual and gentle as the other was sudden and violent, as wondrous as the other was terrifying. Without any direction from the mind I had so rigorously disciplined, my blood volume surged, hormones circulated, milk glands ripened, skin expanded, ligaments stretched, organs shifted. Day after day, I acquainted myself anew with a changed body. The very mass of matter I had once tried so hard to control took hold of the reins, and I relinquished them with unexpected and profound relief. In my mental illness, I felt seized by my body; in pregnancy, I submitted and surrendered to something that felt like grace.

I was sitting at the kitchen table in our sunny rental apartment in Madrid when I first felt the whispering flutter of her limbs. The quality of the air suddenly shifted—*There you are. Hello,* I breathed. Until then, the pregnancy had primarily felt like finding myself in a strange and remarkable experiment. I was fascinated by the changes in *my* body. But now, with a shock of recognition, I felt and saw *her* body, *her* prodding elbows and knees. My illusion of the sovereign mind-self finally shattered; my budding appreciation for the dynamic, intelligent body-self, too, gave way. Behind the contracted self, I saw *selves.* My body was plural, not singular.

Watching her movements ripple across my skin felt like a suddenly visible synecdoche of the maternal-fetal exchange that had been quietly transpiring between our cells from the beginning. With stark immediacy and utter fragility, her movements illuminated the grounding we-ness that precedes and shapes our very being. This was a physical but also an emotional revolution for me; I experienced, for the first time, loneliness as an impossibility. Throughout my days poring over fragile parchments in the archive, boarding crowded trains, walking along foreign streets, I cherished her secret company.

They tell me the child works as hard as the mother in labor; the contractions squeezing my ribs are squeezing her, too. But I forgot all about her during birth; I forgot everyone and everything. Medieval Christian mystics often used and even sought pain to block out all egoic consciousness in order to access the ethereal, unnameable presence of God. Pain "grasps us in the teeth of the moment, destroying for us all sense of past and future."[8] In the teeth of delivery, the words of carefully studied birth books, the calm instructions of my doula, the encouraging squeezes from my husband, were all swept away by the gush of broken water, the slow waves of suffocating contractions, and the scorching blast with which my daughter irrupted into the world.

For all the symphonic joy my daughter's arrival brought, the following weeks of recovery fell into a discordant minor key of throbbing pain. Sensations, again, upended the delicate ecology of my body, heart, and mind. Everything felt raw, displaced, unfamiliar in my body as I struggled to walk, to sit, to dress, and to nurse. The twelfth-century mystic Bernard of Clairvaux, who was quite taken with the metaphor of suckling, clearly never had mastitis. Nights and days blurred together in preparation for and recovery from the dizzying pain and torn flesh of each hourly feed; bouts of fiery infection marked the weeks. Sleep came in fitful snatches often disturbed by perceptual confusion—mistaking rumpled pillows or discarded socks for my infant being smothered under the covers, I'd awaken my husband frantically tearing them off our bed.

My body-self woke, nursed, bandaged, slept, woke, nursed, bandaged, slept; my mind functioned at a low hum of registering and responding to my baby's needs, punctuated by bouts of euphoria or despair. The radical transformation of motherhood left me reeling: at times

I felt dazzled by her existence, and at others, suffocated. Life felt new, but incoherent; like Lazarus resurrected, I was stumbling towards the tomb's opening, my face wrapped in grave clothes yet to be loosed.

After several months, the grave clothes dropped away: the fog of postpartum pain lifted, my heart steadied from the hormonal-emotional extremes, and my mind began to clear. In caring for my newborn daughter, I felt gradually re-ensouled with a self—a mind, a heart, and, most vividly, a body—that apprehended more deeply and clearly. I paused on a walk by the pond while carrying my daughter as she gazed fascinated at a dewy leaf; I saw its gorgeous translucence with new eyes. She cried, and I created a cocoon of warmth and protection with new arms. I finished nursing at midnight and her heavy head fell on new shoulders, the newborn fragrance of her downy hair filled new nostrils, the warm weight of her little body pressed on new nerves. She was born, and I was born anew. It was the first time I fully lived *through my body,* and the joy was so overpowering I would weep; I couldn't even journal my words—I had to sing them, in the dark, by her crib.

Words, in fact, mattered less now. She didn't require my ideas or opinions; she needed my soft voice and gentle hands. But nor was it simply my body she needed, either—my mental distraction or emotional disquiet were as palpable to her as the smell of smoke. She drew out of me an embodied attention, uncluttered by the syntax of subjects and objects.

This new sense of awareness began to spread outwards, transforming the world around me; motherhood not only re-embodied me, but re-embedded me. I remember lying with her on the wicker sofa as a summer rainstorm approached, the porch string lights warm and bright against the darkening sky. Her heartbeat, the percussion of rain, the calls of the whip-poor-wills, the rumbling thunder, the smell of soaked soil, all melded together like the harmonic undertones of a Tibetan singing bowl. I felt the restful sense of belonging from my childhood envelop me, though now suffused in tingling gratitude. In that quality of presence in which spirit and body are fully united in response to the world, I finally savored a "fullness of joy."

ETERNAL LIVES

But that quality of presence committed me to experiencing pain as well. In this newly embodied and embedded sense of self, I began to feel more vulnerable to emotional frictions, even subtle or unintended ones, and their somatic vibrations. The tone of my child's voice when she asked for her dad, not me; the tight pause before my friend's response in a difficult conversation; the icy draft of air when my husband shut the door after a fight; they felt newly charged and formidably complex in ways I couldn't articulate but deeply felt.

I also became more aware that the vulnerability of embedded embodiment worked in both directions; how deeply I affected others in ways that I could not see or fully understand. I remember the first moment this hit me in full force: my oldest, then a toddler, had impulsively hurt her infant sister, and I reacted angrily. As I scolded her, she suddenly clapped her hands over her eyes. My gaze, I realized, was hurting her. These eyes of mine that I couldn't even see, this facial expression I was incapable of viewing and was unknowingly bodying forth, were kindling shame and fear in a beloved child. It was a bitter taste of what the philosopher Gabriel Marcel called the "shadow at the center"— the part of one's self which is inaccessible to the self and *only* perceived by the Other, a proof of our incompleteness and dependence on the Other for our own self-disclosure.[9] I was stricken, and softly took her hands down and wrapped her in a hug, trying to blot it out from her history and her future.

Yet I go on hurting—in the passive and active sense—every day, every hour, simply by virtue of existing in embodied and embedded relationships. I am often tempted to enclose myself within my body, retreat into my own sensations and narrations, and leave those around me to the impenetrable mystery and responsibility of their Otherness. It's all the easier when our therapeutic, political, and cultural ethos invite it. We are encouraged to excavate our "true self" within the recesses of our own body and psyche and barricade behind its unimpeachable authority, behind our righteous boundaries; who needs the Other, except for blame and projection? Philosophy can be enlisted as well; solipsism scoffs at the idea that I can ever know anything outside my own body, let alone the Other. Why not save myself the heartache of trying? After all, how can anyone bear the weight of our unconscious offenses, the vulnerability of infinite disturbances?

It is at this juncture that Christ beckons me, calling me back out of my tomb and into the entangled world of Others, from an embodiment that self-encloses to an embodiment that mediates our inescapable interdependence. By virtue of his own Incarnation, Christ does not allow me to retreat into my particularity, nor ask me to dissolve it into some being-less Being; he asks me to stay yoked, as he does, to the Other: to love my neighbor as myself. For this relational reality and covenant "is eternal lives—to know the only wise and true God, and Jesus Christ, whom he hath sent."[10] To know God is to love.

Yet there's a catch; in bidding us love our neighbor as ourselves, loving one's self is presumed; but elsewhere, Christ bids us to lose the self, to let it die. The only way I can reconcile this is seeing them as referring to different selves. In the parable prefacing that daunting call, he illustrates how a kernel of wheat can either "abide alone" clinging to the stem, or it can let go, fall to the ground, and die. Only then does the seed bring forth much fruit, or, as I now read it, eternal lives. The self that must die is the false self generated by listening only to my own body and my own stories, when I imagine myself self-sufficient and complete, a bounded entity to protect and defend. Eternal lives begin once I let this self fall,

Emily Fox King

trusting the ground to catch it, to break it open and nourish it, and bring forth new ways of being.

Sometimes, I've found this breaking open and dying to be liberating, joyous. It means the death of the lonely self and the birth of new selves midwifed by the Other: "Ah, I never knew this about myself until I met you; until I lost you; until I married you; until I birthed you." It means the death of the stagnant, jaded self, making way for an infinite expansion born of curiosity and attention. Pinned in space and time through my particular body, I multiply, revise, and refine my access to the world through the perspectives and histories embodied in others.

But sometimes, it feels simply like death. And in times when I cling to my anger or my fear, when being alone feels like survival, the only way I have found to face the necessary egoic death is the peculiarly simple and often agonizing practice of meditation. In "still sitting" (a more apt, if unfamiliar, descriptor), I practice what in the therapist's office was impossible for me to achieve: facing the tsunamis of emotion and sensation and keeping my feet on the ground. But the difference is, the ground is not some illusory "true self" intoned by a well-meaning therapist, or marketed by self-help books or invoked on billboards, but the true ground of Being, the ground infused with the light that "comprehends all things," that is "in all and through all things" and "giveth life to all things." Christ is the ground, the matter, the *mater,* in the maternal-fetal exchange of creation, in the birth of new, eternal lives.

It is something I can sometimes directly grasp but not adequately translate. The other day, it felt like this: I was sitting in my office feeling pulled apart: weighted with the residue of a lingering argument with my husband, escaping into heady thoughts of new academic projects, crushed by a sense of finite time and attention against the infinite books to be read, avoiding thoughts of what to make for dinner, yawning from the sleepless night disrupted by my middle child's bad dreams, and queasy about the prospects of trying to resolve the marital conflict in the fleeting window between kids' bedtimes and my own. I began to pack up my bag to leave the office, readying, as I often did, to shove the wild thoughts and heavy emotions in alongside my laptop, and do the next minimally required act to keep life functioning, holding in temporary abeyance the implosion sure to come.

Instead, I stopped. I turned back and sank into my chair, and I breathed. And as I sat trembling before the onslaught of emotions and sensations, something in me gave way. The anger and accusations, the ambitions and anxieties, began to break off the stem and drop. I felt the breath rushing out of me: a gentle, liberating wind sweeping the locks off my throat, my tear glands, my shoulders, and my chest. The walls of my own prison, my self-contained aloneness, came crumbling down around me. I felt the ground beneath me, catching the shards of my egoic self that lay brittle and broken around the tender shoots of new lives. In that ground, there was room for my husband, for my children, for the voices of all the books, and for me. I was ready to go home.

I sense the divine tutorial of embodiment stretching out into eternity—an eternity that, as Joseph Smith envisioned and I now feel, is anything but empty or static. It pulses with new lives, ever emerging, ever embodied, ever embedded. They've already begun. And I can "taste it" like "honey is sweet," and "I know it is good."[11] ✱

1. Viscount Amberley, "The Latter-Day Saints, Part II," *The Fortnightly Review,* December 1, 1869, 682.
2. "Discourse, 5 January 1841, as Reported by Unidentified Scribe," [1], josephsmithpapers.org.
3. Charles Taylor, *A Secular Age* (Cambridge: Belknap Press, 2007).
4. Moroni 8:8, 12.
5. Bryan S. Turner, *The Body and Society: Explorations in Social Theory* (New York: Basil Blackwell, 2008), 186.
6. Doctrine and Covenants 93:33–34.
7. Quoted by William Clayton, reporting an undated discourse given by Joseph Smith in Nauvoo, Illinois, in L. John Nuttall, "Extracts from William Clayton's Private Book," 7, Journals of L. John Nuttall, 1857–1904, L. Tom Perry Special Collections, Brigham Young University.
8. Maureen Flynn, "The Spiritual Uses of Pain in Spanish Mysticism," *Journal of the American Academy of Religion* 64, no. 2 (Summer 1996): 275.
9. Gabriel Marcel, *Being and Having* (United Kingdom: Read Books Limited, 2011).
10. Doctrine and Covenants 132:24.
11. "History of Joseph Smith," *Times and Seasons,* August 15, 1844, 615.

PETER IS STILL WALKING ON WATER

DARLENE YOUNG

At first it was simply the huge gasping HA of joy,
    like a crowd
rising to its feet, like a sudden haul of fish in a net
    that was empty
moments before—a surge of power springing
    him into space,
the thought of a landing wholly absent, thought itself wholly
absent, no sense even of self at all, only
the moment, the moonlight, and that familiar, strange,
beloved face that promised everything—only that.

                                        Years later
in the moments of ceiling-staring before sleep he would tell
himself the story, walk himself through each moment,
the bawl and bluster of wild wind and water and then
the impossible coming towards him, arms outstretched.
It was the future approaching, and all it promised, a peace
that brought a different upheaval, upending everything
he thought he knew—about the world, about himself.

In reliving and reliving that moment, he had learned
to forbid himself the writhing regret, force his mind
away from the flounder, the drenching disappointment
of falling short, that wet hoist back into the boat;
had learned that it does no one any good to carry their own
earlier selves on their backs through life. No, it was not
that shame which kept him awake. Instead, it was this:

What, in that moment, had he felt beneath his feet? What
had he stepped on? Had his soles slapped slippery surface
or sunk two inches down? Had he tiptoed or stomped?
Or danced? He cast and cast again his mind into his feet,
replaying, replaying, searching, imagining, but—nothing,
nothing. Only
that shining face,
that outstretched hand.

David Habben (Colorized by Esther H. Candari)

THE THEOLOGY OF BIRDS

STEVEN L. PECK

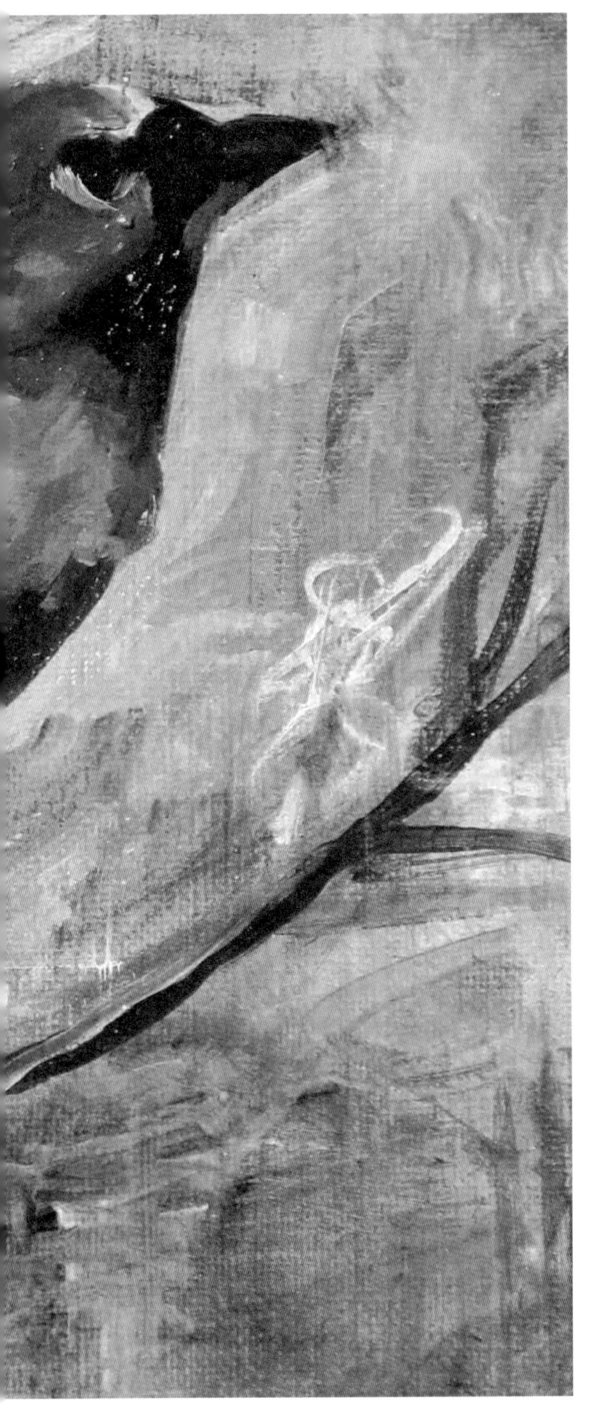

Something that cannot be said in words . . .
Something sweet and unknown . . .
The wind . . . the brook . . .
Something that comes to a trembling fuller tone
Like a waterfall . . .
That little brown creature is singing
A music of water, a music of worlds;
He will fly away south,
But his song stays in the heart
Once it is heard.
— The Hermit Thrush
by American Poet Hilda Conkling (1910–1986)

AS A BIOLOGICAL BEING, I HAVE A rich inner life that is undeniably real and that only I can access. There are some things about what it is like to be me that only I know. I assume it is true for you as well. This also holds for the myriad beings around me, including the little dark-eyed juncos flitting around in the cold outside my window.

All lived experience exceeds our ability to describe it. This is true whether we use language, scientific diagrams, mathematical equations, computer simulations, or a tinker toy model of the universe—any descriptive means. However, the visual arts, poetry, music, and other aesthetic means of expression come closer to capturing and conveying to others the richness of our subjective experience. We wander in a world full of tastes, sights, sounds, smells, emotions, and the feeling of electrostatic vector fields when we walk in thick socks across a new carpet. Likewise, we feel the natural world's effect on us in ways that exceed descriptive articulation.

Having a body gives us an indescribable but felt encounter with a world. We can describe aspects of our field of perception—for example, "There on my right is a crocus creeping up through the soil, its green floral base emerging into my garden." But these words trying to capture this enchanting moment are a mere cartoon of what it was like for me. Much is left out.

The experience is given whole, given at once in a feeling of being. It feels like something. Its components are immeasurable and ineffable. Is it not best described as an enchantment?

Being embodied means that my perception of that growing flower is combined with memories of past nature encounters. My experience is not uniquely constructed just from what my senses perceive. It involves my evolutionary history as a body emerging from earthly processes,[1] including joys or sorrows, reminders of other flowers I might have encountered, and my emotional state from whatever else has happened this day. It is complex, multifaceted, and embedded in both physical and historical realities. This encounter is also unique and will be like no other that has ever existed in the history of the universe—my watching reflected green light rays that are not of use to the plant; the sun at that angle; me tired from having a late night of study the day before; that ant crawling over its surface perhaps looking for small springtails, a common soil insect; the bark of a neighbor's dog, seasoned with the sound of finches, Townsend's solitaires, American robins, and common house sparrows calling from nearby bushes; the wind from a southerly direction cooling me until I draw my hoodie more tightly round me as I listen to the breeze sounding in the branches of my berry-full juniper standing nearby. But the inner experience cannot be partitioned into these separate, sensed encounters with objects and processes constructing the inadequately described aspects of this experience. The experience is given whole, given at once in a feeling of being. It feels like something. Its components are immeasurable and ineffable. Is it not best described as an enchantment?

* * *

I am with my twelve-year-old grandson, Asher, in a nearby canyon. He holds a parabolic-dish mic attached to a recording device. He is aiming it at a singing lazuli bunting in a cottonwood tree. Using techniques I taught him, he moves the disk up and down and from side to side to maximize its sound capture. His eyes are wide, and he is smiling despite the much-too-large earphones sliding around on his head that he holds with one hand to keep in position. We both agree the singing is beautiful. We are experiencing the sound of that bird, and its aesthetic sense of its music leaves me in awe. It is a sublime encounter for me and my grandson.

I don't know what the bird is experiencing. Philosopher Thomas Nagel asks famously, "What is it like to be a bat?" in a philosophy paper of the same title.[2] It explores the deep epistemological divide between experiencing things whose worldviews are conditioned on completely other sensing apparatuses evolved for purposes other than ours. This is often used as a precursor to philosophical hands being raised in surrender at our inability to know with even rudimentary certainty what the lives of other creatures are like. But let's not be hasty. I just claimed, "I don't know what the bird is experiencing." Is that accurate?

True enough as far as that goes, but it is also true that I don't know what my grandson is experiencing. And yet, if taken too far, it would be wildly inaccurate to claim that I know nothing of his inner life. We do share a common evolved neurology. We have nearly identical sensing apparatuses: eyes geared for the same distances and focus and color sensing. We share cultural assumptions about what birds are and what they mean as objects. I remember what it was like to get to listen to birds when I was twelve. So it would be arrogantly reductionistic and inaccurate to claim I have no idea what he is experiencing. Not precisely, of course. I don't know what it is like to be him with his memories and the context in which he engages the world. Yet. I can guess. And I suspect I will not be as far off with him as I would be if I were describing bats.

What of the little bunting? Can I know what it is experiencing? Is it making music? Can I make any claims about the conscious experience of that avian relative? My grandson is two generations away from me—around fifty years. According to data from molecular clocks, the bird and I shared a grandmother about 319 million years ago. Much further away than Nagel's bats, whose common grandmother lived only 94 million years ago. What possible claims about sharing experiences can I make?

Now perhaps this is a bit intellectually reckless, but stay with me. I suspect that this bird, this lazuli bunting, shares an aesthetic sense of the world and experiences joy. We are kin, albeit distant. Even so, kinship has its privileged claims. But first, a pause—a brief interlude with a Japanese form called haibun: text interspersed with haiku.

HUMMINGBIRD HAIBUN

Jakob Johann von Uexküll proclaimed the umwelt—a term coined to capture the notion that all animals perceive the world from an individual perspectival topology, shaping how they encounter their habitat according to their needs. Each organism evolves a set of perceptual apparatuses that structure how and what they sense. We know sight, hearing, smell, taste, touch, and apperception. A host of animals add electric and magnetic senses. Some, like migrating songbirds, perceive the quantum flux in the northern lights.

I am in a shady spot writing an eco-philosophy paper on embodiment. I'm lying on my back under an apple tree, thinking about Uexküll's work, when serendipitously, a hummingbird flies up and down the trunk of the tree and then rests just above me.

A hummingbird sits
still on an apple twig—
looking left then right

I watch as it floats again toward the trunk. Looking for what? These iridescent-feathered birds will occasionally eat small insects and, I suspect, especially sugar-exuding aphids.

How does it sense the world? Its eyes see more colors than I can. Humans are trichromic, with our primary colors mixtures of green, blue, and red. That gives us a few million shades we can distinguish. This hummingbird has another primary color in the ultraviolet. It sees four primary colors and their glorious combinations, giving them hundreds of millions more shades they can discriminate.

Eyes look down
as it hovers above me—
my skin countless hues

What does a hummingbird body know? What is it like to have a heart that beats multiple times while I give a single blink? To feel the world's air currents in the vibrations of its feathers, or to sample nectar on the wing and taste the foundation of its sustenance on its sharp tongue? I watch this one, and it seems curious about the area above where I rest. What is it looking for? Or looking out for—but I laugh. What predator could catch a hummingbird?

I see no flowers it can sup, and the fall migration is about to start. Is it saying farewell or looking for someone with whom to travel? Is it just waiting for the night so it can follow the star patterns south?

Small feet grip a branch
bouncing rhythms in a breeze—
the bird looks straight on

It makes one more circle around my hammock, and as I move my head for a better look, it flies confidently away, then turns behind another apple tree, and I lose sight of it. The sound of its wings still lingers in my ears, but floating over the neighbor's fence, it susurrates out of sight.

The hummingbird flees
at the motion of my head—
Summer wanes apace

I am working on a theology of birds. Which is—what? This little experiment argues that part of being an embodied organism is experiential engagement with the world. It includes the idea of being a singular being among other beings. I speculate that novelty and art enter the world through evolution and through depths that we do not understand nor can we understand scientifically. This is not a religious argument per se, but it does not exclude such, as I will speak of souls and hidden depths of the universe. These constitute a dimension that can easily be called spiritual. I reject reductionism, the idea that the whole can be described as the sum of its parts. I do acknowledge its usefulness for answering specific scientific questions about the physical universe, and even grant that much of the world can be characterized as machine-like and deterministic (for example, when NASA uses Newtonian physics to land a rover on Mars). But the world is far stranger than we imagine, and reductionism gives short shrift to much of the beauty and power of aesthetic dimensions of the world.

As I write from my backyard, I hear a house finch calling from the neighbor's yard. Why is it carrying on so amid the chatter of sparrows in conversation? With the theology of birds, I'm trying to sort out the possibilities that resonate with my experience with the divine to see if I can articulate something sensible. Something meaningful in my daily walk. I think birds will be necessary. I believe many other things will be important. Like evolution. Like science. These will provide the bones of my theological exploration, but like the bones of birds, they need to be hollow so flights beyond the mere mechanical world can lift off. By hollow, I mean they must be light enough not to weigh down the other things that will be important for getting above the earthly mundane. But science will be important. It is inadequate for many tasks, and its values and concerns cannot

Leslie Graff

be bootstrapped from its aims and methods; yet it is still the best thing we have for sorting out the realities structuring the cosmos's framing. So let us agree that science will be essential for our theology of birds. This theology will hold to notions articulated about frequency, dependencies, processes and particles, fields and probabilities,

Some birds sing as we do! They practice for hours. They improvise. They play with themes and melodies. They try things out on other birds and then readjust.

matter and energy, and will embrace both chaos and stasis. But this is only the beginning. We must not succumb to the temptation of thinking science will give all there is to teach us about the universe. Scientism, the idea that all knowledge is discoverable by science, and its shallow materialism must be dismissed as inadequate. Experience is essential to the theology of birds.

If we lived in a deterministic universe, experience would be superfluous. Presumably, a self-driving car has no experiences. But it does not need experience to function. It can do all kinds of things without it. So what does experience add to the click-clack of embodied interaction with the world? Why would it have evolved if the rudiments of survival could hum and whir through existence without this added feature of so many creatures' embodiment?

This consciousness, this seeming non-necessity found in certain animals, led some philosophers to posit that the experience of being consciously aware was an epiphenomenon, something that floats like root beer foam at the top of existence as a carryover from more essential things brains do. However, philosopher Peter Godfrey-Smith has carefully explored the evolution of experience and found that it emerges independently in numerous animal (metazoan) lineages, among them mammals, birds, insects, spiders, and mollusks (including octopuses). We know the brain-correlates of lived experiences for embodied beings—neurology of a particular type; sensual apparatuses that capture "maps" of the objects and processes of the world using sight, hearing, and smell, etc.; and often motility, the ability to move.

Birds provide an example of how experience allows a richer world than seems necessary to interact bodily with that world. Our and their experience exceeds its evolutionary demands. And we two vertebrate lineages have some strangely similar ways of acting in the world. For example, birds sing. Some, it is true, are just running a genetic algorithm when they sing, and their songs do not vary from the genetic program beyond a certain point. But some birds sing as we do! They practice for hours. They improvise. They play with themes and melodies. They try things out on other birds and then readjust their song according to their compatriots' reactions. They play. They perform.

Process theologian Charles Hartshorne was so intrigued by the theological potential of birdsong that he developed a whole theory of beauty based on birds, as he realized that birds have a genuine sense of the beautiful. Daniel A. Dombrowski, looking at Hartshorne's theological aesthetics, elaborates on this:

> We are not being overly generous . . . in seeing the bird's task as strongly analogous to our own: The goal is to lead interesting, beautiful lives both for our own sakes and for the sakes of those (including God) whom we influence. An evolutionary account of birdsong should both predict certain behaviors as well as point out the limitations in its ability to predict.[3]

Or, as I put it above, the aesthetic aspects of birdsong exceed what science can describe or thoroughly examine. Unexpectedly, this avian aesthetic means something important theologically—that joy, play, awe, and the experience of beauty are part of this universe.[4]

In her book *Is Bird Song Music?* violinist and bird researcher Taylor Hollis, who spent years researching and playing music with Butcher Birds in Australia, concludes that birds are doing much of the same thing humans do when creating music:

> Pied butcherbirds' artful combinatorics are on the same page: their songs exceed a rigid set of instructions. Such substantial scope for individual variation in this singing tradition, where repertoire can be pulled out of memory and performed in different circumstances and presumably under different motivational conditions and in different seasons, points to a capacity to manipulate to musical effect.[5]

Musician David Rothenberg, who likewise has accompanied singing birds with human musical instruments, reinforces this notion in his book *Why Birds Sing.* He adds to Hollis's perspective by imagining a singing male bird:

> First listen as a bird might. You're interested in only the sound of your own species, perhaps, and others come across as mere noise. We can never know, we cannot get inside the bird. . . . Or else, imagine a bird enthralled with sound itself. His songs are beautiful, complex, clearly more than what is necessary to get the message across. There must be exuberance, there may be joy. The bird is endowed as a virtuoso and loves to show off, explore, and cry out.[6]

Writing about Blue Manakins in his book *The Evolution of Beauty,* ornithologist Richard Prum talks about the work, play, and improvisation in this species in which three or four males form a dance troupe, led by an alpha male, that practices together for years to get the dance and song just right to impress a female:

> Considerable skill and coordination are involved in putting on these performances. Because the females are extremely discerning, their preferences select for males who have been in male-male social relationships that have lasted long enough to have allowed them plenty of time to practice diligently and iron out any kinks in their performances. Apparently, it can take years of practice to achieve vocal coordination between males that is good enough to attract mates.[7]

In her book *Living as a Bird,* the French philosopher of science Vinchiane Despret convincingly points to territorial displays as an aspect of bird performance. She talks about how these displays, which take on a ritualistic form of aggression, subvert actual aggression and becomes a way to perform aggression without engaging in it:

> Because, if territory can indeed be defined as a spectacular display ground, aggressivity can no longer be the motive, in the psychological sense, or indeed the cause of territorial activity. It becomes instead the motive in an aesthetic or musical sense, conferring on the territory its style, its particular form, its energy, its choreography and its gestures so that aggression becomes a kind of simulacrum. There is a shift from an 'aggressive' function to a different function. An expressive one.[8]

I live with four parakeets. One of them is molting and can't fly, and when I open the cage to let them roam the house, the other three don't fly at all so they can stay close to their grounded compatriot. They are in constant communication, chattering, kissing, responding to each other and the world, and trying out their voices (they love Sufjan Stevens and sing with him with more enthusiasm

Leslie Graff

than any other human artist). Unlike the behaviorists enamored with neurological determinism that grant experience only to humans, I cannot even imagine my bird kin not experiencing things in a rich inner life.

The theology of birds describes our kinship with Earth's creatures who have evolved on this planet with us. We, the birds, and even our divine parents are all part of a material unfolding universe in which embodiment allows us to exuberantly engage with a universe that has evolved toward joy as one of its emergent potentials.

I feel blessed to live in a universe where galaxies, giant gas planets, black holes, moons, and quarks can be combined such that beauty, music, and art emerge—and where at least two wildly divergent lineages of life have evolved in embodied ways that allow both us and birds to experience its aesthetic dimensions. ✸

1. Steven L. Peck, "Latter-day Saint Theology of a Material, Embodied Deity vis-à-vis Evolutionary Conceptions of Embodiment, Agency, and Matter," *Journal for the Study of Religion* 35, no. 1 (2022): 1–35.
2. Thomas Nagel, "What Is It Like to Be a Bat?," *Philosophical Review* 83, no. 4 (October 1974): 435–50.
3. Daniel A. Dombrowski, *Divine Beauty: The Aesthetics of Charles Hartshorne* (Nashville: Vanderbilt University Press, 2004), 68.
4. Henrik Hogh-Olesen, *The Aesthetic Animal* (New York: Oxford University Press, 2019).
5. Hollis Taylor, *Is Birdsong Music?: Outback Encounters with an Australian Songbird* (Bloomington: Indiana University Press, 2017), 277.
6. David Rothenberg, *Why Birds Sing: A Journey Into the Mystery of Bird Song* (New York: Basic Books, 2005), 9–10.
7. Richard O. Prum, *The Evolution of Beauty: How Darwin's Forgotten Theory of Mate Choice Shapes the Animal World—and Us* (New York: Doubleday, 2017), 210.
8. Vinciane Despret, *Living as a Bird*, trans. Helen Morrison (Medford, MA: Polity Press, 2021), 49.

A GRIEF SHARED

SAM BROWN

I WAS EIGHTEEN WHEN MY FATHER died. I'd be exaggerating to say I never knew him. My mom made him leave when I was twelve, and I saw him a half dozen times between his departure and his death six years later. But he'd actually been thriving in my early childhood in Helena, Montana. He had a job then where he felt valued, kids were accumulating on the familiar pace of five per decade, and we had lower-middle-class financial stability. I remember driving in a giant Ford station wagon, delivering newspapers in the freezing pre-dawn darkness, watching him cry when particularly beautiful music played on the classical music station. He sang with a loud baritone that I inherited, and reliable pitch, which I did not. I relished his pleasure in throwing Sunday waffle parties for friends and neighbors. I also remember the stories he made up in the telling, in which we children were the main characters. I no longer remember my name in that fantasy world, other than the sibilant alliteration—savvy Sam or super Sam or the like—but I remember that the protagonist of the story cycle was a boy named Polly Push. The boy got that name because his favorite words were a request that his older sister *Polly* push him on the swing.

With substantial effort, I could uncover other memories, but such are the accessible highlights of our relationship. We were reconciled just before he died as part of the miracle of my late-adolescent conversion. The reconciliation came to be through a letter I received from him in mid-November in my first year of college. By late December, we were with Dad at LDS Hospital, his belly full of protein-rich fluid the color of beer. The hepatitis he got from the kidney transplant that replaced the organs ruined by his poorly managed diabetes had driven his liver to cirrhosis. He joked, thinly, that he was pregnant and expecting twins any day. I remember his sallow, yellowing skin and the horrible thin mustache. It would be a half dozen years before I would understand, medically, why he looked as he did, the typical appearance of someone dying of liver failure. What I knew at the time was that Grandpa said Dad was dying, so I took my siblings in to say goodbye during my Christmas break. He died about a week later: cardiac arrest during dialysis. CPR could not restart his heart, so the team stopped their rhythmic compression of his chest.

I was back at college by the day my father died, in the middle of a Boston winter. I hugged my closest friend at the time, an atheist Jewish woman named Amy, in the quiet leafiness of Harvard Yard. She wept more than I did. She found herself discomfited by the finality of death, imagining what it would mean for her parents to lapse entirely from existence. I was aglow with faith in God, true, but I also didn't have much of a connection to my father as a person. He had always been a startling absence in my life. The fact that the cause of absence was death now, rather than madness or my anger, was immaterial. I suppose I did mourn his death, but that mourning started long before he died and faded quickly once he was safely on the other side. What grief I experienced had to do with my vision of what ought to have been. I was experiencing a generic form of baleful deprivation. I was a fatherless boy. It was the figure of a father that was missing rather than anything specific to the man who just breathed his last on a dialysis machine at LDS Hospital. Such was my early grief.

Later in adulthood, I encountered a new form of grief in the intensive care unit. That's where I practice medicine; I've been working in ICUs for about fifteen years now, drawn to them even before I graduated medical school. They are my home territory, my professional habitat. There is nothing quite like the drama of doing strenuous battle with death. The weapons are life support systems, our wits, and our hearts. The stakes could not be higher.

The statistics say that about one in eight ICU patients will die within the month. It's that severity of illness that justifies the extra attention from

J. Kirk Richards

nurses, doctors, and therapists. That statistic is even a bit optimistic because many of the survivors are people who are in and out of the ICU before we can even blink. It's probably about a quarter or a third of patients we really get to know who will die. We are immersed in death in that place. Without us, many more would die. But even when we try our hardest, people still die. It's biology. So I've made peace with it. I have to manage the grief both to provide excellent medical care and to be a decent human being. It's something I've taught myself to do. I'm pretty good at it. The point is to give people some guidance, treat them well, honor the dying, and grieve in controlled amounts. To grieve every death in the ICU as if it were the death of an intimate is too much. It just is. You'd break. So you mourn a tiny bit with each death, while allowing the families to do the primary work of grieving. With John Donne, you hear the bell tolling and realize that it is calling to each of us at some basic level. But today the bell does not ring for you or your beloved. Grieve too much, and you will lose your mind. Grieve too little, and you will lose your soul. Such is the balance of life and death in the ICU.

By the time I had arrived at middle age, I was well acquainted with grief. I had even written a couple of books about death and the care of patients with life-threatening illness. I was, as they say, a published expert.

But all that counts for little when your wife loses her eye and then her whole body to a rare melanoma over the course of a bittersweet decade of life lived in the shadow of death. I can see why Damocles gave up after a day of living under the dangling sword. The grief that comes from the death of a beloved takes your breath away, clouds your vision, squeezes your heart, and a million other terrible things. It is also sacred, expressing the depth of the bond that has been disrupted. It is seeing clearer than we have ever seen before, even as we are blinded by the suffocating mists of anguish. Both things, as my Kate of blessed memory would say, are true of grief.

The love and the pain aren't the only polarity that grief mediates. There is also, inexorably, the question of individuals and communities.

One-year-and-a-lifetime ago, we are seated around the kitchen table, an ancient Quebecois butterfly table. My laptop balances on the windowsill, behind which stands the floral menagerie-cum-potager that my wife accumulated over the decade we have spent in this house. She loves beautiful things and old things. We, also beloved, sit in the midst of both.

Our oldest child, just back from her first year of college, has joined family therapy for our youngest, who is at a therapeutic boarding school in southern Utah. Therapy is by video conference, and we pivot the laptop camera from face to face, like a low-budget documentary. We're far enough along in her therapy now that it's okay to talk about death. Her mother's death. My Kate's death.

For years, that lethal portent has been the fact too horrible to say out loud for our struggling daughter. Kate grimaces a little with the pain of shifting bony matter inside the vertebral body that we will soon discover is being eaten by her cancer. But also with the reality that she does not love to dwell on the physical and emotional tragedy that is unfolding month by month. Cancer is no simple thing. Sometimes it is hard to say its name aloud, and sometimes it is the needed thing.

"When I was at school a girl in my dorm was talking about it," our oldest explains. "She said it's like having a mission call. Mom is called to serve in the afterlife. That made sense to me. It was really comforting." The youngest nods, trying on the idea that perhaps our loss will be a bit more tolerable if in fact we know Kate will be doing good things with her time away from us. The story even makes a little sense to me—Kate had been away in Paris for a final visit a couple weeks earlier, and I didn't miss her as much then because I knew she was in a place she loved. Maybe heaven will be a bit like Paris. We'll be lonely without her, but confident that she is flourishing.

Even so, I wince. We've heard that story before, many times. Kate and I wrote an essay a decade ago that began with an uneasy engagement of the young-adult novel *Charly*. That titular woman, Charly Riley, is another mother dying of cancer. The novelist paints her afterlife as concrete, busy, and happy in a way meant to put her widowing husband at ease. Kate and I weren't the first to hold *Charly* at an awkward distance. In a book on Mormon history and culture, Lester Bush described a young woman of his acquaintance who wrote a letter to be shared at her funeral, forbidding any reassurance that she was serving an afterlife mission. In my paraphrase, that dying mother was asking an urgent, rhetorical question. *Why on earth would you say that dead people they've never met are more important to me than my children? My calling is to be mother to these children, not to dead strangers.* Kate and I played along with Bush and his friend in that old essay of ours. We knew how absurd the traditional story was. But here is that sorry story from *Charly* and Mormon lore, and it is actively helping our oldest daughter deal with the coming death of her mother.

By then I might have known better than to doubt platitudes and a positive attitude. Honestly, that's been my professional experience in the intensive care unit. I'm often called by human decency to try to say something helpful in the face of an untimely death. Maybe a decade ago, I noticed a louder consensus among thoughtful liberals (my tribe all these years) that the best and perhaps only appropriate response to grief is to emphasize the extent of the tragedy. People shouldn't rush to explain or place the tragedy into meaningful context. They should instead resonate with the pain. Full stop.

The love and the pain aren't the only polarity that grief mediates. There is also, inexorably, the question of individuals and communities.

The old way of focusing on the positive, these critics explained, left people feeling alone and misunderstood. Buried in platitudes rather than succor, they had to struggle through more than their grief. After hearing a particularly passionate exposition of the idea, I decided to give it a try. I did so for about six months. But I noticed that while a few people clearly resonated with the new approach, most stared at me in perplexity. Why would I refuse to reach for a shared language of meaning or reassurance, they seemed to ask, when I'd been around death before? I wasn't a novice, so why was I acting like one? Saying that I had read it on the internet, however true, was not the right answer.

I ultimately abandoned that guiding principle, because it wasn't working. I spend more time now trying to get a sense for people, to hear what kind of language they're using, what questions they

Grief is normal and strong and even a bit beautiful in its pain. It's not just tragic. Grief is a form of love and a connection to meaningful vastness. Grief is a source of solidarity and affection and tenderness.

have. I talk less. And, when I get the sense that such words will be most useful to the people I'm talking to, I say positive and optimistic things. I even use platitudes. Not because I'm denying the grief. God forbid! But because I am meeting the grief with the power of human community and hope. I'm certain I get it wrong sometimes. But better some earnest missteps, in my view, than being the flag bearer for an ideology that grossly misreads most people. I'm wrong less often now that I'm open to more than emotional resonance, no longer merely echoing back well-intended darkness for darkness.

I get why some good people believe that the only response to grief must be to steadfastly acknowledge the depth of tragedy. Much of modern philosophy teaches that life is a meaningless accident. So instead of offering meaning, our job is to stare together at unmeaning. This philosophy plays more and more in public rhetoric these last decades. We need to know that context.

To be clear, this approach isn't entirely wrongheaded. There is something sacred about holding hands in the face of inscrutable suffering. For some of us, the shared acknowledgment of our inability to make sense of something vast can be a great reassurance. When the situation calls for it, as it sometimes does, we should gather together against a baffling misery with nothing but the fact of our loving presence. But we would do well to remember that we can stand together *and* see true meaning. The two are not mutually exclusive.

The more I've stared at these questions from the various sides, the more I think that this new trope—resonate with tragedy and nothing else—is a mandate to treat everyone who grieves as if they were mentally ill. On average, people struggling with mental illness, particularly in our modern cultural moment, crave emotional mirroring, what some scholars term "resonance." I've seen it in my own life and the life of my children. When our psyches exist under certain forms of stress, we want the world to look the way we see it rather than to be deeply understood or to exist in profoundly loving relation. We want people to suffer as we suffer. Misery craves company. So people of a particular cast of mind want reassurance that the tragedy, the trauma, is real and irredeemable. I've had moments myself that feel just that way, plenty of them. And I've heard those words hundreds of times from people I know and love. It's hard not to remember an emotion expressed so powerfully.

Still, as I've been watching closely, I think that's usually depression talking. I've learned that much from all the therapy sessions with my daughter, who sought (unsuccessfully, thanks be to God) to end her life as a pained exit from the anticipated grief of her mother's advancing cancer. I know how real and strong and important emotional mirroring can feel—can be—for some of us. I've felt it myself. There are days when I just want bleak resonance with the extremity of my sadness; those are rough days indeed. But that's not most days, not even most sad days.

Having partaken of both emotional states at great length, I can see the difference between grief and mental illness. Grief is normal and strong and even a bit beautiful in its pain. It's not just tragic. Grief is a form of love and a connection to meaningful vastness. Grief is a source of solidarity and affection and tenderness. It is a turning outward as much as inward. It can also, of course, be annihilating. Particularly when it intermingles with or even transforms into depression, anxiety, psychosis, or the other plagues flowing from Pandora's box. Mental illness wears many faces, but it includes despair, self-hatred, and rootless pain. It is not a form of love, but a force that threatens love. It is hopeless.

All these years into intimate familiarity with grief, I'm not persuaded that treating us all as

J. Kirk Richards

J. Kirk Richards

if we were mentally ill does anyone much good. Pushing ourselves to believe that tragedy is pure trauma does violence to the world in all its splendor. What I'm proposing is rather harder than the two extremes we hear the most about: reciting Hallmark cards with our fingers in our ears or hopelessly (if companionably) resonating to despair. What I'm proposing is that we share grief.

I remember when Kate's cancer recurred six years ago. We were watching general conference a couple months later, and the stories about cancer were about people dying despite fervent prayers for rescue. We felt a bit exasperated, as we had hoped that the sermons would be uplifting and hopeful. After laughing uncomfortably, we debated whether to be angry. We realized that there were people listening who were already on the other side of a cancer tragedy, but we knew that there were people who'd had their prayers answered in sad and terrible ways and they needed to get some companionship. We as a family would have been better served by happy stories about freedom from a death sentence. But we didn't get that. We digested this fact together: our needs were not met while others' were. We realized that we must share the Church, share the words and stories. In love, we belong to a body that sometimes will not work for us because it is serving others with distinct needs. In the midst of our bereavement, we will have to make accommodations. We will need to share grief.

This sharing of grief has another face, one that for me, has been among the hardest and holiest work of my life. As a cancer husband and then a widowing single father, I realize that I am often asked—whether I want it or not—to be the vessel of a community's worry and dread. With the best of intentions, no small number of relative strangers have rushed up to me to express the depth of our tragedy when all I wanted was a world where Kate was still physically present. The pain of such awkward encounters has often been acute, and initially, I tended to flee in anger and pain. I can't remember when I finally figured out that I had another option. Instead of running away, I could admit that I was called sometimes to hold grief for others. It was hard work, and work I didn't want to do. But, as I started this new work, I came to see that it was holy. The effort to share grief pulled me out of myself. It did not make my grief any easier; it was not a treatment. But it was sacred practice, and in the pursuit of the sacred stands the sublimely troubling dream of heaven-on-earth. And that is a dream worth fighting for.

I would never hold another bereaved person to this standard. If I shirk this duty, I am not a bad man. It is fair for me to ask others to share my grief by giving me space and tolerating my bad manners when they overstep bounds. But there will be times, many of them, when I have the strength. And when I have that strength and I exercise it on behalf of others, I feel an extra measure of power and grace. Among the many strangely beautiful gifts of this bereavement has been the calling and capacity to give from my deep woundedness. That grace is the painful promise of a shared grief.

Sometimes shared grief can feel too much to bear; there are limits to the burdens weary shoulders can carry. Kate told me as we started to watch the different chemotherapy treatments fail, one after another, that she'd rather have people say hopeful or kind things to her than to tell her how tragic her life was. Things were not going the way she wanted medically, to be sure, but she did not think of her life as a tragedy. One well-intended friend told Kate that this phase of her life was excruciating. Kate bristled. She was busy trying to live as well as she could with the time she had left. There was richness and beauty and poignancy. She had little desire to luxuriate in the trauma of cancer. The constant din of excruciating tragedy was not true as Kate saw it. Her life was hard, and it was glorious.

I've found this true for myself as I've walked this grief, even admitting that I'm a more melancholy and pessimistic soul than Kate ever was. Occasionally, I want someone to resonate with the grief, to speak the tragedy, but mostly I want buddies in the mountains, gentle company for dinner, visitors who have something good or useful or interesting to say. Sometimes even someone who needs the gravity of my grief to soothe their souls. I don't want pontifications or expatiations. More than anything, I am grateful for help with parenting and an expression of affection for Kate or me or the girls. There isn't a one-size-fits-all approach here; there is the sharing of our hearts.

And I think that's where shared grief points us: watching and wondering, call and response, testing the waters. And above all the awareness that we are all bound together in our shared frailty, our common tenderness. We are bound in the promise that every life will end and every mortal hope will fade into the dust. And we are bound in the covenant that, in all our grief and grievousness, we are glorious and holy, the people of heaven. ✱

TEMPTATION

ELIZABETH
PINBOROUGH

after Shane McRae's "The Hastily Assembled Angel Also Sustains the World"

Mend this moment—
Our Son is falling.

Beneath the temple's pinnacle—
the holy city's highest holy—

we wait.
On Jerusalem stone
we array
ourselves for a pause—bells, pomegranates
weight fringe to earth—

we orbit *now.*

A thrum pitches our invisible crowd
past here, past *how:*

Catch him.
Catch him, lest
he fall.

We, arms encircling (each and each),
keep expediencies, run alongside,

under, over all

that could so viciously run awry. *Catch*
him, catch him, the Son is falling.

Gather time
in intractable
knots.

Above, Messiah spars the tempter (matched
beyond match), to sieve errors in reason,

stay execution—

a while yet. Not long ago, He passed
planets in the dash to womb's

throne, passed
continents and
ages,

to meet the meridian, to suture
the center point of history to His

own body—

to stitch the cracked veil with lily stems.
He weighs salvation against the cost

of bread *now,*
riches, then
power.

Wayfarer, wayfarer, do you behold
twin paths—bearing kings' scepters

or riding a Passover ass?

After forty days, Imagination is ravenous
for bread. Wrath would taste of grain

tumbled by a mill
stone, dirt-ground
bread.

Waiting is manna. Wings sieve currents,
wake air above, beneath. Light lathes our

circumference,

slippers on stone, heads upturned to
the plunge. He feels the heft, a gold

orb in one hand,
baptismal
dove
in the other, feathered covenant—
chimes, wings, an intelligence to

spell the devil

of his tricks. *Behold, my beloved Son,*
echoes down—mercy unwinds.

Get thee behind me—
a quantum moment
when sight
writes the end—when script becomes
scripture. Still, we none of us look

away—

Not one of us
looks away.

KALEIDOSCOPES OF MEMORY

Finding God in Broken Things

MEGAN ARMKNECHT

". . . History may be servitude,
History may be freedom. See, now they vanish,
The faces and places, with the self which,
as it could, loved them,
To become renewed, transfigured,
in another pattern."
–T. S. Eliot, "Little Gidding," from Four Quartets

THE AUTUMNAL CHILL WENDS its way up the dilapidated stairwell, following us through the darkened doorframe and into our Soviet-era apartment. We strip off our galoshes, raincoats, and gloves. We laugh as we talk about a funny interaction that morning. We had both been scolded by a Ukrainian babushka—me, more particularly—for the infraction of not properly wearing hats.

Why is she not wearing a hat? the wrinkled woman had asked me, pointing at my companion. *It is for her health and you are the older one—why isn't she wearing a hat?*

I had shrugged—She doesn't want to, I had replied. How was I to force someone to wear a hat?

"I just don't like hats," my companion says nonchalantly, as we move into the kitchen to heat water. A rainy November morning requires herbal tea.

The kitchen, like most of the apartment, is old. How old, we are not sure, not by historical nor by mission age. One of our neighbors says that this block of apartments stood before World War II. When we see him in the *dvor,* in the apartment courtyard, he regales us with stories of his grandmother—how she survived the Nazi occupation, how this small corner of eastern Ukraine was full of death, destruction, and life.

My companion exits the kitchen momentarily to go to our bedroom to grab milk, where, strangely, the refrigerator rests by my headboard. Who made the decision to put the refrigerator in the bedroom, I will never know, but there it stands, making our bedroom an odd extension of the kitchen, home to both bagged dairy products and morning prayers.

This apartment is both in and out of time, with and without history. I only know the missionaries who came right before us—two elders who had written detailed "whitewash" notes before they were transferred out of this area and moved on to other fields.

And perhaps the term *whitewash* is apt. With no one to tell of beforetimes, we are free to make our own stories, our own history here. We are the first sister missionaries to live in this apartment,

Artem Rohovyi

to use this kitchen with its frosted window looking out over a road named after a revolution, leading to the prison. This is my companion's first area, her first apartment—the beginning of her story, full of possibilities. For both of us, it is a new city—a new start. As the first sister missionaries here, in a strange way, it feels like we are the first women to ever live in this apartment, which of course cannot be true, can it? But in the golden autumn light, we feel like the only ones, disconnected from the larger past, while preparing breakfast together in a small corner in eastern Ukraine.

Zion is the "pure in heart," but my heart is far from pure, however willing. My willpower proves powerless against the contradictory desires of my own heart, let alone against bridging the chasms which divide human experience.

And still, this space contains multitudes—more than I can recognize as I sit down at the kitchen table, turn on the CD player, the Mormon Tabernacle Choir intoning softly. The cupboards are full of missionaries past: of ranch dressing packets and taco seasoning from thoughtful Cache Valley mothers, of Taylor Swift calendars, of *Ensign* cutouts of a blond, European-looking Jesus posted onto the wall . . . walls which once-upon-a-time might have held a portrait of Lenin or Stalin, or else listened in as trusted confidantes ridiculed Brezhnev while sharing the literature of dissent with a side of kvas and shelled sunflower seeds.

My companion and I work in the kitchen, lost in our own narratives and crafting narratives for those we try to serve. Will Tomara agree to read the Book of Mormon? Will Lena finally answer our phone calls? Will Sasha come to church? Mornings in the kitchen are for hope—two American girls, far from home, happy in their companionship and dreaming of miracles, dreaming of Zion in this eastern land. How will Zion be built? We are not exactly sure, but we believe the promise that willing hearts prosper in Zion.[1] If we are anything, we are willing.

Not all mission mornings are like this. They simply cannot be. Another companion of mine frequently recited the mantra "It won't always be like this" to remind me that even bad times end. My own experiences as a missionary testified of ups and downs: of wounds inflicted by other missionaries, of crippling homesickness, and of disappointment after disappointment; but also of generosity, of good Ukrainian Saints wiping tears away from my eyes, of golden fields of Ukrainian sunflowers against a striking blue.

It won't always be like this; nothing lasts forever.

The leftover missionary paraphernalia we discover while cleaning out dusty drawers also speak of this almost Newtonian law: *Elder,* penned one missionary to another,

> *I know you're having a hard time, but just hold on. And remember these lines from Jimmy Eat World:*
>
> *"It just takes some time*
> *You're in the middle of the ride,*
> *Everything, everything will be just fine*
> *Everything, everything will be alright, alright."*
>
> *Love you, man.*

Finding the note feels like trespassing. I know both elders (though I do not know when or even if they served here . . . perhaps this was a note left behind during a missionary exchange). I know their reputations, whether good or bad. But the note softens me. It was written to a missionary who had, months ago, hurt me. A missionary who I felt had turned a blind eye to how my then-companions bullied me. I still cannot forget what happened that summer, and I am not ready to forgive, but something shifts inside of me, and for a moment, I see him not as an antagonist, but as a fellow wandering, hurting soul. I put the note down, embarrassed to infringe on this offering of friendship and afraid to delve into my own fears.

How will Zion be built? Again and again, the Lord says that Zion is the "pure in heart," but my heart is far from pure, however willing.[2] My willpower proves powerless against the contradictory desires of my own heart, let alone against bridging the chasms which divide human experience.

Theoretically, aspiring to the ways of the citizens of Enoch's city inspires me to understand the poetry inside of others, to see them as my brothers and sisters rather than strangers or enemies. In reality, I balk at throwing away my weapons of war. My own avarice, others' pride, and the ignorance which blinds us all mock the promise of Zion.

And yet, and yet. I still receive glimpses that unity and love are possible. I find them unexpectedly: in a letter not addressed to me, in a November morning in Kharkiv, Ukraine, in a kind word on the street: "I am not interested, girls, but I admire you for being here, all the same." *It won't always be like this.* So I savor the morning, trying to hold onto a moment that quickly turns into memory.

Memory and history are fickle. The moment I think I understand them, they slip out of my grasp, surprising me with their audacity, reminding me that they refuse to be owned. To assume that memory and history are fixed entities is dangerous, but it is also dangerous to ignore them, or to let someone else tell our stories for us. The stories we tell about ourselves, our nations, our families—they matter.

"History may be servitude, history may be freedom," wrote T. S. Eliot in "Little Gidding," as part of his magisterial *Four Quartets.* It is a sentiment which resonates within me for reasons beyond my understanding, something I feel more than I know how to explain. Perhaps it is because of my own history, of seeing how the stories I tell myself can blind me to or remind me of responsibilities to those around me; perhaps it is because of a personal belief that we cannot change the future unless we confront the past.

Years after sitting in that kitchen in Kharkiv, I will sit with a man (a man who will become my husband) and watch a Chilean film, *Nostalgia de la Luz* (*Nostalgia for the Light*), about the varied searches for truth in the Atacama Desert: the search for the mysteries of the cosmos in the desert sky, and the search that mothers, wives, and sisters undertake, looking for the remains of disappeared, assassinated loved ones in the desert ground.

Artem Rohovyi

"The light we see from the stars is actually hundreds of years old," explains a Chilean astronomer. "The light we see is already past. The present is so brief. Blink, and it disappears."[3]

The light we see is already past. Memory is alive, pulsing through us, connecting the present to the past, but also decomposing the second we blink away from the present. History interprets what is left from the past, analyzing the memories of others, trying to explain patterns, processes, and change over time. *History may be servitude, history may be freedom.*

Right now, the present filters my memories of Ukraine. I cannot think of that sunny kitchen in Kharkiv without wondering if it, too, has been destroyed. I remember the people of Makiivka,

Artem Rohovyi

of Kharkiv, of Donetsk, and Mariupol, the kerchiefed *babushki,* the smiling families, the coal-stained miners, the faces I knew and the ones I did not, and I wonder what has happened to them—wonder what is happening to them.

I cannot remember walking through the spring streets of Mariupol without seeing them now—destroyed, bombed out, kitchens cut in half. My memories are like a children's science book with transparent pages stacked on top of each other, the better to see the inner workings of a clock or the functions of the human body systems. The last page shows simply a skeleton, but add the next-to-last transparent page on top of the skeleton, and you see the nervous system. Add the next, and you see the organs, until page by page, you arrive at the beginning, with a picture of a smiling child, kicking a soccer ball.

Now, I see the skeletons. I see the bare bones of apartments, I see demolished maternity hospitals. But go back, and I can see myself on those streets, in those apartments, with those people. Go back further, and I can imagine those streets during the Soviet Union under Nazi occupation. Go back further, and they are no longer streets, but fields. How does God hold the past, present, and future simultaneously before Him, like a river of glass? And how does He hold the hurt we inflict on each other, on ourselves?

I cannot hold it all, but I do have glimpses. I see it as my own memories spread before me, painted with brushstrokes of past, present, and future; I feel it as my remembrances of places and people I used to love, as my past and present experiences with them. My hopes and fears for the future transfigure and renew their faces.[4] I remember a moment at Little Gidding, the very parish which inspired T. S. Eliot's musings on time, memory, loss, and love. For an afternoon, I traveled with Sam (the man with whom I had watched *Nostalgia for the Light*) and his good friend Neil through the summered English countryside.

Sam and I were not yet engaged, but very much in love, and eager to share beloved memories and places with each other and create new memories in those beloved places. Cambridge, England, was one of those places for both of us, and a place that Sam wanted to introduce to Neil. I sat in the backseat as we drove from Oxford to Cambridge, listening to Neil muse about resurrection, watching the fields shift between gold and green.

We took a detour to Little Gidding, a village in Cambridgeshire with a small Anglican chapel. This chapel had served as a muse to many poets, and we passed that way because of what we had read, and what we had felt as we read.

The oak-paneled walls of the chapel gave a rosy feel as the June sunlight pierced through the stained-glass windows. A hush came over our conversation as we read embroidered transcriptions of poems and epitaphs:

> *You are not here to verify,*
> *Instruct yourself, or inform curiosity*
> *Or carry report. You are here to kneel*
> *Where prayer has been valid.*[5]

We stood in a holy place, a place where our prayers mingled with the prayers and supplications of countless others throughout the ages, from wandering kings to determined tourists. This place was not only holy because of the past, but because we, ourselves, living and breathing, with bonds of friendship and love stood in that place with our own hopes, fears, and dreams. We stood in a place of timeless moments, within walls which had witnessed both transcendence and banality.

Later, the three of us took a carefully crafted selfie outside of the chapel, trying to create a memento, trying to hold onto the present already slipping away. I could not know then what the future held. I could hope that I would marry the man who had his arm around me, but I did not know what specific joys and sorrows would follow us; I did not know that that summer would be the last time I would see Neil in person; I did not know how to love either of them the way their souls deserve. I loved them as much as I could at that moment, and I hope I love them more now.

Again, I turn the page of my book of recollections to Ukraine (a place which materializes often in my kaleidoscope of memory), to a place I loved as I was able in the moments I lived there, to a place I hope I love more even now. If I open to a specific page in the summer of 2012, I find a five-story Soviet apartment building, most likely built during the time of Khrushchev. If I open the next translucent page, I see myself there, a twenty-one-year-old missionary, sunburned, flea-bitten, and deeply sad, kneeling in a dusty Soviet kitchen, with July sun streaming through floral curtains, crying out to God in despair and brokenness, feeling the impossibility of serving a mission, of finding God in faces made both familiar and unfamiliar.

And though one might not see the change from that page, I know what I felt that day, broken and worn, carrying a weight of sorrows and expectations. I know the song I heard, whispered through mountain canyons, across the Atlantic Ocean, over sunset plains, into a post-industrial Ukrainian city, the words which filled a missionary's heart with the awareness of God: that God loves broken things, broken people, broken me, that He is the lover of souls, the comforter of Zion, and the healer of her lonely, wasted places.[6] ✸

1. See Doctrine and Covenants 64:34.
2. Doctrine and Covenants 97:21.
3. *Nostalgia de la luz (Nostalgia for the Light)*, 2010, directed by Patricio Guzmán. This quote is a paraphrase of what the astronomer said; it is how I remember it.
4. See T. S. Eliot, "Little Gidding," lines quoted in the epigraph.
5. T. S. Eliot, "Little Gidding."
6. See Isaiah 51:3: "For the LORD shall comfort Zion: he will comfort all her waste places, and he will make her wilderness like Eden, and her desert like the garden of the LORD; joy and gladness shall be found therein, thanksgiving, and the voice of melody."

Joseph Discovers the Plates

ANNIE POON

BUYING JEWISH WHISKEY

NATHAN B. OMAN

IN A LOVELY SPRING GARDEN IN suburban Philadelphia, I handed cash and a handkerchief to my friend's rabbi. It was the first time that I, an observant Latter-day Saint, had ever purchased whiskey. For the next two weeks, however, I would own a large store of booze, along with a number of half-used boxes of breakfast, and a lease on a very nice apartment in Jerusalem. At the suggestion of my friend Chaim Saiman, I had agreed to act as a friendly Gentile, purchasing the unused chometz (leavened foodstuffs) and its storage locations that the members of his synagogue were prohibited from owning during Passover. At the conclusion of the holiday I could, if I so chose, sell the whiskey back to its original owners.

As law professors, Chaim and I share an interest in jurisprudence, law & religion, and contracts. As observant believers, we are both fascinated by the place of religion in the secular world and the way that adherents manage the negotiation between tradition and modernity. The result has been a years-long running conversation on law, contemporary politics, faith and commerce, and, inevitably given Chaim's dual training in yeshiva and law school, halakhah, the vast corpus of Jewish law. When Chaim explained to me that at Passover it was possible to avoid the need to dispose of one's whiskey and other valuable chometz by selling it for the duration of the holiday to a Gentile, I had a new ambition. Legal scholars have long studied how parties use contracts to bargain around troublesome rules. I was fascinated by the idea of contracting around divine law. When I explained to another friend and faculty colleague why I was driving from southern Virginia to Philadelphia in the middle of the week, he said, "Law, religion, and contracts. It's like a religious ritual specifically designed for Nate Oman."

As I understand it, the legal basis for my trip to the Pennsylvania garden begins with Exodus 12, which describes the first Passover and sets forth the rules to be followed thereafter. In verse 15, the text reads, "Seven days you shall eat unleavened bread. On the first day you shall remove leaven out of your houses, for if anyone eats what is leavened, from the first day until the seventh day, that person shall be cut off from Israel." The exposition of this rule in Jewish law begins with the earliest halakhic text, the second-century CE compilation known as the Mishnah. The rabbinic debates recorded there explore the contours of the rule in Exodus. To ensure compliance, the house must be scoured for chometz with a candle, and all leavened products burned. To deal with any residual chometz, one must go through the legal ritual of disclaiming ownership, declaring that the chometz is now dust and therefore owned by no one. The debates in the Mishnah were then subject to further commentary and debate in the Talmud. The Talmud in turn has been continuously analyzed and systematized, such as in the Mishnah Torah of Maimonides, a process that continues unabated to the present. When must the ritual search for chometz begin? What constitutes chometz? (For example, alcohol distilled from grain was brought within the prohibition.) And so on, a thousand debates on each issue over the centuries. As I understand it, the well-established consensus among Orthodox exegetes is that an observant Jew is not allowed to own any chometz during Passover, nor can chometz be stored on the property of a Jew. Centuries ago, however, a problem arose for Jewish distillers. They owned large amounts of chometz, but government regulations made it difficult to simply destroy their stock for Passover. Thus was the workaround of the sale to a friendly Gentile born, a workaround gradually expanded to all of those who wished to avoid burning valuable chometz every spring.

While seemingly baroque to a nonbeliever, the layering of these rules over the centuries illustrates a basic structure of the religious condition.

THE
BOOK
OF
MORMON

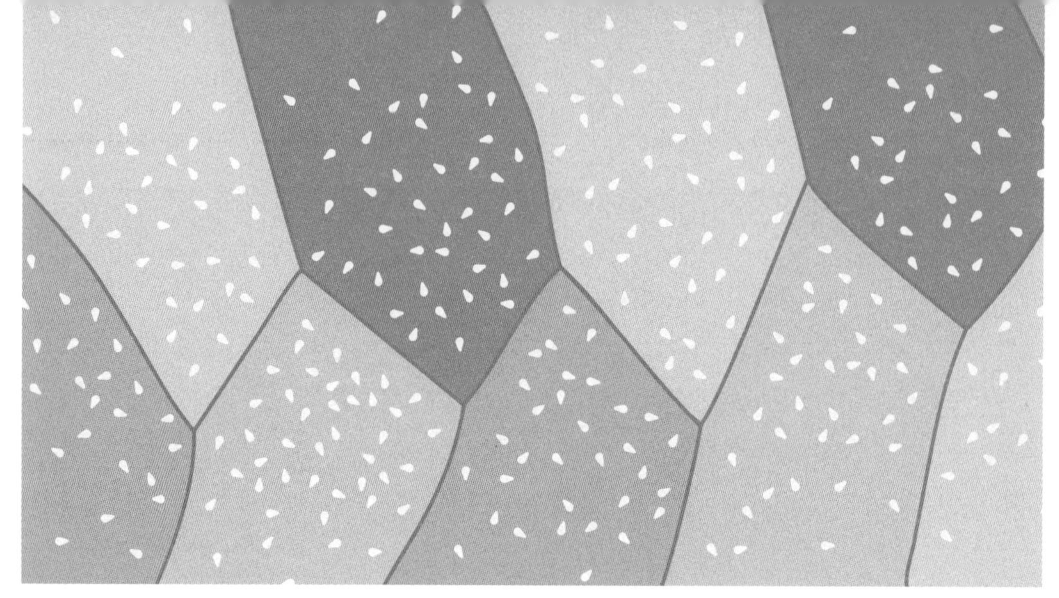

Hannah Wilson

To be a believer in the modern world is to live in a strange land. It is not that modernity is relentlessly hostile to faith. It is far easier for minority religious communities to live faithfully in contemporary liberal democracies than in any other kind of regime in human history. Our society, however, is not constructed around religious faith. As the Catholic philosopher Charles Taylor has pointed out, secularity isn't so much a society from which faith has been extracted as one in which faith is optional. Within secularity, faith is contingent in a way that it wasn't for previous generations both because of social pressure to religiously conform and because, in a real sense, a life without faith was unthinkable. Most people simply lacked the necessary conceptual machinery to consider a world without the God of their fathers. Secularity is the loss of that sense of necessity and the construction of a social world that aspires to be indifferent to religion. A believer, however, lives in a world where the reality of God continues to sit at the center of existence. The mismatch of the world of belief and the world of secularity constitutes the experience of faith in modernity.

Jewish law provides a marvelous example of this dynamic. Every legal system creates an imaginary world. The common law, for example, imagines a world divided by clear lines of property and planted thick with the obligations of tort and contract. The world in which we actually live never quite corresponds to the law's imagined reality. Legal remedies strive mightily to bring the two into alignment, but good lawyers understand that this effort will always fail in the end. There will always be a gap between legal entitlement and what the legal system can actually deliver as a practical matter. The halakhah is a particularly extreme version of this dynamic. To study the Mishnah and the Talmud is to enter into an at times fantastical jurisprudential world. In this world, the Temple continues to stand in Jerusalem, and pious Jews bring their offerings to the priests to perform the sacrificial rituals. The land is dotted with sanctuary cities and other legal oddities. The Sanhedrin continues to sit and the intricacies of its procedures mete out justice to Israel. All of these laws continue to be studied in exhaustive detail in modern yeshivas.

To call the world of Jewish law imaginary or fantastical is not, I hope, to insult or belittle it in any way. It is only to point out the way that the halakhah creates an entire world whose existence would be unguessed at by a foreigner to the legal texts. However, after a lifetime of devotional Talmud study, it is a world that lawyers and hedge fund managers in suburban Philadelphia, members in good standing of America's technocratic elite, can enter with ease.

The life of Orthodox Judaism in part seems to be an effort to inhabit the world of halakhah in the face of a social world that is very different from the one envisioned by the law. Part of how one does this is simply by studying, discussing, and debating the law. Indeed there is a real sense in which much of the halakhah exists in order to be studied. For anyone who has even a passing familiarity with a functioning legal system, it is clear that much of Jewish law exists as a vehicle for jurisprudential discussion rather than as a system of operative rules. But the halakhic world isn't inhabited purely through classroom debate. One also enters that world by following those rules of Jewish law that have been blessed by tradition and experience with concrete practical significance. Indeed, as I understand it, much of the work of response and commentary over the two millennia since the Mishnah was first written has been an effort to mediate and manage the tension of living in both the concrete world of any particular historical moment and the world of halakhah simultaneously. In other words, as a living practice halakhah is a way of being a Jew in a world where being Jewish is optional. There is thus a sense in which Orthodox Judaism, far from being an insular or reactionary retreat from secularity, represents a kind of virtuoso performance of faith in a secular world. Indeed, Jews have been living in a secular world, in Taylor's sense, for far longer than Christians. They are better at it. They have more experience.

I think that this kind of performance is on display in the effort to bargain around God's law. There is a temptation for both believers and critics to imagine faithfulness in fundamentalist terms. There is some pristine original template for living the faithful life, and "real" religion consists of unbending adherence to its strictures. Such fundamentalism, however, is an illusion. The pristine template never actually existed, it is always a past constructed after the fact with the troublesome bits excised from memory. More importantly, fidelity is always dynamic, a matter of managing allegiance to an evolving tradition that is continually both resisting and accommodating the world. Even those who purport to be following a fundamentalist path are doing this. The question for a believer is thus always how does one adapt a tradition while accepting its authority and maintaining fidelity to it.

One can think about this question by analogy to the process of legal change. The great nineteenth-century jurist and historian Henry Sumner Maine claimed that legal systems change in one of three ways: by legislation, by equity, and by fiction. Legislation is an idea familiar to laypersons, but equity and fiction in the legal context have specific meanings. Equity refers to a loose interpretation of a rule in order to achieve substantial justice. Fiction refers to the process of adapting legal rules by agreeing to pretend that their conditions have been met when in fact they have not. Good Victorian that he was, Maine thought in terms of progress with fiction being the most primitive form of legal change and legislation representing the most advanced stage. Like most Victorian narratives of progress, this one doesn't hold up terribly well to scrutiny, but Maine was on to something in his taxonomy. These are, in fact, the ways in which legal systems change in practice. Applied to divine law, however, the tool kit can become fraught.

Christians are generally fond of equity. They purport to look beyond the surface of rules to see their inner spirit, a spirit that can be applied with considerable flexibility. Hence, Christians read the Hebrew Bible through the lens of Paul's hyper-abstraction in which the true "spirit" of the rule can be its negation. To take an extreme example, Paul argues in his epistles that the true spirit of circumcision consists in not being circumcised. This allows for flexibility, to be sure, but one can understand the skepticism of a Jewish reader as to whether Paul is in fact being true to the law revealed on Sinai. Indeed, one of the vices of Christian spirituality is its tendency to abstract from tradition. All historical contingency falls away in the search for a transcendent and universal spirit. This creates a constant risk of self-negation. I suspect that this is especially true for the kind of Evangelical Protestantism that dominates much of American Christianity. Essentially Calvinist in its theology, American Evangelicalism often emphasizes spirit over law and the personal, subjective experience of being saved over the demands of liturgy or strict behavioral codes. This subjective focus can risk a drift toward a stance of "spiritual but not religious." A certain numinous psychology can replace theology, and the language of therapy and self-help can eclipse the drama of sin and repentance.

Mormonism presents a similar danger of self-negation, but it does so through religious legislation rather than equity. Latter-day Saints are marked as heretics from Christian orthodoxy in

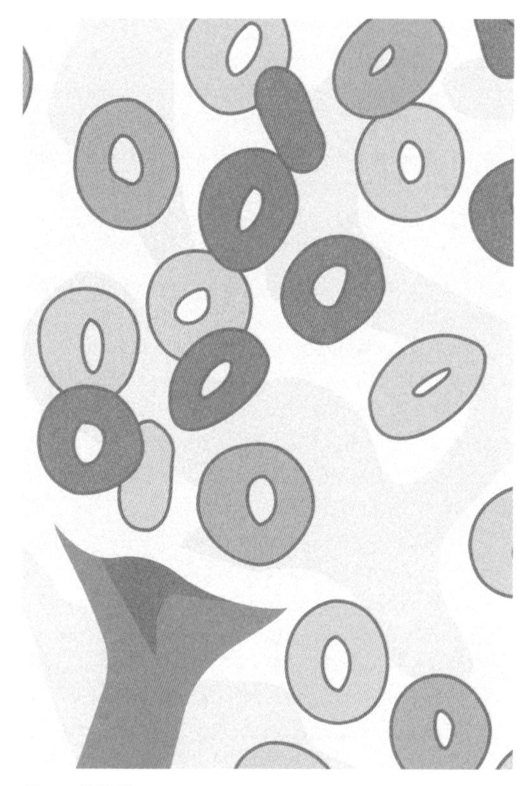

Hannah Wilson

part by their belief in living prophets and continuing revelation. The idea of a hierarchy that can speak with God and speak for God opens up the possibility of religious legislation in a way that doesn't exist, I suspect, for most Christians and Jews. To be sure, the hierarchy's claims to such expansive authority risks abuse, and a God who replaces one revealed law with another revealed law may be puzzling. If one risks the paradox of an eternal God whose demands can change, however, the mechanics of religious accommodation, even religious revolution, become easier.

The approach taken by my tradition has its own risks and pitfalls. On one hand, it can tend toward a dysfunctionally expansive fundamentalism in which every statement of the ecclesiastical hierarchy or institutional church becomes freighted with the authority of divine revelation. The result is that a belief that would seem to promise an unusually dynamic form of religion can, in practice, become rigidly conservative and sclerotic. Ironically, however, an opposite danger also exists. Continuing revelation locates the present between a past filled with revelations that have been superseded and a future filled with revelations that have yet to be given. This creates a dynamic that has a tendency to dissolve all religious claims in the present, particularly religious claims embedded with the concrete experience of the Latter-day Saints themselves. Thus what begins as an apparently extreme claim to authority can ironically turn on itself with the authority of the future claimed against the authority of the present by invoking the example of the past.

Armed with an appreciation for the dangers of equity and legislation, legal fiction looks more attractive. The rabbi to whom I conveyed the cash in exchange for the chometz insisted on the juridical reality of our transactions. The moment was embedded in a series of legal formalities designed to emphasize the complete transfer of the chometz to my ownership. I was assured that I had every right to take and consume the whiskey if I wished to do so. He made it clear, for example, that I had the right to enter the Jewish homes whose pantries I had leased and make off with my Cheerios and booze. The exchange was structured as both a cash sale and a bartered exchange (handkerchief for whiskey) to eliminate any difficulties under Jewish law as to my ownership. It turns out there is some doubt as to how to make a binding contract with a Gentile, and the redundant contractual structures were a response to that ambiguity.

I was also told that for the transactions to be valid as a matter of halakhah, it must also be valid under the governing non-Jewish law. Accordingly, I signed a document that purported to be a sale of goods under Pennsylvania law. On this latter point, I will admit to some skepticism. Despite Chaim's diligent lawyering, title to the chometz may have remained with the original owners under Pennsylvania law. Our mutual understanding of the deal looked much more like a lease or a secured loan than a sale. While we were careful not to say so, it was understood by all present that I would be selling the chometz back at the end of Passover. There is a long legal tradition of using dummy sales for transactional purposes other than the transfer of property. Perhaps I was really just renting the chometz for a short period or, alternatively, making a small cash loan with future advances secured by the chometz as collateral. Both are real possibilities under American commercial law, which tends to treat transactions according to their economic reality rather than according to the labels that parties give them. This is a potential problem, as with both a lease and a secured loan my Jewish friends would retain title to their chometz during Passover.

To be sure, there are enough doctrinal complications in the contract Chaim drafted that it might survive the acid wash of the Uniform Commercial Code's functionalism. In contract law, the parole evidence rule can cover a multitude of sins. Certainly, one could argue in good faith that the contract has enough validity under the secular law to be valid under Jewish law. Still, the entire transaction had more than a whiff of the legal fiction about it, a mass of formality designed to say that we are doing one thing while actually doing something very different.

In my mind, it is the double-mindedness of the legal fiction that is brilliant. Sitting in the suburban garden in Philadelphia, it was impossible not to feel the authority of Jewish law. Indeed, several members of the synagogue were there to witness the transaction with their children for precisely that reason. The forms and signatures literally had no other purpose than to comply with the demands laid down in Exodus. The dynamics of equity and legislation that tend to erase the very traditions from which they spring were wholly absent from the transaction. If anything, the very particularity of the legal formalities mitigated against the Christian danger of dissolving religion into spirituality. Legal formalities work precisely because they are strange and serve no purpose outside of the law. The purpose of a formality is to clearly differentiate to participants between actions that have a legal significance and those that do not. No one, for example, accidentally files a real estate deed in their local circuit court without understanding that they are performing a legal act. There is always a risk, however, of legal formalities becoming too familiar. As a legal formality becomes widely used outside of the legal context, it decays, losing the ability to differentiate between legally significant action and legally irrelevant action. In order to work, a formality must be weird. When the law at issue is divine, properly functioning legal formalities will be oddities that make it impossible to forget the claims of God. They are ritual acts that exist only to comply with divine law. At the same time, there is a sense in which the entire transaction selling the chometz existed to avoid the harsh requirements of that law. The continuity of the suburban whiskey collections were maintained. The fiction manages the problems of fidelity and evolution, allowing the tradition to change without negating itself.

There are, of course, limits to bargaining around God's commands. A law that collapses completely into fiction is terminally ill, but judiciously used legal fictions create a suppleness that allows one to bend without breaking, change without forgetting. This is precisely the challenge of secularity. A world in which religion is optional is one in which it can be forgotten. The threat to religious survival in secularity is less the polemics of the irreligious than the indifference of those who have forgotten how to be religious.

The danger of Christian or Mormon strategies of evolution is that they lend themselves to forgetting. Protestant Christianity can exalt a subjective encounter with the spirit in a way that can all too easily dissolve into subjectivism. The idea of continuing revelation, on the other hand, tends to render every Latter-day Saint claim to authority contingent, gnawing away at its own foundations in a way that risks the collapse of the entire tradition. There are virtues to ritual, formality, and fiction that both traditions would be wise to find ways of cultivating. The very oddity of selling Jewish whiskey to a Latter-day Saint makes the forgetting of tradition impossible. It's part of the genius for change without forgetting that has made the survival of Judaism possible in a world that for Jews has been secular since at least the destruction of the Second Temple in 70 CE. A healthy respect for and fascination with that success, along with my friendship with Chaim, led me to the garden in Pennsylvania and will, I hope, lead me to buy more Jewish whiskey in Passovers to come.

Next year in Philadelphia! ✸

"SOLAR BARQUE"
WINTER 2023

REVELATIONS OF DIVINE LOVE

Approaching Infinity with Julian of Norwich

ANNABELLE CLAWSON

I DIDN'T HAVE A STRONG REASON for visiting Norwich, England, last October. The medieval city is often overshadowed on tourists' itineraries by charming places like Oxford and Brighton. But I wanted a short getaway before beginning a master's program at the University of Cambridge, and Norwich was nearby and seemed interesting enough.

The first place I visited was the church of St. Julian, a modest pebble in comparison to the mountainous Norwich Cathedral. Unlike the other churches dotting the city center that boasted towering spires, intimidating stone, and intricate ceiling carvings, the church of St. Julian was unassuming. In a word, it was quaint: cobblestone walls beneath neat rows of shingles, sloping predictably in an inverted "V," and small windows of unstained glass.

Inside, I found a small chapel with a capacity for maybe fifty people, plain white walls, and an altar draped in forest-green velvet. On a table near the entrance was a stack of paper, hand-cut into strips not unlike the quotes I'm sometimes asked to read aloud in Relief Society. I took one, reading the following:

> In this vision he showed me a little thing, the size of a hazelnut, and it was round as a ball. I looked at it with the eye of my understanding and thought, "What may this be?" And it was generally answered thus: "It is all that is made." I marveled how it might last, for it seemed it might suddenly have sunk into nothing because of its littleness. And I was answered in my understanding: "It lasts and ever shall, because God loves it."

The words were attributed to Julian of Norwich, a fourteenth-century mystic and anchoress at the church of St. Julian. Her real name is unknown, so she is typically referred to by the church's name. As an anchoress, she lived a portion of her life (at least twenty-two years, according to scattered surviving sources) "anchored" to the church in prayerful solitude. She lived in a small cell attached to the nave, from which she never emerged—although a tiny window about the size of a mail slot allowed her to watch mass and receive the eucharist. A servant would have brought her food each day. Perhaps in her

Lisa De Long

cell there was a window to the outside world where she received visitors.

The church I was standing in was not the same church in which Julian lived over six hundred years ago. Her cell was destroyed sometime in the sixteenth century, and the remainder of the church gradually met the same fate. Through the centuries, walls and windows crumbled, collapsed, and were reconstructed; a bell was fashioned on the church's tower; and different elements of the building were repaired in isolated restoration projects. During World War II, the church was bombed and destroyed, necessitating a complete rebuild. Nevertheless, I felt a deep sense of the sacred in that humble patchwork church.

VISIONS IN THE WILDERNESS

This wasn't the first time I had encountered Julian of Norwich. Two years previously, I had read her work in a medieval literature course at BYU. Her *Revelations of Divine Love* is a record of sixteen powerful visions that she had when she was about thirty years old.[1] The visions occurred one after the other on a night when she was awfully ill. Once she recovered, Julian recorded her visions, which she called "shewings," in what is now called the "short text." Undoubtedly, her occupation as an anchoress compelled her to meditate and expound upon her visions—two decades later, she produced the "long text," a more meticulous version of what she had composed previously, with extensive theological commentary. The short and long texts together became the *Revelations of Divine Love.*

My first impression of Julian of Norwich was somewhere between awe and incredulity. I found that her visions shared common elements with other familiar theophanies: like Nephi, she saw the Virgin Mary and the crucified Jesus; like Moses and Joseph Smith, she struggled against the devil; and like Alma the Younger, she was transformed by God's immense mercy. Her *Revelations* are flooded with unapologetic declarations of a God who endlessly loves us. And Julian, like other prophets in and out of the scriptures, felt an urgency to share the things she saw (and it's a good thing she did—hers is the earliest surviving work in English written by a woman!).

Julian's words were a cascade of truth that profoundly resonated with me. But as pleasantly startled as I was by her *Revelations,* my mind seemed to slide into questions about their legitimacy. I knew these questions didn't stem from how her words settled in my heart—I was inspired and enlightened by her visions—but rather how they seemed to stir things up in my mind. Julian lived during what Latter-day Saints call the Great Apostasy. Then how could she have seen Jesus and spoken with God? Better yet, how could she have so eloquently described a vision of three heavens, a doctrine I believed was unique to my faith? I even felt some discomfort about her gender. Nowhere in any of my religious studies had I learned of a woman who had prophetic visions to this extent. Would it be a greater blasphemy to call her a prophetess or to deny the palpable prophetic quality of her writings? I wanted to believe Julian, and I also wanted to believe in an apostasy. I just didn't know how. So, unsure how to proceed, I placed this cognitive dissonance on a high shelf in the corner of my mind, among other Questions I Will Ask God One Day, and forgot about it.

An answer snuck up on me about eighteen months later while reading Fiona and Terryl Givens's book *All Things New: Rethinking Sin, Salvation, and Everything in Between.* After highlighting several prophetic figures who lived after Jesus and before Joseph Smith (including Julian of Norwich), they suggest that we soften our definition of apostasy "from total eclipse to wilderness refuge."[2] Perhaps it's better to think of the apostasy as a period of time in which the Church was "in the wilderness" and the Restoration as the process by which the Church is gathered and brought out of exile. In this line of thinking, the Restoration didn't reinstate something that had been wiped off the face of the earth; rather, it brought the Church out of the wilderness, picking up pieces, filling in gaps, and recontextualizing gospel truths.

This reframing allowed me to reconcile Julian's *Revelations of Divine Love* with the Great

Apostasy in a productive way, strengthening my belief in both. When I returned to Julian a second time in Norwich, I felt a surprising connection to her. A reverence. Whatever had kept me from fully appreciating her work before had since evaporated. This time, her *Revelations* struck me with greater force, urging my spirit in new directions.

AT THE FOOT OF THE CROSS

I ducked under the Romanesque door to enter Julian's reconstructed cell. It was as plain as the church, with a simple altar beneath a wooden carving of Jesus on the cross. On one wall, the closest to the nave, was a shrine dedicated to Julian where visitors could light candles in tribute to her. Above the shrine was a stained-glass window depicting Julian kneeling beneath a crucified Jesus. At the time, I understood the image to be a metaphor capturing Julian's devotion. Only after I purchased a copy of her *Revelations* on my way out of the church—with the intention to read them more thoughtfully than I had in my busy BYU years—did the nearly literal meaning of the stained-glass image become clear to me.

In her *Revelations,* Julian witnesses Jesus's crucifixion and death as if she were present on that devastating Friday two thousand years ago. The excruciating detail in which she relates the Passion is perhaps the most evocative element

Lisa De Long

Lisa De Long

of her work, including her striking descriptions of Jesus's broken body—"the sweet skin and the tender flesh, with the hair and the blood, was all raised and loosened from the bone, and where the thorn tore open the flesh in many places, it looked like a cloth that was sagging, as if it would soon have fallen off"[3]—and his bleeding head—"The great drops of blood poured down in globules from under the garland, seemingly from the veins; and in their coming out they were brown-red, for the blood was very thick; and in their spreading out they were bright red."[4]

In my Latter-day Saint upbringing I had never encountered such uncomfortably realistic descriptions of the crucifixion. I wanted to skip over them in embarrassment and focus more on abstract theological discussions. But Julian saw a purpose, even a necessity, in observing these "horrifying and dreadful, yet sweet and lovely"[5] images from the foot of the cross: all who seek redemption must understand the Savior's suffering and death wholly and intimately. Like other devotional texts of the late medieval period, rife with graphic depictions of the crucifixion, Julian's *Revelations* invites people to experience the infinitude of the Passion.[6]

In the Book of Mormon, Amulek teaches that "there can be nothing which is short of an infinite atonement which will suffice for the sins of the world" (Alma 34:12). Associating the Atonement with infinity can help us better understand the scope of Jesus's redemption and salvation. Infinity cannot be encompassed within a mortal form, neither can it be beheld with mortal eyes. Yet, Jesus suffered the Passion in his mortal body: "how sore you know not, how exquisite you know not, yea, how hard to bear you know not" (Doctrine and Covenants 19:15).

But there must be some way that we can represent this suffering, however clumsily or inefficiently—some way to evoke infinity in a manner that moves us. Otherwise, we are left with a minimized notion of infinity, rendered two-dimensional in our sheer inability to understand it. In describing the indescribable—the infinite sacrifice of the finite, human Jesus—Julian's morbid narrative gives a taste of what infinity entails. This illuminates an essential truth: Jesus is the bridge between the finite and infinite, between mortality and immortality, and between corruption and incorruption (see 1 Corinthians 15:53–55). Julian writes that we must journey onto an infinite plane in order to fathom how much Jesus loves us:

> I saw in truth that as often as he could die, so often he would . . . truly the number of times was more than I could grasp or imagine, and even my mind could not comprehend it at any level . . . But to die out of love for me so often that the extent surpasses man's reason, that is the highest gift that our Lord God could make to man's soul.[7]

It is in the infinity of the Atonement of Jesus Christ, and the utter incomprehension of his sacrifice, that we comprehend his love for us. At the foot of the cross, all children of God can "eternally marvel at this high, surpassing, inestimable love that almighty God has for us."[8] His infinite suffering and infinite love are not mutually exclusive: To behold his suffering is to behold his love.

Julian wasn't there that day at Calvary, rubbing shoulders with the Virgin Mary, Mary Magdalene, and other disciples of Jesus. But she didn't need to be there. An infinite Atonement means that none of us need to be there to experience divine love. At the same time, an infinite Atonement means that all of us need to go there, spiritually, at some point—not to gain divine approval but to discover a forgiveness that has always been there. Julian's *Revelations* prompted me to imagine, for the first time, what it truly would have been like to be there. To "view his death" (Jacob 1:8) in its most gruesome and realistic form. To place myself among the few who stayed near and watched his life drain out of him that night. It may be impossible to comprehend the infinitude of the Passion, but Julian took me closer to infinity than anyone else.

"I SHALL DO NOTHING BUT SIN"

I quietly left Julian's cell, wandering back to the table near the entrance of the church. I took a copy of *Revelations of Divine Love* available for purchase and found a seat in the nave, thumbing through the pages. For twenty minutes, I opened to random sections, reading a few pages before flipping someplace else while other visitors milled about the tiny church, taking pictures by the altar and sauntering into Julian's cell.

In Julian's twelfth revelation, she says, "I often wondered why by the great foreseeing wisdom of God the beginning of sin was not prevented: for then, I thought, all should have been well." Bear in mind that Julian has just witnessed in vision Jesus's crucifixion and death, an experience so visceral that she deemed it the worst pain she's ever felt. Thus, this question about the necessity of sin isn't just about sin as a barrier between humanity and God; it's also about sin as the currency with which Jesus's suffering is measured. In other words, why couldn't we have just not sinned so Jesus didn't need to atone for all of us?

God's answer to Julian speaks volumes in its simplicity: "It is necessary that there should be sin; but all shall be well, and all shall be well, and all manner of thing shall be well." In this response, God's saying, "Don't worry too much about sin or the state of your soul. In the end, everything will be okay. I'm going to take care of you. You will be with me." This "all shall be well" refrain shows up consistently throughout Julian's Revelations.

One of the most beloved Book of Mormon scriptures is 2 Nephi 2:25: "Adam fell that men might be; and men are, that they might have joy." It's a catchy, feel-good passage teaching that Eve and Adam's fall didn't destroy God's purposes. The fall is why we're all here, and we're supposed to enjoy being here! However, too often this verse is quoted in isolation, yielding only a partial understanding of Lehi's point. If we continue into verse 26, we obtain a more complete picture: "And the Messiah cometh in the fulness of time, that he may redeem the children of men from the fall." The fall of Adam and Eve is essential for the plan of salvation, but it is not our salvation. Jesus is our salvation. Without Jesus, Adam and Eve's sin is irredeemable. Without Jesus, there is no joy.

Like Lehi, Julian discusses the Fall and the Atonement in tandem: "God's Son fell with Adam, into the depths of the Virgin's womb . . . to excuse Adam from blame in heaven and on earth." That reconciliation in heaven and earth is the testament of God's love for us: we can be free from blame not just on the day of judgment but also today. Sin makes space for redemption and carves out a capacity for joy—and we can feel that here and now. Eve and Adam understood this, noting that were it not for their transgression, they would never have known the joy of redemption—a joy which can be felt in this life

His infinite suffering and infinite love are not mutually exclusive: to behold his suffering is to behold his love.

and in eternity (Moses 5:10–11). While the fall of Eve and Adam bears eternal consequences, its effects are only temporary because of Jesus Christ: spiritual and physical death can both be overcome through him.

Julian understands her fallen state, but she is not deterred or ashamed. She says, "I shall do nothing but sin, yet my sin shall not prevent his goodness from working." This passage is powerful and beautiful, but it generates significant questions. How does someone qualify for God's blessing? Is it not true that God "cannot look upon sin with the least degree of allowance" (Doctrine and Covenants 1:31)? What does it take to be saved? At first, I thought this was some kind of divine paradox. But then I saw that it was only a misunderstanding of God's true nature. Is God's desire to save humanity sparked only by the kindling of piety? Did Saul's sin prevent God's goodness from working? What is God's goodness, if not to save us from despair, fear, pain, and sin?

Julian shifts the focus from blame and shame to hope and faith in Jesus Christ. She acknowledges that living a sinless life is impossible but stresses that God doesn't demand sinlessness. This isn't to say we are meant to remain in a state of sin, but rather to emphasize that God doesn't want us to become too preoccupied with our failures. Sin is a temporary fixture in our mortal existence, but Jesus has made a permanent dwelling in us, an eternal connection and redemption with our souls. Because of him, God's goodness is not just within reach; it's within *us*. Like the Israelites in the wilderness, we only need to turn our heads, to look and live. This suggests a reframing of reconciliation: Sin doesn't separate us from our Heavenly Parents; it only prevents us from seeing them.

But sin is still sin. It causes pain, it fills us with remorse, it complicates relationships. However, the suffering that stems from sin is not to punish us. Rather, it's to carry us to Calvary. And once we are there (and we all deserve to be there), by the immediacy and infinity of the Atonement, our pain is displaced by comfort and our sins erased. Thus, our sin-induced suffering is only temporary, a brilliant juxtaposition against Jesus's infinite grace. Paul expresses this paradox beautifully, saying, "where sin increased, grace overflowed all the more" (Romans 5:20).

Sometimes, I forget that sin is what's temporary and redemption is what's endless. I mistakenly imagine that Jesus extends forgiveness in carefully measured portions that only last until I sin again. But when I realize that "I shall do nothing but sin" and at the same time I understand the impermanence of this sinful state, then I can "sing the song of redeeming love" (Alma 5:26)—because his love is greater than my sin ever was, or ever will be.

CLOSER TO INFINITY

Although I spent a total of maybe forty minutes at the church of St. Julian, I have thought about her almost every day since then. I went home with a copy of her *Revelations of Divine Love*, which I've studied carefully over the last six months. I have also held onto that flimsy paper with the quote about the hazelnut.

If Julian's *Revelations* had one message, it would be that of God's love. Indeed, that's what she's trying to say with the hazelnut metaphor: we are so small that we can fit into the palm of God's hand, but God still loves us, and that love endows our existence with significance. Julian's *Revelations* were a call for me to simplify my faith at a time when I desperately needed to do so. In that simplification, I experienced a flood of relief simultaneous with a surge of enthusiasm—both inspired by God's love for me.

Julian's visions offered me a new perception of God. The deity she described didn't coincide with the deity of my understanding: a God who demands justice, a Savior who pays my debt, a Spirit that departs when I do wrong. Julian's Godhead was different. She spoke of a God who wants to save me, a Savior who inspires me to worship God, a Spirit that never leaves, because God's love is endless. At one point in my life, I would have shaken my head at Julian's approachable, merciful Trinity—if her characterizations were true, then salvation became too easy and sin too accessible. But at this particular point in my life, after years of faith deconstruction and religious instability, Julian's Godhead was a welcome thunderstorm in my parched spiritual landscape. ✸

1. Julian of Norwich, *Revelations of Divine Love*, ed. Yolande Clarke, trans. G. Warrack (London: Society for Promoting Christian Knowledge, 2017).
2. Fiona and Terryl Givens, *All Things New: Rethinking Sin, Salvation, and Everything in Between* (Meridian, ID: Faith Matters, 2020), 173.
3. Julian of Norwich, *Revelations of Divine Love*, 55.
4. Julian of Norwich, *Revelations of Divine Love*, 17.
5. Julian of Norwich, *Revelations of Divine Love*, 18.
6. Jennifer C. Lane, "'Come, Follow Me': The Imitation of Christ in the Later Middle Ages," in *Prelude to the Restoration: From Apostasy to the Restored Church*, ed. Steven C. Harper et al. (Salt Lake City: Deseret Book, 2004), 115–29.
7. Julian of Norwich, *Revelations of Divine Love*, 67.
8. Julian of Norwich, *Revelations of Divine Love*, 16.

PRAISE GOD WHO MADE FENCE LIZARDS

JAMES DEWEY

that twitch & shed their tails then regrow them like arroyos
in spring praise God who designed gingko trees with
leaves like Hawaiian skirts dancing praise God who
rolled iron ore nuggets & opals like eyes & crimson
jasper in sandy washes praise God who bloated rivers
that blush at sunset & sidewind like the slippery snakes
on their banks praise God who sent glacial rivers out
of icemouths churning & frothing like chocolate milk
praise God who plotted constant motion in ocean to
spit on sitka spruce & sculpt basalt arches a giant
crocodile tail trailing out to sea to praise God who
concocted this tidal river ebbing back & forth a lover
caught between hills she wants & sea she should praise
God who built this breathless pair of translucent peach
geckos scurrying above me on the ceiling to protect
my typing fingers from hungry mosquitoes hush-
buzzing praise God

MY SOCIALIST WALLPAPER

The Democratization of Design in the Age of Social Media

ADRIENNE CARDON

I FELL IN LOVE DURING A LONDON study abroad. Disappointingly, it was not with a fetching young footballer with an adorable accent and great hair. It was with a dead socialist, William Morris.

It was love at first sight. My nineteen-year-old eyes fixed upon an exquisite wallpaper hanging in the Hammersmith home of the nineteenth-century Renaissance man. Be still my heart. The pattern that wooed me, Pimpernel, is an ornate woodblock print that's been enchanting countless others since its 1876 debut. It's dazzling down to the smallest details. The tempestuous tangle of vine. A floral motif snaking its way through flowers, buoying them. The deeply rich greens and specular golds in the colorway. The texture of it, and the sheen. All of it spoke to me. I promised myself I'd someday hang it in my future home.

But when a famous Instagrammer put it in her house in 2021, suddenly, I no longer wanted it in mine.

Why did the thought of sharing this particular wallpaper put such a bitter taste in my mouth? Could I truly only find pleasure in exclusivity? And what would the man behind the design have to say about all of it?

Wallpaper is undeniably having a moment, with US sales projected to nearly double in the next five years. To the chagrin of resell-obsessed realtors nationwide, homeowners are craving a more permanent throwback to simpler times. Maybe we've realized we want the warmth of our grandmother's walls. Maybe we've had enough "sad beige." Whatever the reason, the nostalgia is real.

My wallpaper moment starts and ends with its most enduring designer, William Morris. Born in Essex in 1834, this celebrated triple-hyphenate—poet, philosopher, designer—is largely credited as the father of the arts and crafts movement, the influential design philosophy whose tenets and ethos would eventually pave the way for other twentieth-century architectural styles like the Bauhaus and prairie movements.

Our somewhat magical introduction occurred in 2003 at Kelmscott House, his former West London domicile turned museum. In its height, Kelmscott hosted all of London's movers and shakers (including playwright George Bernard Shaw, who also described the house as magical). In this century, it's an enchanting treasure trove that houses many of Morris's outputs—from

William Morris

That smoggy, coal-smudged Dickensian image you have of 1800s London? That's what Morris despised. Destitution butted up against the opulence that created it.

weavings to artistic treatises to furniture, plus a bounty of jaw-dropping wallpaper. I was a millennial kid in a Victorian candy store.

Most curiously of all, to round out his rather serried curriculum vitae, I learned Morris was an inveterate socialist, a literal poster boy for the cause. Wholly unaware at age nineteen that nineteenth-century socialism was actually fairly common, I resolved to further de-exoticize this unfamiliar political theory as I continued to consume his art.

There could be no disputation that his prints were ethereal, undisputed masterpieces, but I soon became equally intrigued by the designer himself and his theories on home and the democratization of art. It was clear to me even as a teen that my design preferences would be influenced by his works, but I could not have anticipated that his thinking about the place of art in a capitalist world would be so important in my homebuilding.

Anna Mason, a former curator at the William Morris Gallery and a leading expert on the arts and crafts movement, offers an explanation of his socialism as framed through his political agitations.

"He spoke out against the suppression of free speech, police brutality, class bias in the judicial system, the sexual exploitation of women and girls and the wanton destruction of the environment. The root of these evils, he argued, was a system driven by profit."[1]

This anti-capitalistic, anti-industrial movement of art that Morris encapsulated—what was it really all about? What did socialism mean to Morris, the philosopher? What did socialism mean to Morris, the man of letters? More curiously, how exactly did he square his deification of originality and craft with the class-busting commonality of socialism?

And selfishly, could I find vindication in his work for my petty irritation at the thought of sharing?

Born on the blistered heels of the industrial revolution, Morris eschewed mass-produced factory goods—soulless replicas without craft or beauty. He insisted life didn't have to be sordid or unattractive, as he thought modern London living had become.

"What is there in modern life for the man who seeks beauty? Nothing," Morris lamented. "The age is ugly."[2]

Morris exhibited this predilection for beauty from a very young age, often studying and sketching the flora and fauna native to his countryside village, a practice that undoubtedly would influence his future designs. Born into a wealthy family, Morris's idyllic childhood offered a stark contrast to the early industrialism of the era—a Victorian economy running at full steam, apparently with no brakes. The market's invisible hand seemed to fulfill the biblical dictum that "whosoever hath, to him shall be given, and he shall have more abundance: but whosoever hath not, from him shall be taken away even that he hath."[3]

Morris's multiplying abundance was art, and he was somewhat insulated from the social issues of city dwellers. He nurtured his love of nature, combined with an intense interest in medieval literature, well into his late childhood, mostly unaware of the inequitable evils that plagued much of his homeland. But not for long.

By the time Morris went to study at Exeter College at Oxford—where he would refine his artistic talents and ignite a passion for political theory—John Stuart Mill had already published *Principles of Political Economy.* Charles Dickens was busy turning out novels that pointedly critiqued the huge gap between the wealthy (like the Morris family, whose fortune came from copper mining) and the poor (those who were doing the mining).

Morris proved an eager student and quickly became an admirer of political writers like John

Ruskin and Christian socialist Charles Kingsley. As he continued to learn about the horrifying conditions of many laborers, his art began to entwine with his burgeoning politics.

"Art cannot have real life and growth under the present system of commercialism and profit-mongering," Morris declared.[4] "The contrasts of rich and poor are unendurable. Feeling this, I am bound to act for the destruction of the system which seems to me mere oppression."[5]

Though he despised the rampant inequality of his time, his political leanings were ultimately swayed as he considered that industrial life was appalling not only on moral grounds but also on artistic ones.

That smoggy, coal-smudged Dickensian image you have of 1800s London? That's what Morris despised. Destitution butted up against the opulence that created it. A society sick with its own glut.

London had become a sore for sighted eyes.

Dark, dingy, and unsafe factories were altogether inhumane—and the inferior products they churned out were proof of it.

"Will you not be bewildered, as I am," Morris pondered, "at the thought of the mass of things which no sane man could desire, but which our useless toil makes—and sells?"[6]

Morris would have despised the modern "big box" store aesthetic from a moralistic ground. He would have bought local, championed things

William Morris

of beauty and craft. He would have abhorred Amazon and been enthralled by Etsy. Been more Bernie Bro than Bezos Bro.

Buoyed by his early artistic successes, he boldly staked a claim in the political arts, focusing on building healthy creative communes where focus was placed on fine craftsmanship and the humans responsible for it.

"All the minor arts were in a state of complete degradation especially in England, and accordingly in 1861 with the conceited courage of a young man I set myself to reforming all that."[7]

This included shouting often and loudly against classism that led the poor toward sickness and destitution. Workers, Morris intoned, were not cogs in a machine, scraps of metal destined to sweat and die in poor working conditions in mills and factories. Laborers were people, human men and women with noble purposes to fulfill and art to make! Worthy of lore and veneration. And jobs. His socialism found practical expression as he routinely hired skilled craftsmen to work in his studios, his type foundry, his print shops, his workshops, and in his conservation efforts as he rebuilt many churches across the Continent.

William Morris

Morris dreamed of a society based on trade and common good fulfillment, almost like a medieval-inspired commune. The litmus test of a healthy society shouldn't be profit, he argued. It should be purposeful, meaningful work, and beauty. Always beauty.

"History has remembered the kings and warriors, because they destroyed," Morris lamented. "Art has remembered the people, because they created."[8]

Morris's ideas were well received among the intelligentsia in the abstract, but whether they'd find tangible expression was another question. How, after all, can one preserve actual craft and technique in the face of an increasingly mass-produced market? How to realize these ideals?

Morris turned to his social circles to work out the practical application of his theories, which included a bouquet of pre-Raphaelite artists including Edward Burne Jones and Dante Gabrielle Rosetti. With their added endorsement it wasn't long before Morris became the face of the newly formed Socialist League.

Morris's brand of socialism was a sort of spiritual fervor and vision for humanity—spurred less by financial considerations and more by a protective love of art and nature. Seeing the very real threat modern industrial capitalism posed to both, he worked tirelessly to spread his ideas to both the rich and the poor.

Wielding increased public influence, he unleashed treatise after treatise, pamphlet after pamphlet on socialism, and many on art, which to him were inextricably linked. And though he saw the massive scale of profit-driven ugliness, he knew he'd only truly find success lurking in smaller, actionable ways.

He'd start with London.

No, smaller.

Communities.

Not quite small enough.

A home.

There it was. The home, the natural place to birth a utopia.

A home-centered, socialist-supported revolution.

Morris's writings turned to a widespread reexamination of the very concept of home. In *Lectures on Art and Industry* he pondered, "If our houses, our clothes, our household furniture and utensils are not works of art, they are either wretched make-shifts, or what is worse, degrading shams of better things."[9]

Why shouldn't we fill our homes with things of purpose and beauty? Morris wondered. *Why should the plate we eat off be a less significant product than the accomplishment of a soldier?*

"If I were asked to say what is at once the most important production of Art and the thing most to be longed for, I should answer, A beautiful House," Morris wrote.[10]

"You may hang your walls with tapestry instead of whitewash or paper; or you may cover them with mosaic, or have them frescoed by a great painter," he continued. "All this is not luxury, if it be done for beauty's sake, and not for show: it does not break our golden rule: Have nothing in your houses which you do not know to be useful or believe to be beautiful."[11]

This emphasis on the beautiful home caught on. Morris rode this wave of enthusiasm into furniture design, founding the London firm Morris, Marshall, Faulkner & Co. in 1861. During his tenure at the firm, he designed his most iconic piece, the Morris chair, a comfortable wooden easy chair. These chairs required considerable handiwork and knowledge to construct and were customizable with many fabrics of Morris's own hand, or those created by his daughter May.

They were also unpatented so that other craftsmen might build their own by hand, using Morris's design as a blueprint and customizing their own details and woodwork.

In his patent-frenzied entrepreneurial era, the desire to "open source" his work was more than notable. It was revolutionary. He had very intentionally laid this ground for his democratization of art. If you can't afford to pay someone to make you a Morris chair, here are the instructions: make your own—your home deserves it.

"What business have we with art at all unless all can share it?" Morris wrote to the editor of the *Manchester Examiner* in 1883.[12]

He wasn't just OK with people cribbing his work, he encouraged it.

The Morris chair became a staple not only in his native England but soon all over the world, and reproductions were attempted by top furniture houses in Europe and the United States and even by architects like Frank Lloyd Wright.

Morris had made good on his promise to make beauty abundant and available to every kind of home, from estate houses to row houses—old money machines and the nouveau riche and the proletariat. He preached his brand of socialism into English society through art.

Having achieved his mission of freeing us from the tedium and impersonality of the machine, there remained still another philosophical question to answer: how can the beauty of our homes be unique, but common?

Six years after I fell in love with Morris, I fell in love with another man. I ended up marrying this one. As newlyweds, we scored our own unique piece of real estate—a 1910 bungalow rental with no air conditioning and tall ceilings and original molding. It was 850 square feet of charm. It wasn't as grand as Morris's Kelmscott House, but it *was* exactly one block from a donut shop. And it was ours. (The neighbors' sewage that occasionally crept up from ancient pipes into our bathtub? *Not ours.*) When it was time to look for more space to accommodate our growing family, our realtor kept steering us toward new constructions, because people "in our demographic" "want to build."

We didn't. We could realistically afford a new construction in a new subdivision, but almost nothing about that was appealing. I was obnoxiously proud about wanting something other than white kitchens with matching walls. I genuinely gravitated toward things that felt unique, and snobbishly chided people who settled for what I considered boxy, soulless spaces. I dreamt of mature trees, the warmth of wood and a hint of history. I wanted art glass and oak and patina. I wanted a place of worship, basically an old church.

We ended up in a 1988 split-level.

It *was* in a great neighborhood close to everything, triangulated perfectly between Target, the library, and the freeway, at the end of a long cul-de-sac where our future children would roam wild and free. It still wasn't our arts and crafts dreamhouse. But it boasted a brick chimney facade, colonial-style windows (OK, they were drafty), solid oak cabinetry, and good hygge. It would more than do, and we were lucky to have it.

Life around us was moving at top speed, but our decorating pace was glacial (it took us four years to hang our first picture). With one income and zero free time, our days were spent with back-to-back babies, the droughts and floods of self-employment, and more than a couple of literal floods from faulty plumbing. We had no means or energy to work on our house. We became incidental adherents of slow decorating.

Mid-pandemic, our social calendars suddenly cleared. Armed with funds from some careful savings goals, we decided to tackle a few home projects we'd told ourselves we'd "get around to."

I knew what I wanted to do first. The wallpaper.

After years of fixing things out of necessity, it felt luxurious to think about doing a project that was purely aesthetic, whose sole purpose was to create beauty. And though it was a wallpaper print I'd loved for nearly two decades, I was also thrilled to hang something so special, such a unique expression of my soul. And something nobody else had.

I ordered the paper, and we blocked out a few months out to install it. Dusty dreams were at last materializing.

Then, to my anguish, during my sad ritual of late-night scrolling, I saw it. The Instagram-famous decorator posted a picture of her daughter's newly designed bedroom. And there it was, peeking out from the adjacent bathroom. Pimpernel. She'd used the wallpaper. *My* wallpaper. In the same colorway.

I was unreasonably upset. I sent snarky text messages to two designer friends. All the feelings of "I found it first!" flooded in, along with worst-case-scenario self-pitying, "Great, now everyone is going to put that paper in their home!"

How could a man like Morris, after all, be OK with any of his work becoming so common as to live in every other Instagrammer's home, his singular patterns potentially at risk of becoming the "live-laugh-love" of wall hangings? How could he possibly tolerate the image of his wallpaper being so casually "liked" to the point of an algorithm churning along toward its be-all and end-all of advertising revenue?

But then, the most terrible realization of all. I was doing the exact opposite of what Morris had preached. I wanted beauty for myself—but I was enraged at the idea of anyone else having it, too.

"I do not want art for a few," Morris once wrote, "any more than education for a few, or freedom for a few."[13]

Morris would have been so disappointed with me. I was disappointed with me. For years he talked about democratizing art, and here I was, griping about sharing it and carrying on one-sided arguments with the woman who "discovered" him.

Instinctively, I know art is for everyone. Beauty belongs, as Morris knew, not only to the noblesse (or Insta-famous) but to the baker and the barber too. Even before I knew much about Morris, I appreciated these philosophies. Faced with some tough self-reflection, the question lingered. Do I still hang it? Or should I return it and try another of his more obscure prints?

"You loved it for fifteen years," my interior designer friend said. "You should hang it. It's yours."

How strange it is to live in this time, an era where we know what everyone's homes look like, homes we've never once set foot in. Our virtually connected culture has afforded us glimpses into the interior lives of the rich and famous and also regular folks across a wide demographic divide. We fill up our Pinterest boards with kitchens we love and gleefully judge the design choices made in those we don't. The pressure to create a beautiful home can be smothering, but that doesn't mean a beautiful home is an unworthy venture. There is real necessity in surrounding ourselves with soul-speaking art and artifacts.

For Morris, it was all about nature. His textiles reflect his love of flowers, plants, and the little creatures who inhabit them. His art was very personal to his upbringing and his tastes. And bless him, he had the generosity of spirit to share it with everyone.

I'd been adequately called to repentance but still wondered—what of originality? What of unique craftsmanship? There is virtue in diversity, after all. While we don't need identical art, we do need to encourage the appreciation and enjoyment of it wherever we are able. "The arts are necessary to the life of man," Morris explained.[14] Art is salvific.

Morris even went so far as to equate the end of art with the end of civilization. When it came to building his socialist utopia where class lines

William Morris

vanished and beauty reigned in each and every home, Morris knew and reiterated one important truth: we are only as beautiful as the worlds we create and share.

One gentrified house in the middle of a slum isn't going to cut it, not in a utopia. Our communities should be full of art and expression, and one house in need of repair is in our collective interest to improve. Beauty, like kindness, multiplies on a broad scale.

Perhaps this is why walking along a small, well-kept neighborhood street is so satisfying, so joyful. Home after home that are connected through human intention and human labor make the world a lovely place. I suspect this is why we care so much about the walls that house us, the art that enlivens us. We're not owed originality, but we owe it to each other to share the art that inspires us.

I hung the wallpaper in my front room that spring.

I feel joy every time I walk by it. I no longer care that it also hangs in the bathroom of a little girl I'll never meet. I hope it brings her joy, too.

New visitors are quick to comment on it, and a good few prod me for details. They politely indulge me as I give them an excited (not brief) history, and they follow along when I ask them to come up close and inspect it. Put their hands on it, position their eyeline at the parallel, examine the textural pop and the way the light waltzes across the gold. I have no idea what they're quietly thinking at this point, but I'm genuinely delighted I can share something so lovely.

If I'm lucky, I hear a small echo of Morris himself, musing quietly about the endless abundance of art:

"Speak not, move not, but listen, the sky—it's *full* of gold."[15] ✸

1. Anna Mason, ed., *William Morris* (London: Thames & Hudson, 2021), 23.
2. Mason, *William Morris,* 392.
3. Matthew 13:12, KJV.
4. William Morris, "Letter to Andreas Scheu," September 5, 1883, in *The Letters of William Morris to His Family and Friends,* ed. Philip Henderson (London: Longmans, Green and Co., 1950), 187.
5. Mason, *William Morris,* 53.
6. William Morris, *Useful Work versus Useless Toil* (London: Socialist League Office, 1886), 24.
7. Mason, *William Morris,* 164.
8. William Morris, *Hopes and Fears for Art* (Boston: Roberts Brothers, 1882), 44.
9. William Morris, "The Lesser Arts of Life," in Reginald Stuart Poole et al., *Lectures on Art Delivered in Support of the Society for the Protection of Ancient Buildings* (London: Macmillan and Co., 1882), 182.
10. Mason, *William Morris,* 161.
11. William Morris, *Hopes and Fears for Art* (London: Longmans, Green, and Co., 1908), 109–10.
12. William Morris, "To the Manchester Examiner," March 14, 1883, in *Letters of William Morris to His Family and Friends,* 165.
13. Morris, *Hopes and Fears for Art,* 34.
14. Morris, *Hopes and Fears for Art,* 42.
15. William Morris, "Fair Weather and Foul," in *The Collected Works of William Morris* (Cambridge: Cambridge University Press, 2012), 366.

SPARK BIRD

Or How to Save the World

JEREMIAH SCANLAN

THE GEESE DIDN'T MAKE SENSE. I spotted them in passing from my car window, Canada geese strutting on dead grass—and they left a spike of dread in my chest. Were they supposed to be here? Shouldn't they have all migrated south by now—wasn't that what geese were famous for? I had read about the current biodiversity crisis for the first time over Christmas break, and as I returned to Utah for my final semester of college, I was thinking about what I could do to help. Now it seemed the world I had only just decided to commit myself to was already unraveling, undone by the newly ordinary sight of Canada geese relaxing in a park in the middle of winter.

Two books and two flocks form the inciting incident of this story. The first flock you've already met. The first book, the horror novel *Annihilation*, was the reason I had been spooked into learning about the biodiversity crisis over Christmas break. I discovered the second book when I got back to my apartment, popped open my laptop, and tried to research geese. I found myself in front of a PDF of *Let's Go Birding!*, written by one Ted Floyd, editor of *Birding* magazine. A cheery quick-start guide to birdwatching, it positively vibrated with Floyd's enthusiasm. I was supposed to be researching geese, not picking up a new hobby, but the book drew me in.

And then, after only a few pages, Floyd brought me up short. "Stop reading this little book right now. For real. Stop reading and go outside."[1] Start with an American robin, he suggested. And just observe.

The book and the geese together had cast a spell on me, and I decided I would let it carry me just one step more for today. I stepped out of my apartment and started walking. The day was warm, the streets still lightly dusted from a recent snow. Turning down a new street, movement caught my eye. I looked up—

And there, hopping on a gutter among dripping icicles, were the most unexpectedly stunning creatures I had ever seen. With clever black masks underneath cheery crests, their bodies were buffy tan on top with a yellow belly, ending in graceful coattails of gray and black wings tipped in red. And there wasn't just one, but a flock of six or seven of the robin-sized birds, hopping between the rooftops and the trees, chattering with each other in friendly whistles, entirely oblivious to the fact that I was standing there on the sidewalk with my mouth hanging open.

"Are not two sparrows sold for a farthing?" Jesus said. "And one of them shall not fall on the ground without your Father" (Matthew 10:29). Or, as a recent stake conference speaker put it, God knows where every sparrow will lay its head to rest tonight. Whereas I had just barely noticed the geese in the park, or learned that these birds on the rooftop even existed, creatures for whom I had no name. It was as if, after holding back for so long, nature had suddenly decided to spill all its secrets at once and had sent this troupe of adorable little bandits to invade the room where I had all my life plans carefully arranged.

Where they promptly started smashing all the furniture.

When I got back to the apartment, I learned that Canada geese had figured out that they didn't have to bother to migrate if they could find a nice spot of mowed grass to relax in. I also learned that the rooftop robin hoods were called cedar waxwings. Ted Floyd's book explained that birders had a name for that kind of dazzling first contact: *spark bird.* Before I closed my laptop for the day, I had ordered a pair of binoculars and a field guide.

The worm of worry remained inside me, but now I had a plan. When the earth was finally put together, "God saw everything that he had made, and indeed, it was very good" (Genesis 1:31), yet I had just learned through direct experience that I knew very little about what made the earth good. If I was going to figure out what God might have us do about our compounding ecological crises, I would have to start *seeing* the world for the first time. Not just learning about it, but *experiencing* it, trying to soak in with my own eyes and ears the reasons why God so loves it. Birds seemed like a great place to start.

As if, now that I'd seen a cedar waxwing, I could ever go back.

BIG YEAR

Birds—would you believe it—were everywhere. It turned out that any time I set out with my binoculars, I was bound to discover something I'd never seen before simply because I'd never bothered to look.

There were of course the urbanite birds: plucky robins, workaday house sparrows, raucous scrub jays. But I was also astounded at how, with very little effort, I could drive to a golf course or an industrial pond or the foot of the mountain to see the kinds of creatures that I thought were only supposed to appear posing in Audubon paintings: great blue herons, egrets, Steller's jays, sandhill cranes.

My favorite haunt became a path along Utah Lake only fifteen minutes from my apartment—Skipper Bay Trail, according to my freshly downloaded birding app. Soon I was visiting several times a month, and nearly every time I went, there was something new to see. Red-winged blackbirds swaying on the tips of the grass in the warmth of the sun. Flycatchers and kingbirds swinging to and from their perches to nab insects mid-flight. Black-billed magpies pranking each other in the bushes and squawking like squeaky toys. A soaring red-tailed hawk eyeing us all. The torrent of discovery swept me along—pouring down, as it were, from the windows of heaven, such that there was not nearly room to contain it.

There was also a whole new birder language to learn: *bins, LBJ, pish, chase, dip.* I learned that many birders kept a *life list* of the different species they'd seen and that each new species was a *lifer.* A year where you set out to see as many species as possible was your *big year.* My own life list grew by the dozens. By the time I graduated in the spring, I had seen over forty species. By the end of the year, I would have one hundred and ten.

The more I looked, the more astounded I became. I couldn't believe that God had toiled over something as captivating as a Virginia rail just to hide it in the marsh grass. Or bothered to dream up something as hilarious as a California quail scurrying across the road. And He hadn't planned on telling me about any of this?

Except, of course, the birds had been shouting their presence from the rooftops. And as my wonder at the world unfolded, so did my anxiety. Every new species was a new friend, and someone new to worry about, another knot in a tangle of

Yamamoto Baiitsu

problems. The more I fell in love with birds, the more I needed solutions for them.

TWITCHER

People much smarter than I had been trying to untangle these knots for centuries, so I dove into the best books to discover what they had found.[2] I made quick progress at first, finding the categorical arguments easy to reject. No, the earth was not just made for plunder. No, humanity should not try to pay for its sins by committing mass self-extinction. But my to-read pile grew as long as my life list, then longer, while the answers did not become any clearer. Even the touchstones of environmental ethics that I agreed with emotionally or spiritually always felt too vague and incomplete. The great conservationist Aldo Leopold, for instance: "A thing is right when it tends to preserve the integrity, stability and beauty of the biotic community. It is wrong when it tends otherwise."[3] The vibes are spot on. I'm still not sure what it means.

The scriptures didn't have straight answers either, full of seemingly contradictory commands, vague directives, and manipulable guidelines. To take just one well-worn example, the Doctrine and Covenants instructs that the earth—"the fowls of the air," no less—has been "ordained for the use of man" (Doctrine and Covenants 89:12). When read alongside Genesis's exposition that God has given humankind "dominion over the fish of the sea, and over the birds of the air, and over the cattle, and over all the wild animals of the earth, and over every creeping thing that creeps upon the earth" (Genesis 1:26), it's reasonable to understand why someone could believe the "use of man" to be purely or primarily economic. Yet the Doctrine and Covenants makes it clear that use also encompasses "to please the eye and to gladden the heart . . . and to enliven the soul" (Doctrine and Covenants 59:18–19). Where does that leave us? I couldn't decide. Constructing a satisfying environmental ethic out of gospel teachings felt like trying to assemble a five-course meal from a pantry full of delicious but contrasting ingredients, some as malleable as rice, others as specific and potent as horseradish and watermelon. When Enoch heard the earth mourn for the filthiness upon it, I couldn't help but read his pleas to God as his own despair over being at a loss as to what to do. "O Lord, wilt thou not have compassion upon the earth?" he asked repeatedly. "When shall the earth rest?" (Moses 7:49, 58).

My putative ethical reasoning was unexpectedly put to the test when a family of stray cats appeared in the storage unit next to where I parked my car. Someone had set out water for the kittens, and the mother hissed ferociously whenever I got too close. Later, I saw the mother prowling the parking lot and realized with a stab of worry that she was hunting the covey of quail I'd recently discovered hiding in the apartments' flower beds. I'd seen the chicks running after their parents like dirty cotton balls possessed by magnetic properties. Who was in the right? Didn't the mother have to feed her kittens? Quail were hardly a threatened species, but weren't their adorable young just as entitled to life as the cats? Should I try to scare the mother off? Contact the owners of the storage unit and ask them to turn the cats over to a shelter? Call animal control myself? I dithered for weeks. Then, one day, the cats were gone. I realized I hadn't seen the quail in some time, either.

Meanwhile, the river of new lifers had narrowed to a stream, then a trickle. The kingbirds I'd been so dazzled by at first weren't as surprising the third, fourth, or fifth times I visited Skipper Bay Trail. Fall migration surged through with a brief blast of fresh air, then it was back to the winter birds: the year-round robins, the juncos, the house sparrows in the usual bush by the hair salon. Discovering new species required further and further visits afield. I felt my attention slipping, the initial thrill wearing away, my desire to act waning because I couldn't figure out a satisfying direction to exercise it in.

Twitcher is the term for a birder who subscribes to rare bird alert listservs and drives hours to catch a glimpse of an off-season rarity or misdirected vagrant. The title is, if not outright derogatory, a bit of a verbal side-eye, a criticism of a type of bird watching that seems to be nothing more than a sport, a competitive, obsessive hobby rather than a wholesome or merely eccentric one. As fall gave way to winter, I signed up with the Sageland Collaborative, a local conservation group, to help survey rosy finches, an adorable yet elusive species that descends from the Rocky Mountains during the winter as snow swallows up food sources in the higher altitudes. Without better data, experts aren't sure how the species is faring because of climate change. I flew home to Pennsylvania for Thanksgiving, and rather than sticking around for the extra week or so until Christmas break began, I scheduled a flight back to Utah so I could make sure I met my monthly survey date. At this point the anxiety overcame me that, despite whatever I told myself, I wasn't doing this for the birds anymore, that the magic I had thought so inexhaustible had disappeared. Maybe I had become a twitcher, and was now condemned to return to a disenchanted life. Or, worse, maybe I had mistaken novelty for astonishment, and there had never been any magic in the first place.

I never did see a rosy finch. The year after, I moved back east for grad school and a new phase of life, trading the scrub jays of Utah for the blue jays of my childhood. Settling in a new place meant new birds to discover, which was exciting. But leaving behind the birds of the West was also clarifying. Looking back, I saw that the wonder, the beauty, the *fun* of birding had never diminished, even when I'd worried it had. Even when I saw the same birds outside my apartment window every day, I hadn't stopped loving them, even if I didn't know what they needed from me.

Ogawa Haritsu

PATCH

One of the things I love most about the restored gospel is its insistence on improving the here and now, of planting the abstract in the dirt. Or, as Rosalynde Welch put it in a beautiful essay, "if heaven is here, then it's all low altitude."[4]

In birdwatcher slang, your *patch* is a spot that you visit frequently. It can be a favorite trail, a park, a spot by a lake. It can be your backyard. The tiny world outside your window. Except that once you start paying attention to your patch, it never stays tiny. When you slow down and start to pay attention to individual birds, you can't help but become absorbed. In their movements. Their habits. Their lives, so completely full and apart from your own.

My favorite place to go birdwatching is the backyard of my parents' house in Pennsylvania, where I grew up. I like to sit in the sunroom and watch the robins. Every summer, they are there. Running in the grass looking for worms. Nodding off in the sun on the driveway. Singing *cheerily, cheer up, cheer up,* from the trees I climbed as a kid. The juveniles from the year before have returned as adults, and they are feeding new juveniles, just as shaggy and needy as the adults had been last summer. "A small place, as I know from my own experience," Wendell Berry has said, "can provide opportunities of work and learning, and a fund of beauty, solace, and pleasure—in addition to its difficulties—that cannot be exhausted in a lifetime or in generations."[5] Is it any coincidence that a robin features so prominently in Rosalynde Welch's essay? They are the very definition of low-altitude wonder.

When I'm sitting on the sunporch, I trust that better answers to our modern crises will come—whether those crises are social, political, ecological, or spiritual. When I first saw the geese in the park, I needed to know what to do about it. But the most important answer, the most important *action,* I've discovered for myself was to start paying attention in the first place. Not just through education or research or keeping up with current events, as important as those things are. But by watching the same backyard, street, or lakeside trail for five, ten, fifteen minutes at a time.

And when I started paying attention, I realized I had things slightly backwards. Paying attention, it turns out, is not just for gathering the data to solve the problem set of eternal salvation. It is, on some level, salvation itself. "By our attention we gain the world and the world becomes a home," philosopher L.M. Sacasas has written. "What we get, simply put, is nothing short of the world itself."[6]

Put differently, a little like grace, the world has already saved you. As a manifestation of God's love, how could it not? Thus, being in right relation to the world might start with constantly encountering that reality in its solid, little ways. In your patch. Only then will you gain the world. Only then will you encounter the kind of grace that inspires transformation, not out of fear for what you can't do, but out of love and gratitude for what has already been done for you.

After a bruising first year of grad school, I flew to Utah to visit friends. Despite their love and encouragement, I was stressed, unhappy, worried about the dizzying direction of my life and theirs as we all went our separate ways. I borrowed a car to drive out to Skipper Bay Trail and sat by the side of the lake, watching the birds far out on the water. The birds weren't new that day. They hadn't been for some time. But the peace I was looking for found me there in the wind and the waves. I knew it could be the last time I visited the trail for years. Maybe for the rest of my life. But there would be another patch. I would find it. ✸

1. Ted Floyd, *Let's Go Birding!* (Delaware City: American Birding Association, 2009).
2. To name a few: *A Sand County Almanac,* by Aldo Leopold; *Desert Solitaire,* by Edward Abbey; *Vesper Flights,* by Helen Macdonald; the *Southern Reach Trilogy,* by Jeff Vandermeer.
3. Aldo Leopold, *A Sand County Almanac* (New York: Oxford University Press, 1949).
4. Rosalynde Welch, "Airborne at Low Elevation," Wayfare, Winter 2022.
5. Wendell Berry, "Faustian Economics," *Harper's Magazine,* May 2008.
6. L. M. Sacasas, "What You Get Is the World," *The Convivial Society,* December 27, 2022.

FALLING INTO PARADISE

GEORGE B. HANDLEY

NOBEL LAUREATE DEREK WALCOTT begins his epic poem *Omeros* with a story of a festering wound that won't heal. The story is rich in symbolism: the wound was inflicted by the anchor of a sunken slave ship, and the plant that ultimately provides salvation grew from a seed that had been transplanted from Africa, borne by a swallow. The wounded fisherman bathes in water suffused with this plant inside of a rusty cauldron that had been a part of a former slave plantation. Walcott describes him emerging as if from a baptism, like a second Adam in a new world. For the characters of the poem, healing does not come from repression or neglect of history's wounds or from perpetual cries for revenge, but from accepting and transforming the meaning of the conditions that those wounds left behind. Walcott's native island of St. Lucia becomes, then, not a cursed vestige of a violent colonial history but instead what he calls a "self-healing island."

Many years ago now, following a surprise opportunity to interview Walcott in a public forum, chance events had led to him becoming something of a literary mentor for me. His bald assessment of some of my poetry was that I was trying too hard to "sound like a poet," and he urged me to write prose for a while, to try to quiet my voice down, to be anonymous. I dutifully spent the next year drafting prose about my meditations on the Provo River, an experience that became the most deeply satisfying writing I had ever undertaken. However, I was completely unprepared for Walcott's response. He wanted to know where all the pain in my writing came from. His questions persisted until he learned of my older brother's suicide when I was eighteen.

"Ah, well that explains it," he responded.

"I really don't know what you mean." I was surprised by how annoyed I felt, but I tried to disguise it.

"Pain behind the prose—I can feel it. Have you ever written about his death?"

"No."

The truth is, not only had I never written about it, but as the years had passed, I found talking about it increasingly difficult and rare.

"Well, then, now you know you have to write about it. It will be the hardest but most important writing that you will ever do."

"That is not going to happen," I said.

"You will thank me later, but you must do it," he said calmly. I was angry at his intrusiveness and his insistence. But after our conversation that night I had a dream that brought me strange peace, and I awoke knowing I would have to write about my brother. As I began in earnest, repressed details came back of that terrible December day, which sent me to my parents and my surviving brother to fill in the blanks. Though difficult and tearful, those conversations were some of the most important our family had ever had. They resulted in an essay about my brother's death that later became a chapter in my book, *Home Waters.*

As I was preparing for the final publication of the book, a trusted friend read it and told me that I was waiting too long in the book to tell the story of my brother and saying too little about my family in general. The poignancy of that event, he felt, almost felt dishonest to delay for so long. Putting it earlier in the narrative, however, was going to be logistically very difficult, and it also raised more existential questions for me. Was I writing a memoir or a book about a river? What, finally, was my story in the expansive context of where I lived?

As I tried to answer these riddles, one fishing memory emerged and found its way into the first chapter. I was sitting in my car with a friend just after moving to Utah. Heavy rain had chased us off the river, and we were waiting to see if it would clear. I found myself telling him the story of my brother's suicide, something that was at that time still hard for me to talk about. He then startled me with the story of his own mother's suicide. As I wrote this scene for the book, I described myself looking out the window at the rain on the

Tali Hafoka

river and hearing my friend say, "*This bullet that ripped a hole through his head and through your life is the reason why you crave friendship and why you love this river.*" No sentence I had ever written up to that point was more painful to write or more truthful, and it was the last sentence I added to the book.

Walcott had been right. There was a reason, a deeper personal reason, I was drawn to the river and loved to write about it. I was wounded and needed healing. It didn't convey the whole story to say my brother "killed himself." He died of an illness. His body betrayed him. His chemistry failed. Something took from him his ability to enjoy the pleasures of an embodied life, and as best as I could figure, it was nature itself that had taken it. This left his suffering without an answer. The question was: why, if nature was the very reason for my suffering, did I think it could heal me?

Nature already knows how to heal itself. It persists in the face of the insults and injuries we inflict upon it, something not unlike Christ's command to turn the other cheek. This shouldn't ever be interpreted to mean, of course, that we *should* injure nature or that we can't do irrevocable damage to it; in fact, its meekness, like that of children, only highlights the injustice of our abuse. Many believers and critics alike have misunderstood Christ's call to meekness as a call to weakness, to indifference or acquiescence to injustice or to pain. This is a profound distortion of the truth. Christ does not right wrongs like a mighty knight errant, but when we turn to Him in our brokenness, He *rewrites the meaning of our story.* The facts of our lives do not change, but His power seems to rearrange the furniture of our minds where facts have settled, freeing them from the appearance of inevitability and of fixed meaning.

Section 88 of the Doctrine and Covenants offers a clue as to how intertwined Christ's healing power is with the natural world. The revelation tells us that Christ is in the light of the sun and of the moon. He is the light that gives shape and color and form to all things. He is the present force, the loving guarantor of a continuous creation. And while this miracle takes place around us daily, we scarcely notice, ironically, because we are too busy nursing the very wounds Christ's creations can heal. Or too busy repressing them, running away from them. I sometimes wonder if our greed and materialism are just symptoms of our unhealed wounds. Instead of turning to

Tali Hafoka

Christ, we use and abuse nature as a material resource to numb the pains of life even while we praise its exotic beauty.

Some drugs heal, but some, of course, only shield us from pain without getting at the root cause. Our faith in Christ can bring healing, but we can also use it as a palliative no different than any other painkiller or material luxury. I have often worshiped a false god who I hoped would simply erase my past and my pain, erase my mistakes, and place me back in that mythical Eden that we imagine lies outside of time and beyond this earth. But instead, the living God provides many small edens on this earth, moments of real and raw and imperfect beauty (is there really any other kind of beauty?) that penetrate me and raise me to new levels of consciousness.

I don't know how to distinguish such moments from the many experiences of forgiveness that my faith in Christ has brought me. In nature and in repentance both, it seems that my sorrows and my sins are not so much taken from me, as if they never happened, but transformed, as if I just mistook their meaning. In my moments of highest exultations on a river, on a mountain, in the deep forest, watching the sun rise or set, like Walt Whitman I let loose my own barbaric (and holy!) yawps in celebration. I am convinced we humans haven't fallen out of paradise. We have fallen into it. The so-called cursed conditions of this life are the very conditions of our healing and redemption. This planet is our self-healing island.

Maybe we have misunderstood what it was Jesus was offering. He spoke of a kingdom but

insisted it started within us. If I knew I would die tomorrow, I would spend my last day praising God for the paradise he gave me here with my loved ones in the loved places we lived. I see no reason to believe that paradise in heaven will be any different than it has been here. Here it has always been mixed up in my own imperfect and particular life, the bruises and tragedies and heartbreaks that have broken me open to God's glory. Elation is proportionate to sorrow but then surpasses it, just enough to know that it is not an illusion. To paraphrase William Blake, this earth's beauty has taught me to weave joy and woe together into the finer garment of my life.

At the end of my journey of composing *Home Waters*, I began to speak of the "healing power of nature" as a refrain. I now see how much more generously available this healing is, even or especially when it isn't attached to the name of Christ in any overt way. Millions of God's children feel healing daily from the beauty of the earth, the perception that life is a miracle, or the heart-swelling that is inspired by a joy that reaches beyond common understanding. And no small measure of our human creativity in poetry, music, or art is a response to such experiences. So generous is the Creator that it hardly seems to matter, at least initially, that people understand the source of such healing. It is as if He gives all without any demand for recognition, without any precondition. He is the ultimate anonymous artist.

But something happens when we finally find the courage to say His name, to recognize His suffering on behalf of all Creation, and to praise

Him in His creations. The earth that was our exile becomes our heaven. And what can we do in response other than to recognize, appreciate, share, and steward His generous gifts of the Creation? We find more healing, more joy, and more courage to take up Christ's cross, to learn

My burdens weren't lighter because nature helped me to forget. My burdens were lighter because I finally realized that nature was helping me to see, understand, and accept them.

His capacity to suffer all things. The Czech philosopher Erazim Kohak expresses this poignantly in his remarkable book *The Embers and the Stars: A Philosophical Inquiry into the Moral Sense of Nature:*

> When man goes into nature, it must be a place of remembering, not of forgetting. Away from palliatives and distractions, the pain does not subside: it stands out in all its purity, purged of all self-justification and self-pity. What remains is pain, pure and clear as a bright crystal. There is no distraction, no escape. And yet something does happen, slowly, silently. The grief does not grow less beneath the vast sky, only it is not reflected back. Artifacts reflect grief. . . . The forest is different. It lives, it absorbs the grief. . . . When humans no longer think themselves alone, masters of all they survey, when they discern the humility of their place in the vastness of God's creation, then that creation and its God can share the pain.

Oh how I treasure these words. What truthfulness they convey to me. The very rocks around me on the trails I hike are not so impervious and solid that they cannot absorb and share my pain. I could build a mansion of beautiful walls and furniture, and every object of my vanity would reflect my pain back at me. The created world, on the other hand, is alive. It forms an embedded network of shared grief that becomes, slowly and silently, a shared joy. Immersive experiences in the vast expanse of a forest, an ocean, a mountain, or standing in the middle of a river lighten our burdens. Who does not know this is true? At first, I didn't really understand why this was the case. I had only a vague sense that this was just a symptom of better physical and mental health. It was, but that health signified something transformative and healing at work deep inside me. My burdens weren't lighter because nature helped me to forget. My burdens were lighter because I finally realized that nature was helping me to see, understand, and accept them. Memories came to the surface, like deep slivers that had to find a way back out. As Walcott surely must have intuited when he urged me to to confront my brother's death, I was coming to nature in the same spirit that I was coming to my Savior, as a broken vessel. And in proportion to my sorrow, my joy deepened. And then surpassed my sorrow.

The strange and wonderful logic of the Atonement is that the cause of our wounds also holds our cure. Nature reduces us, humiliates us, pulverizes our ego and our sense of our own centrality. But, enlivened by God's breath, this becomes nature's gift, its recompense. Like Job or Moses, as we witness the creation, we discover our nothingness and our newfound and healing significance in the same moment. This does not leave us callous any longer to the suffering of nature or of our fellow beings. Once we become properly yoked with Jesus, we are expanded and become more than our atomistic selves. We become our brother's keeper and stewards of all of His creations. The natural world brings gifts without price, recompenses of wonder and elation and solace. I know of no more adequate response to such generosity than devoted, compassionate love for every one of His creatures. ✱

Derek Walcott (left) & George Handley (right)

MY LADY OF

DAYNA
PATTERSON

after Lance Larsen

My lady of March in Brooklyn and a leisurely lunch of fettuccine funghi at Forma's. My lady of the subway rat. My lady of walking through Manhattan with my daughter and architect brother. My lady of him pointing out the art deco, the sloped sides and stepped back stories to allow in the sun. My lady of Central Park. My Lady of Strawberry Fields. My lady of the busker who sang us a McCartney song while we all agreed John was our favorite. My lady of Van Gogh's Starry Night, textured paint like embroidery, whorled stars, black cypress in the foreground connecting heaven and earth, piercing higher than the village steeple. My lady of my daughter holding my hand as we pass from room to room, my brother trailing behind. My lady of swapping tennis shoes when my girl's feet begin to ache. My lady of ibuprofen and acetaminophen. My lady of the poor man's tour of Ellis: the Staten Island Ferry. My lady of Lady Liberty's blue-green patina caught in the waves and waning light. My lady of her copper plating once shiny as a penny. My lady of the multitudes who wanted her painted over and the multitudes that resisted her painting. My lady of verdigris the work of 130 years. My lady of her original torch cut away, windows installed, flame coated in gold leaf. My lady of an immigrant's perspective and my ancestors who passed beneath her gaze. My lady of give me. My lady of Lazarus. My lady of Manhattan skyline at night, stars vacuumed from the sky shimmering in the dark shards of buildings, an earthbound galaxy in its own milky haze. My lady of all the graffiti. My lady of the tattoo shop, steady whine of the tattoo machine, bodies bared to this ancient ritual of ink and skin. My lady of sushi. My lady of lobster rolls. My lady of purple fries and wasabi mayo. My lady of the roe that popped gently against our teeth like tiny bubbles. My lady of the high empress cocktail with grapefruit spritz and bamboo spear of lychee—a mouthful of stars. My lady of not enough and too much and pavement and steel and pipes belching steam, clouds curling up into the dark. I'm here, lady, and even here, lady, I find your plenitude, tree roots cubed by concrete, green tips cascading up, flaring into night.

DOCUMENTS FOR THE NORTH AMERICA ARTICLE

GABRIEL GONZÁLEZ NÚÑEZ

Artwork by Jorge Cocco Santángelo

SENDER: Lloyd Chehda, Cristalina
TIME: Monday, November 19, 2009, 2:57 pm
RECEIVER: Curbelo Ventura, Jorge
SUBJECT: Documents for the North America Article

Dear Anciano Jorge Néstor,

I am writing to you about the article that, as decided in the last council meeting, we will publish in print and also on the Church's website as a PDF for the 75th anniversary of the beginning of the preaching in North America.

I have gathered the material you requested so that you can be at ease knowing that what you write will be accurate.

I should also point out that there is a record in the Apostolic Archive indicating that around 1851 a missionary was sent to some destination in North America, but there is no further information. Nothing is known about his name or, for that matter, the fate of his expedition. I guess the fact that no one kept a good record of this goes to show just how far removed the northern end of the continent was from the concerns of those early Saints. I will continue searching, but for the time being, there may be no option but to make no mention of that unknown missionary.

Should you have any questions, just let me know.

Sister Cristalina
Executive Secretary
History Department
The Church of Jesus Christ of the Saints of the Last Days

FROM THE ENCYCLOPEDIA OF MORMONISM; ENTRY: "MISSIONARY EXPANSION"

The Church of Jesus Christ of the Saints of the Last Days was founded on April 6, 1825, in Misiones Orientales, Paraná, under the leadership of Prophet Omar Ibayú. A few months earlier, he had been expelled by the people of his town for having received the Book of Mormon, and then he organized a church after the pattern set by the saints of former days. That very same day, the first missionaries put on their now characteristic black soutanes and began the labor of preaching in towns across Misiones Orientales. They then went into other provinces. In 1838 the first missionaries were sent to Paraguay, Brazil, and Tahuantinsuyo. Then in 1841 the first missionaries were sent to Argentina. By 1845 there were missionaries in Colombia. Through the efforts of these early missionaries, many converts joined the Church in the other provinces of Paraná, as well as in parts of South America. The growth of the Church in cities like Purificación and Buenos Aires led to some controversy in the heart of the Church about whether to preach or not to those who had no Lamanite blood. In 1847 the voice of Jehovah was made known to the Prophet Omar regarding the matter through a dream. In it, the Lord confirmed to him that the gentile nations, too, should receive the gospel, in the same manner that the Romans had received it from the ancient apostles.

EXCERPT FROM THE PERSONAL JOURNAL OF BROTHER ENRIQUE MARCELO RESEK RÍOS

May 4, 1936

We held a farewell mass here in Washington, at the Aguilars' home. I can't believe that we've been in this land for six months now! And I can't believe that we are about to leave! As requested by Anciano Domingo Antonio, I was the mass's celebrant. This was bittersweet to me. On the one hand, communing with the Saints filled me with the Spirit, but on the other hand, I was burdened by the thought of the trek we will begin tomorrow, first by train to New York, then by ship to Montevideo, and finally by train to Navú. I did my best to celebrate in a most excellent way so as to set a lasting example for our brothers and sisters Aguilar, Monroy and Echo Hawk to follow after our departure. I extended the welcome greeting, we sang the Gloria together, I invited Brother Rafael to say the prayer, we sang the Kyrie together, I prayed over the bread and passed it, I prayed over the cup of wine and passed it, I did a reading from the New Testament (Revelations 14:6) the fulfillment of which I explained in my homily, I gave Anciano Domingo Antonio time for a few words, and then I concluded the mass with a closing blessing. I was greatly impressed with the words spoken by Anciano Domingo Antonio, who was moved upon by the Spirit, for he could not otherwise have uttered such a solemn prophecy. I feel it important to make a record of it:

"The work of the Lord is but a handful of seeds in this land that is so far removed from the light that the Book of Mormon promises, but the day will come when these peoples will find the light of truth. The work will grow here as with the shape of the ombu tree, first sprouting in one place and then with branches that will reach outward as if they were roots in search of water. From this city we will reach the entire country and the neighboring countries too. The North American Mission will be a power in the Church."

FROM A REPORT PREPARED BY THE CHIEF APOSTLE FOR THE THREE, JANUARY 1934

As you are aware, Brother César has delivered to us on your behalf the two letters that arrived from Washington, United States. We read them in our last Council meeting, first Brother Jorge Aguilar's and then brother Rafael Monroy's. We did so in the spirit of prayer. We were greatly impressed that two families of Mexican converts would happen to meet in the capital of a Gentile nation. If only the Aguilars or only the Monroys had moved there, this would not be as impressive, but in this case it is two families of converts that left everything behind in their homeland, all of their own accord, and ended up meeting in a foreign land. We were also impressed to learn that many Indians are moving from the state of Oklahoma to the city of Washington in search of economic opportunities. After reading the letters, we prayed once again. We felt an unmistakable confirmation from the Holy Spirit that the Lord Jehovah is creating the necessary conditions for preaching the restored gospel in North America. Such conditions did not seem to exist until now.

FROM A TEXT PUBLISHED ON HISTORIA.IJSPD.ORG ABOUT THE FIRST MISSION TO THE UNITED STATES

In 1860, Apostles Daniel Fernando Hortal González and Víctor Santiago Vásquez Arredondo traveled from Church headquarters in Navú, Misiones Orientales, to Richmond, North Carolina, which was then part of the United States, in order to begin preaching. These missionaries were unsuccessful in establishing the Church and were unable to baptize anyone. Their labor was met with rejection and filled with discouragement. Such was the case to a great extent due to their lack of English-language skills and to the war of independence that about that time broke out in their preaching field. They concluded that translating the Book of Mormon into English was not a viable task for them and that during such violent times it was not safe to proclaim the Church's position that slavery should be gradually abolished everywhere in the world. As a consequence, after three fruitless months, both Ancianos returned to Navú. There they made a report, first to the full Council of the Twelve Apostles and later to the Council of the Three Pontiffs, in which they recommended that some prudent time be allowed to pass until more favorable conditions existed in North America. In the words of Anciano Daniel Fernando: "I feel compelled by my service in North America, yet I also feel conflicted because I cannot help but always come to the same conclusion. Only once the Book of Mormon is translated into English, only once we hold that book in our hands, will the key also turn for the gentiles that Prophet Omar turned for us when he translated the book into our Spanish."

FROM A LETTER BY ANCIANO DOMINGO ANTONIO RODA MARTÍNEZ TO HIS WIFE, NOVEMBER 25, 1935

My dearly beloved Cata,

I am finally able to sit down and write to you, my eternal wife. There are so many things I would like to tell you, so many things I wish I had lived with you by my side. Perhaps the day will come when those of us sent by the Lord may fulfill the holy apostleship with our companions at our side. But for now, all is according to the will of the Holy One of Israel, who sent me to these lands I never thought I would see. And while it is all rather exciting, I do miss you.

Now, mind you, I am not complaining about the company of my brother Enrique or of Teófilo. As you well know, they are quite agreeable, especially Enrique, to whom I am bound in the unbreakable bonds of Our Lord's apostleship. Without the company of these my two companions, the voyage on board the Camões would have been very difficult to bear, especially since I do not fancy traveling by ship.

Anyway, we disembarked at the port of New York on November 18th. That was a sight to behold! The city is large, and standing on the ship's deck, I was impressed by the many skyscrapers there. I suspect that just as I was surprised by everything I saw (the ships, the crowds, the movement of people), many individuals were in turn surprised by us. For example, on the train to Washington, I noticed several times that some passenger or another would stare at us. Anciano Teófilo believes it was the habits we wear. Perhaps he is right, because in the week we have spent here, I have noticed that priests in this country wear suits and ties, which gives them the appearance of businessmen.

We arrived in Washington that same day, and the two missionaries we had sent to this city a few months before were at the station to receive us. Along with them stood a young Indian man called Echo Hawk (whose name the missionaries translated into Spanish for us.) His Spanish is quite impressive, which he learned in his native Oklahoma trading with the Mexicans. He is the only proselyte we thus far have in these lands. He was baptized on October 29th in a river called Potomac. In these parts the fall is very cold around this time of the year, so we are all inspired by the faith of this braided, hat-wearing young man who would not wait a single day more to be buried in the water in order to find new life in Christ the Lord.

That night we also met the two families that wrote requesting the missionaries, namely the Monroys and Aguilars. They are young, with small children, and the light of the gospel shines on their countenances. They treat us with much deference and even invited us to stay in their homes. In fact, as I write to you we are spending the night at the Monroy home. We have felt quite welcome with them, and we have laid our hands on each and every one of them to invoke blessings upon their heads.

Oh, that you could meet the Saints here! That you could see this picturesque city!

[...]

FROM THE PERSONAL JOURNAL OF THE PROPHET TÉOFILO, WHEN HE WAS A SEVENTY

XII/24/35

Today, December 24th, 1935, at about 6 in the evening, in a grove of leafless maples and within a stone's throw of the Potomac River, it was my privilege alongside Anciano Enrique Marcelo to exercise our faith when our brother Anciano Domingo Antonio knelt and clasped his hands to dedicate the lands of North America for the preaching of the gospel. Night was falling, and a cold breeze blew sharply into our faces, but even so, the fire of the Holy Spirit descended upon us. After the dedicatory prayer, we broke out in Latin chants (as is our custom in such solemn occasions) and also in Spanish songs (as is becoming more commonplace).

FROM THE TALK "OMAR IBAYÚ AND THE BOOK OF MORMON," GIVEN BY ANCIANO EDUARDO RAIMUNDO IN THE CHURCH'S JANUARY 1995 GENERAL CONVENTION.

As a young man serving a mission, I learned the importance of Omar's prophetic vision to translate the Book of Mormon into a modern language. I was one of the earliest missionaries to serve in the United States. During my whole mission I only had but three proselytes. Early on, it was just my companion and I, with the help of two families of Mexican converts. Other missionaries arrived later, but for several years that was more or less what it was like for everyone. Now, let us compare that with last year, when nearly 40,000 people were converted in that country. What was different? Well, the only thing my companion and I had in English was the Bible, so we could only use the Book of Mormon with the handful of people who spoke our language. Those who spoke English had no interest in a book they could not read, so we were mostly working with the South and Central Americans who lived there. This changed after two of our proselytes, brothers Echo Hawk and Eduardo Raimundo Balderas Ibáñez, finished translating the Book of Mormon into English. Then came the great harvest, first in the rest of the United States and then in the Confederate States and in Canada.

FROM THE 2008 CHURCH STATISTICAL BOOK, ENTRY: "NORTH AMERICA"

. . . In the three countries, the Church now has 3.5 million members, nearly 700 dioceses, and 18 temples . . .

SENDER: Curbelo Ventura, Jorge
TIME: Monday, November 19, 2009, 5:14 pm
RECEIVER: Lloyd Chehda, Cristalina
SUBJECT: Re: North America Article Documents

Dear Anciano Jorge Néstor,

Dear Sister Cristalina,

Thank you for sending this my way. I skimmed over it just now. It will be very helpful when I get around to writing the article!

Coincidentally, I was on the phone yesterday with the brethren in the North America East Sector. They told me that nowadays it's impossible to track down the exact spot where the dedication of North America took place. Nonetheless, it seems we have a general idea of where that was thanks to the descriptions in the journals of the Ancianos. The Church historian over there has worked really hard to find that general area, which now is some sort of park on the outskirts of Washington. Of course, the place itself is not as important as the fulfillment of Anciano Domingo's prophecy. When I travel to the United States next month, we will place a historical marker in that park.

Sincerely yours,

Anciano Jorge Néstor
Council of the Twelve
The Church of Jesus Christ of the Saints of the Last Days ✸

THROUGH A GLASS DARKLY

Memory and Windfall Pears

ISAAC JAMES RICHARDS

part of peace and all of ear. Pressure,
and release, a life in one word: pear.
Speak again, green god, in Adam's
vowels; I hear, and it is sweet.
—from "To a Pear" by Jim Richards[1]

MY LEAST FAVORITE SPRING-cleaning assignment was picking up the pears—soggy, rotten, winter-logged pears that had fallen off our tree just before the first autumn freeze. The tree was unpruned, the pears bitter, so we didn't pick them when they were ripe; we just let them pile up on the ground and gathered them up every Saturday before mowing the lawn. Usually, we got most of them before they were covered with snow, but there were always soft, darkened exceptions to be found the next March.

One spring cleaning, however, my four younger brothers and I had been granted an occasion to procrastinate. Instead of gathering pears, we eagerly crowded around in a circle in the basement, watching my dad remove the glittering relics of his childhood from a dusty cardboard box. I suspect that my mother had encouraged my father to sort through his old keepsakes and identify any that were no longer meaningful repositories of memory so that they could be discarded. To be honest, I cannot remember any of the thrilling knickknacks my father produced from that magical old box—except for one.

"Oh . . . my . . . gosh!" my father exclaimed, laughing in shock and surprise. He gently pulled his hand from the box to display a tiny green and yellow feather, no bigger than a tie clip. Still laughing, my father struggled to articulate an explanation through gasps for air.

"This . . . is a feather . . . from my pet parakeet . . . Tommy!" His eyes were wild with excitement, nostalgia, and wonder.

The memory ends. This is all that remains. I remember the box. I remember exactly where we were on the carpet in the basement. I remember my dad's constant laughter, the tiny feather, and I even have some semblance of why this moment became so permanently impressed upon my mind. You see, when I saw this material remnant from my dad's childhood pet, the feather became a kind of forbidden fruit—it opened my eyes to a new level of consciousness. Though I was a child, my sense of time, memory, and aging had been heightened. I had glimpsed a shadow of my father's former life. The feather was like a

Carly White

talisman, a symbol of death, a token of love, and a time capsule all at once. Seeing it, or rather, seeing my father's reaction to it, broke some kind of innocent spell within me. Perhaps I was just growing up, but in hindsight this archaeology of my father's past, this discovered treasure, marked a point of no return.

Memory features prominently in Plato's dialogue Phaedrus. In it, Socrates recounts the legend of Thoth, the Egyptian god of writing, who created hieroglyphs to improve the memories of the Egyptian people. King Thamus disagrees with Thoth and accuses him of ascribing to words a benefit that is the opposite of what writing really does. For King Thamus, writing produces forgetfulness rather than memory—for who needs to remember something that has been written down? While Thoth saw the hieroglyphs as a repository of memory, King Thamus saw writing as a vacuum of forgetfulness.

To my surprise, Tommy the Parakeet made a reappearance in my life more than a decade after my father rediscovered that feather. I had graduated high school, served a mission, and was now married and attending BYU. My wife and I had just made the four-hour drive from Provo to Rexburg for the Christmas break. It was late on a Sunday night, and everyone had gone to bed except for my father and me, who stayed up talking. Through the living room windows—dark panes of glass—I could see ten inches of new-fallen snow sparkling underneath the porch light, which was just bright enough to illuminate the railing of the deck before vanishing into darkness.

Somehow, we began talking about poetry, publications, and graduate school. I was considering getting a master's degree in English at BYU, like my dad. I was probably asking for some advice on where to begin with this whole writing thing. As a result, my father went into his study and brought out a stack of old literary magazines and poetry journals—places he had published in. We began perusing them together and talking about which outlets were more competitive than others. This part of the memory is crystal clear: I was holding a copy of BYU *Studies Quarterly,* volume 38, issue 3, when I came across my father's poem, "Adam's Song," that won first place in the BYU *Studies* 1999 poetry contest. This time, I was the one who was laughing, as I read, incredulously:

> Tommy was the first pet I had in Eden,
> *par'a·keet"* seemed to fit—*small parrot*
> *with long tail, the color of apple, new leaf,*
> *and lemon; harsh, irritating song.*

As I read those words, bending the spine of the journal between my hands, touching the faded paper, whatever magic spell that had been broken all those years before was humming gently in

Carly White

the air again. My notions of time, memory, and aging resurfaced. It was as though the poem was a portal through which I fell headfirst into that memory of a decade before. Once again, my father and I laughed together, and I asked as to the whereabouts of the little feather.

"Gone," he said with a shrug.

I gathered the windfall pears each spring with rawhide gloves and a black garbage bag. If you ever need to gather windfall pears, you should remember to hold them gingerly, so they do not squish and slush into moldy mush in your palm. I know from experience that winter-rotten pears hold enough juice to soak through Walmart gardening gloves, even leather ones. Once, I accidentally stepped on a pear that was syrupy slick, hidden beneath a pile of thawed leaves. The oblong orb squirted paper-thin in an instant, sending my foot sliding across the grass. I fell smack on my rear, jeans smeared with oozing, sugary pulp.

Once, I accidentally stepped on a pear that was syrupy slick, hidden beneath a pile of thawed leaves. The oblong orb squirted paper-thin in an instant, sending my foot sliding across the grass.

The encounter with Tommy in "Adam's Song" launched my reading of my father's poetry. This process was a journey all its own. Whatever faint understandings I had of time, memory, aging, and the father-son relationship were no match for the magic of the written word.

Nephi said, "I desire to behold the things which my father saw" (1 Nephi 11:3). That scripture gradually took on new meaning for me, especially as the parallels between my father's life and my own grew stronger each passing year. I felt a natural affinity for my father. I often confused pictures of him as a child for pictures of myself. Same blond hair, same glasses. Growing up, the refrain from my relatives was: "You must be Jimmy's boy!"

To be sure, there were plenty of differences. He played hockey while I played tennis. He was the fourth child of ten, I was the oldest of five. Still, we had many interests in common. I went to the BYU Jerusalem Center like my dad, and the night before I left, he pulled out a box of old Jerusalem souvenirs. That box must have escaped the spring cleaning, for inside was a yarmulke, his old Jerusalem Center nametag, and other mementos. We peered inside that box together on the exact same spot of carpet as before, right outside the storage room in the basement.

By the time I was a graduate student and PhD-bound, I had taken to saying, "I'm just trying to see the things my father saw!" whenever I recognized another point of connection between our lives. This sentiment was taken to its limits when my great-aunt invited my wife and me to stay in her basement apartment, on Apache Lane in Provo, after our wedding. That same basement apartment was where my father and mother lived when they were first married. In fact, it was where I was born, and the apartment my father would have been living in when he wrote "Adam's Song" and other poems during his master's degree. It wasn't until I began reading his poetry, however, that the phrase "see the things my father saw" took on a whole new meaning.

Carly White

Look! There I am, tasting my first breath of air from the womb. Look! There I am, crying in the crib, gripping my father's pinky. Look! There I am, riding happily on the back of a horse. Look! There I am again, pretending to be asleep so my father will carry me in to bed from the car after a long road trip. Look again, I'm the Boy Scout laden with badges, the boy exploring a beachside cave while my mother frantically screams my name, the boy waking his father with notes of piano practice on an early Saturday morning.

Of course, I know that I might not be the main character in all these poems. Some of them may be about my brothers. Some of them I am more certain about than others. Some, as my father has gently reminded me, are just fiction. There are some, however, which are sure. For example, "A Few Questions—Involving Pears—For My Newborn Son," was published in BYU *Studies Quarterly* in the year 2000, before any of my younger brothers were born. It begins:

> So how do you like the air? The way it
> hums on your skin,
> moves through your nose in quick shots,
> or cools the lungs
> with the scent of fresh pears.

The unpublished poem "Pacifier" uses my name as it recounts my dad trying to wean me off that plastic comfort: "with scissors I cut / the nipple off." Then there's "Kissing Boys," which begins:

> When was the last time I kissed him,
> my eldest son, on the mouth?
> I can't remember.

Here my father's poetry is an anti-memory; he uses words to describe a transition that he cannot remember.

* . * *

Pears recur throughout my father's poems, but even before I read them, pears were my favorite fruit. This is probably because my grandmother would send us two boxes of Harry & David "Royal

Riviera" Pears every autumn. Those pears are a memory all their own. They would arrive like costly emeralds, gently packaged in a sturdy cardboard box marbled with pine-green designs. Those treasured pears were padded with olive-green foam, wrapped in golden foil, and cushioned in sage-colored tissue paper. Those pears were so sweet, your tongue could feel the grains of sugar in their slushy flesh. Those pears were better than candy, white gold like platinum, priceless.

My dad told me that he remembers drafting the poem "To a Pear" as part of a graduate school exercise at the University of Houston. He placed a pear on the table and freewrote for one hour, later shaping the best stuff together into a final draft. In Plato's *Phaedrus,* there are etymological connections between poetry and memory. The word for poetry, *poeisis,* has a general meaning of making something—specifically making a composition of words. Similarly, the word *mneia* means to make or compose reminders, and it is almost a fusion of the words mneme (memory) and poeisis (to make or compose poetry). Think of the phrase "making memories" as an act of creativity or composition.

Besides reminding me of those delicious autumn pears, I like "To a Pear" because of its insights about memory. Speaking of a pear, my father writes that "To cup you / is to pray" and "To pray is to remember / life before this life." Similarly, for Plato, things perceived in mortality are mere forms of a prior existence, and recognition of truth or beauty is simply a remembrance of former contact with ideal forms. My father adds, "I have not forgotten, / pear, you are a universe." In this worldview, memory is tantamount to the ability to recognize or discern truth. According to both Plato and "To a Pear," memory is recognizing, in the imperfection of this world, a shadow of a perfect and former ideal.

We know God is a Father, and many have said that God is a poet. All I can say is that having had a poet for a father, I have a new relationship with scripture. After all, the earliest scriptures were simply writings from parent to child, like Adam's "book of remembrance" (Moses 6:5). The difference of course between reading my father's poems and reading scripture is that the former is particular and uncanonized, the latter general and canonized. Since God's scripture is for all his children, it is hard to remember that they are also "just for me." I find it interesting that some of people's most meaningful interactions with scripture are described precisely as those types of moments, moments when they did feel that it was written just for them—about them.

Carly White

Reading my father's poems, I can feel this individualized love so strongly, as well as the pain of his sacrifices on my behalf. In "Petrology," my father writes:

> You can only lie at night
> on the floor beside his crib,
>
> hold a finger out for him
> to grasp until his crying
> ends and yours begins.

Carly White

These poems by my father do a variety of things to my memory. In some cases, I remember the events of the poem vividly, like when my brother cast his line into the lake and caught an old sock full of sand instead of a fish. Other times, the poem may bring to my remembrance something I had entirely forgotten. Then there are poems like the one just quoted, where I could never have had a memory of being in a crib but reading about those words makes the scene a part of my life's fabric in the form of a faux memory. In the poems where I am but an infant, I often view the scenes in third person—not through my own eyes, but through the eyes of some omniscient onlooker who can see my father and myself in the same frame.

Now, when I read God's poems—his psalms, aphorisms, verses, stories, and songs—I read them as if he wrote them just for me, about me. Of course, my memories with Heavenly Father are among the haziest of all. I can see myself in the premortal life only in the way that I can see my baby self in my dad's poems—by conjuring the scenes from the words. In this life, we see only "through a glass, darkly" (1 Corinthians 13:12). But one day, of course, "face to face" (1 Corinthians 13:12). With the perspective of eternity, however, perhaps our faux memories are not false at all, and words can help us glimpse beyond the veil. I wish I could remember what it felt like to grasp my father's finger between the bars of a crib. That memory is somewhere. Perhaps it will come back to me.

The mouth

has always longed to taste this true
and primal paradox—
Take, eat. Only you
are sin and virtue, as Eve knew.

Like her, fruit, make me wise. Give me
a swallow of cold knowledge.
Bright temple, I have fasted
and confessed. Now let me in.

—from "To a Pear"

Which metaphor shall I use for this mysterious thing called memory? Is memory a box, like the boxes that held Tommy's feather, the pears, and Jerusalem souvenirs? Is memory the feather itself? Is memory like poetry or scripture, helping us see the things our Father saw, helping us see the way He sees? What image could capture simultaneously the materiality and yet the ephemeral nature of memory? How does one describe the way a memory transforms and is transformed? Ah, I've always admired the stubborn materiality of those pears, hiding underneath soggy leaves and piles of snow. Some memories, despite the passing of time, like windfall pears after harshest freeze, refuse to disappear. Others, like a poem or the dripping white flesh of an overripe pear, dissolve on the tongue and vanish, leaving only an aftertaste. And when I try with gloved hands to gather my memories into a plastic bag, I can feel them squishing and changing shape as I go, as I put them down on paper. There they are—my memories, shadows of true forms—strewn across my mind like so many misshapen and deteriorating pears scattered about the lawn. I have tasted the sweetness of a fresh pear and desire others to partake also. Here, you should try one. There, now you can see. ✸

1. Jim Richards, "To a Pear," in *Fire in the Pasture: Twenty-First Century Mormon Poets*, ed. Tyler Chadwick (El Cerrito, CA: Peculiar Pages, 2011).

DIVINE VULNERABILITY

Healing the Human Family

THOMAS McCONKIE

A FEW YEARS AGO, MY WIFE AND I started working with a therapist named Bruce, a self-effacing Buddhist master who is shinily bald and has wrinkled jowls that evoke the sleeves of a wizard. His eyes are clear and his gaze penetrating. When he laughs, there is nothing but laughter. He gets to the heart of the matter with the kindness of a bodhisattva and the fierceness of a samurai.

Gloria and I realized that there were some issues coming up in our marriage that we weren't easily going to resolve on our own. Personally, I felt relief that I could share some of my frustrations with a third party. Hopefully, I thought, my wife would be willing to listen to me better if a trained professional assured her that what I was saying was important.

In our first session, after pleasantries and introductions, Bruce asked us the therapist's equivalent to "what seems to be the problem?" I generously volunteered to explain that there was a real sore spot in our marriage. "There are times when I'm really passionate about something, and I want to share, but I notice my wife gets distracted a lot when I'm sharing. Sometimes it feels like she doesn't really care."

Bruce listened deeply, then reflected back, "I hear you saying that when you're sharing something that's really important to you, but then feel like your wife isn't fully present with you, it's a very disturbing experience."

"Yes, exactly," I said. "If I can't share my excitement about life with my wife, then who can I share it with?" At this point, only ten minutes or so into the session, I felt a whole-body sense of self-satisfaction. I'd articulated my frustration fully and someone had finally understood it. Now for checkmate—Bruce will explain to Glo how important it is for a spouse to be a good listener, especially when your spouse is sharing something that means a lot to them.

Unexpectedly, Bruce put the question to me: "Thomas, I wonder if you'd be willing to give up the fantasy of a life free of disturbance."

My jaw must have involuntarily swung wide open like the overhead storage bin on an airplane during severe turbulence. A dead silence followed. I was stupefied. After I returned to my senses, a profound clarity hit me with no further explanation needed: I realized I had unconsciously made it my wife's responsibility to protect me from any disturbing experience in our relationship. I had

Ivan Kramskoi

told myself the fiction that if I was feeling disturbed, surely it meant that someone had done this to me, and that it was their job to make me feel better. In a single deft stroke, Bruce had cut through my drama and revealed a completely different way to be in my marriage: My wounds, my disturbances were my own, and nobody else was responsible for them. (Of course he wasn't saying that when my vulnerabilities are triggered I can't ask my loved ones for help. I can and I should. But if my go-to instinct is to blame people when I feel threatened, then I'm doomed to a life of constantly trying to control other people's behavior.) I was never the same after that moment. My wife assures me our marriage hasn't been the same either.

With the help of a highly skilled therapist, I was able to see that the everyday disturbance of not feeling valued didn't start with my wife and therefore wasn't likely to end with her either. That pain goes back to the foundations of human vulnerability itself.

From that moment on, I had an intention to stay curious each time I felt devalued. Rather than fixating on the story I had about how my wife needs to be a better listener, or how my friends ought to appreciate how helpful I am, I practiced staying in my body, staying with the very uncomfortable sensations that came up whenever I didn't feel esteemed and valued. In doing this, I've learned at least two important lessons. First, when I feel disturbed, the temptation to avoid responsibility and blame my discomfort on others is almost overwhelming. Second, with practice I can actually learn to rest in my vulnerability, letting intense experiences rise and pass through my body like waves. After the intensity of the disturbance passes, I'm in a better position than ever to act with intelligent love, to do the most loving thing I can possibly do in the next moment.

Briton Rivière

THE DEVELOPING SELF

Bruce revealed to me how vulnerable I am in intimate relationships to not feeling esteemed. To fully appreciate the range of what he calls "core vulnerabilities,"[1] it's helpful to first understand the developmental territory of our most basic biological needs. By definition, to have needs is to be vulnerable.

From even before we're born, we have a need for the basic conditions of warmth, nutrients, and adequate rest. In addition to crying when they're too hot, too cold, hungry, or just plain tired, newborn babies are drawn to the voice, presence, and touch of their caregiver. From the very earliest stage of life, we start with a need for safety and security.

Just as foundational to our need for security is our drive to seek pleasure. In a sense, pleasure is a derivative of the conditions that ensure our safety and survival. For example, it's incredibly pleasurable to get a good night's sleep in a comfortable bed. It's pleasurable to eat delicious food and to have a healthy body that's free of any discomfort. From before the time we're born, this need to seek pleasure and avoid pain is innate to our biology.

Just as early, our sense of self starts to form. There is now a "me," and everything else that is "not me." This emerging self is hungry for esteem and affection. From the first moments of our fledgling selfhood, we need to know that we're wanted. To not be wanted or not belong is to face certain death. Most adults wouldn't last too long left completely on their own in the wilderness. How much less an infant? Right at the heart of all human relationships is essentially a biological need to belong.

From about twelve to eighteen months in healthy development, we start to actively exercise our will and come into a sense of *power.* "I want that!" we yell from the top of our lungs. Wanting what we want, we're very clever at working out the best ways to get it. Sometimes we unleash the all-out charm offensive, overcoming Mom or Dad with blunt-force cuteness. Other times we'll deploy the meltdown technique. Not only do we learn to get what we want, we also learn to discern when we've met our match. We can tell when Mommy means business and when we might push a little harder for some extra screen time or a lollipop. In other words, we learn not only control, but submission.

We are born completely vulnerable to the conditions of mortality. And to the extent that our needs are not perfectly satisfied each time one arises, especially in early life, we will feel a disproportionate level of disturbance as we move into adulthood.

CORE VULNERABILITIES

When our foundational biological needs feel threatened in any way, when we experience privation of any kind, the body has evolved to respond with a certain measure of panic. It sends us highly intense signals that our *very survival might be threatened.* We feel disturbed to our core.

Our neighbors have a rescue dog, who likely spent some of his early days on the streets. He's now a thriving adult dog with loving caregivers. But they still need to keep the supply of dog food well out of his reach, or he'll get into the bag and literally gorge himself until he's sick. He probably spent so long being hungry as a pup—feeling as though he was at the brink of death—that the hunger signals he gets now are especially intense, even exaggerated. In other words, he would do *anything* to avoid feeling hungry. To him, hunger pains mean imminent death. It's irrational—he's been food secure for many years now. All signs point to his next meal coming right on time. But deep in his canine bones he feels something very different: *There is never enough.*

To some extent, no matter how loving or perfect our homes were where we grew up, we all have an inner rescue dog. We all experienced privation on some level—this is the nature of embodied life—we are vulnerable by design.

We don't have conscious memories of crying in our cribs as infants, the sting of hunger shooting lightning bolts of displeasure through us. In those moments, we didn't have a mature mind that could reason that we'd likely be a little uncomfortable till Mom woke up. Rather, our direct experience was that we were on the brink of starving to death. The intelligence of our animal bodies produced an appropriately intense response, and as a result, we wailed with all our might to draw the caregiver close, to soothe the blaring sting in our world with the warm, fatty goodness of mother's milk.

From early life, the natural man (i.e., instinctual self) forms memories of a world of lack. These are unconscious memories that are coded at the cellular level of the body. In our adulthood, these somatic impressions give rise to mental-emotional patterning that is primed for the experience of *not enough.* We see through the eyes of mortal scarcity, and everywhere we look we see deficit.

If I often felt a lack of security when I was young, I may be more prone to that experience later in life. I might eat more than I need to at a given sitting to avoid the vulnerability I feel when I'm hungry. Or if my fixation takes a different pathway, I might be stingy with my resources, feeling deep in my body that I don't have enough to share with others.

Maybe I was deprived of pleasure or exposed to unbearable pain when I was too young to defend myself. Moving into adulthood, I might be addiction-prone, seeking pleasure and avoiding pain to an unreasonable degree. The ocean of suffering that seems to lie just beneath the thin surface of my everyday mind threatens to well up and drown me. So I err on the side of pleasure-seeking to the point that I'm almost totally unwilling to have a direct relationship with pain.

If I felt deprived of esteem growing up, I might be especially vulnerable to seeking out affection and approval. The more I go looking for approval, the hungrier I get for it. And social media exacerbates our vulnerability around esteem. It's now easier than it has ever been to get immediate visual feedback on how people feel about me: How many views, how many likes did my last video get? Captivated by this substitute version of true esteem, we risk losing touch with our innate and divine value.

And then the need for power: To whatever extent I didn't have the experience of being powerful in early development, I might fixate on the need to be in control later in life. Maybe my parents struggled to provide a proper holding environment for me when I was young. I never felt quite like I could control my own space. Now when I feel a loss of control in adulthood, I panic and look to control things I have no business trying to control—my adult kids, the real estate market, people's opinion of me.

I've emphasized the nurture side of vulnerability, but we're each born with a biological predisposition to feeling certain vulnerabilities more than others. This is the classic nature/nurture dichotomy in psychology. Some of us may have more addictive personalities by nature and therefore react more intensely to the denial of a pleasure. Others of us who are more relational by temperament might be more vulnerable to a loss of esteem from others.

In any event, we have basic biological needs that are simultaneously our deepest vulnerabilities. We often react ineffectively to these mortal vulnerabilities in an attempt to escape our own suffering. Given this predicament, it would be convenient to have a language for this distinctly human psychology.

ENERGY CENTERS

In a brilliant move, Father Thomas Keating has integrated the developmental territory we just explored—core vulnerabilities and all—to life in the gospel. He realized that what Paul referred to as "lower nature" and the "natural man" can be understood not only theologically, but psychologically as well.

Father Keating describes this territory in terms of *energy centers,* a term he adopted from the work of the author Ken Keyes Jr. The original metaphor is vivid. In physics, the center of gravity is the point in a body where the mass is concentrated. This mass generates a gravitational pull. Gravitational fields can be weak or strong, depending on the mass of the body doing the pulling. We know from modern astronomy that gravitational fields can become so intense in the case of black holes that not even light can escape their field.

So it is with our core vulnerabilities. The signals of the body can be so intense when these vulnerabilities are triggered, it is as if they exert a gravitational pull on our higher nature. When the signals are intense enough, they completely consume our attention and energy in the vortex. We become fixated on the apparent emergency and routinely lose our capacity to make freer, wiser choices.

The energy centers in this sense are essentially one big energy suck. That is, when we're caught in the instinctual drives of the natural man, we invest our time, attention, and resources to escape the vulnerability we're *already feeling* in the body. We pursue symbols of security such as money and possessions in order to feel safe. We seek empty pleasures like scrolling on our devices and endless consumerism. We try to win the esteem of both ourselves and others by always being busy and constantly striving for accomplishment. We express a shallow sense of control by shouting over one another whenever we disagree. There is no end to these appetites. The more attention we feed these energy centers, the more massive they become. The more massive they become, the more difficult it is in each successive moment for us to escape their gravitational pull.

Because the body is developmentally foundational to our humanity, the heart and mind are especially vulnerable to its disturbances. Like any three-story building, if the ground floor has

structural issues, the upstairs neighbors are going to feel it. Being aware of the activation of the energy centers helps us sense any tremors before they escalate into dangerous earthquakes on the upper floors. We learn to detect the very instant our basic needs feel threatened—when the shaking begins—and to seek more stable ground.

When we're not alert to what's happening in the body, before we know it, a disturbance has recruited energy from the mind and sent us into a flurry of anxious thoughts. The body then feeds on those thoughts and becomes even more disturbed. Or disturbance from the body seizes the heart and divides it with painful emotions. Those emotions then trigger similarly painful thoughts, thus agitating the body even more. In this way we generate our own private hell many times over in a single day.

As our awareness becomes more stable, however, we learn to soothe ourselves at the level of the body before these disturbances scatter the mind and divide the heart. How do we soothe ourselves? It is simple in concept but difficult to do in practice: We learn to be willing to feel what we're actually feeling in the body and to trust the Ground of our being. That might sound abstract, but it is actually extremely concrete. Lehi embodies exactly this trust when he speaks to his son Jacob in the wilderness: "thou knowest the greatness of God; and he shall consecrate thine afflictions for thy gain" (2 Nephi 2:2). In more psychological language, as long as we are embodied beings, we are going to feel disturbance and signs of threat. But generally, the signs of threat aren't indicating any real threat. We just *feel* threatened. We can trust the body's process and let the tremors rise and pass without spinning elaborate dramas in the mind. When we're in our private hell, we think: "This isn't OK. I can't be here. I need out." When we're in heaven, it's just the opposite: "I *am* OK. This too is consecrated." This is freedom.

Recall my unconscious rationalization in marriage therapy: *If my wife would just pay attention to me how I want, when I want, my need for affection and esteem wouldn't feel threatened, and I wouldn't have to feel disturbed so often.* In other words, rather than directly inhabit my vulnerability, I tried to control my wife's behavior in an ongoing fantasy that one day I would be free of any disturbance.

As we bear one another's burdens, we imitate our embodied God who weeps and become more godlike ourselves in the process.

The moment we feel intense sensations building up in our bodies, our instinct is to escape. In an effort to escape the reality of our embodied vulnerability, we often say things and do things that are harmful to ourselves and to others. We justify our actions because we feel at a deep level that if we don't do something to escape, we'll be overwhelmed with pain, or possibly harmed beyond repair. In a gospel context, we can understand this psychological process as the drive toward *sin.*

SIN

The Greek word in the New Testament that we translate as "sin" is *hamartia.* It implies "to miss the mark, to err." But what mark are we missing when we sin? Where do we err in the vulnerability of these human bodies?

In a word, we risk worshiping the finite at the expense of the infinite. As human beings, we have basic needs that we can pursue endlessly in an attempt to avoid the basic fact of embodied vulnerability. There is nothing wrong with needing safety, pleasure, esteem, or power. In fact, we could say that these are all divine gifts we're given to enjoy in human life. The problem is, we are all too prone to getting sucked into those black holes. The energy centers chant only one mantra: "This is good, but I'd give it all for a little more." The appetite of our lower nature is insatiable. And because we can never get our fill at this level of reality, scarcity is the law of the land. In the Tao Te Ching it reads:

Fill your bowl to the brim
and it will spill.
Keep sharpening your knife

and it will blunt.
Chase after money and security
and your heart will never unclench.
Care about people's approval
and you will be their prisoner.
Do your work, then step back.
The only path to serenity.[2]

What is purely irrational yet demonstrably true is that the more security we seek *beyond a reasonable point*, the more we feel like we don't have enough security. When we idolatrize our basic needs, they become hollow gods who are impotent to satisfy the true hunger of our souls. We're then left with the doomed task of trying to satisfy ourselves. In our worst moments, we'll justify any kind of behavior it takes to escape the specter of being swallowed alive by our core vulnerabilities. Sin in this sense is a vain but understandable attempt to avoid our deepest suffering.

In his formulation of original sin, St. Augustine duly notes our tendency to miss the mark, to act out. But he then goes a step too far in my opinion by imputing something corrupt about our humanity itself. With our new understanding of sin as a natural tendency to avoid vulnerability, we can easily imagine a new telling.

In a Latter-day Saint formulation of sin, we can start with a reverence for the physical body and acknowledgment that our biological vulnerability brings with it certain liabilities. But these are precisely the liabilities we're given to work with in order to gain mastery over the physical realm. Vulnerability, in other words, is not a bug, it's a feature. We have the opportunity as embodied beings to willingly accept more and more vulnerability—both individually and collectively. As we bear one another's burdens, we imitate our embodied God who weeps, and we become more godlike ourselves in the process (Moses 7).

The word "vulnerable" comes from the Latin "vulnus" and literally means "wound." Thus, it is not sin and a corrupt nature that we've inherited as human beings, but an Original Wound. By willingly embodying this Divine Vulnerability, we learn to descend below all things. To the extent that we're willing to not only endure but embrace our personal Gethsemanes, we curtail sin's capacity to tempt us. After all, if we're willing to feel absolutely every experience that the Divine consecrates for our sanctification, what need is there to act out? What power does sin have to tempt us in the end? Christ is the living incarnation of this path.

ENERGY CENTERS IN SCRIPTURE

There is a vivid depiction of the energy centers in Matthew 4, where Jesus goes out into the desert in prayer and fasting for forty days. It's easy to skip to the end without letting the gravity of what is happening fully sink in. When I view this account through the lens of the energy centers, I see a clear path that Christ has shown us to further participate in our own theosis.

Whatever we personally take the Devil to be, we can say that he is cunning. He knows right where to hit us. There Jesus is, out in the wilderness, hungry, alone, and weakened. The Devil says to Him, "If you are the Son of God, tell these stones to become loaves of bread."[3] Remember, the prime directive of the body is to get comfortable and to stay comfortable. Few of us know how intense our disturbance would be if we fasted for days and weeks on end. This is energy center number one: safety, security. The Devil tempts and mocks Him, as if to say: "You have all the power in the world. Why go hungry when you could have a bite of bread right now?" Jesus responds:

"People do not live by bread alone,
but by every word that comes from the mouth of God."[4]

There is relative happiness, and there is happiness beyond conditions; the pleasure of having agreeable life circumstances versus the joy independent of circumstances altogether. Jesus is clear which master He serves and overcomes the first temptation.

In the second temptation, the Devil takes Christ up to the top of the temple and says what amounts to, "If you're such a big shot, throw yourself off from this temple, and all of the angels, all of your pals will show up and they won't so much as let you stub your toe."

This clearly touches on the energy center of esteem and affection. The Devil plays on the very human need to feel important, to feel that we've got a posse at our back. Putting His trust in God alone, Jesus sees through this guile:

> *"You must not test the Lord thy God."*[5]

In the third temptation, the Devil pulls out all the stops. He takes Jesus to the peak of a very high mountain and shows Him "all the kingdoms of the world and all their glory," *and basically says, you could have power and dominion over all things, if you first submit to me.*

Jesus knows, however, that if He seeks power, the seeking will never end. His heart will never unclench.

> *"You must worship the Lord your God and serve only him."*[6]

This account was written nearly two thousand years ago, yet the patterns remain timeless. Our core vulnerabilities are our greatest temptations. When our basic needs are threatened, we get intense signals from the body telling us there's an emergency. From there, we have a strong tendency to freak out and rush to a short-term solution to escape what we're feeling.

By overcoming each temptation, by confronting each core vulnerability of our humanity, Jesus chooses the only true happiness there is. How appropriate that His ministry should start right here in His moment of victory over the Devil:

> *Jesus came to Galilee, proclaiming Good News from God. "The time is ripe," he said, "God's realm is already so close to you. Turn towards it. Trust this Good News."*[7]

In fact, the Kingdom is closer than close. When we are no longer afraid of our own vulnerability, when we are at-one with the joy and sorrow of our embodied humanity, we find an entirely new center of gravity in Divine Reality.

Though perhaps not as dramatic as the scriptural account, we are faced with similar temptations every day of our lives. To view the modern desert of temptation, look no further than the string of billboards lining the freeways. Almost without exception the messaging is designed to amplify our innate sense of lack. The ads tell us we would be happier if we made more money working from home, looked more beautiful by getting plastic surgery, had a drink while surrounded by beautiful people of influence, or went to the Bahamas to unplug.

How are we doing in our own desert? How often are we driven to satisfy the insatiable needs of the energy centers? Are you starting to see now that there is a part of you that will never feel safe and secure enough? A part of you that will never feel enough pleasure and avoid enough pain? The task is simple but difficult: Let your eye be single to God's Glory. Let this sanctifying Light infuse the most vulnerable parts of yourself again and again. In exactly the most disturbing moments of your life, you can train yourself to open up, relax, and trust that something from beyond is making you holy.

RIGHT RELATIONSHIP WITH THE ENERGY CENTERS

Life is actually disturbing us all the time. It's provoking us all the time at the level of our basic vulnerabilities. We think if we use more force, more cunning to get conditions back to a place where we don't feel so upset, then we'll finally be OK. In fact, this agenda is a program for misery. As long as we are unwilling to feel the vulnerability we're *already* feeling, there will be no end to how much we struggle to escape our current experience. The energy centers will grow more massive and devour even more of our attention and energy as they do so.

As long as we are sensitive, embodied beings, we will feel disturbed on and off for the rest of our lives. This is what Bruce meant when he asked me with a Zen master's sternness if I would be willing to give up my fantasy of a life free of disturbance. God wants us to get the message too. We are vulnerable in our humanity. We will be constantly tempted to blunt what we're feeling by acting out

Nicholas Roerich

and engaging in short-term strategies that make us feel a little better now but a lot worse in the long run. It's sin by any other name.

Remember that in a sense, sin is a wrong view that denies Divine Reality and the abundance that *is already right here.* Sin is what feeds the energy centers and our chronic sense of lack. More than a punishable act, sin is a lost opportunity. Think of the last time you did something you would consider to be sinful, whether big or small. Were you not avoiding some uncomfortable experience in the body, doing something that you thought would bring you a little bit of relief in the moment, only to realize that acting out made things even worse than they were before?

The more we respond to the energy centers with a conviction that we must escape from what we're feeling, the more we'll come to believe that we aren't capable of embracing our original wounds with love and acceptance. The more we act out from the energy centers, the more we reinforce the aspect of our humanity that feels alienated from God.

When we relate to the energy centers from a new place, however, they become a passageway into Grace. Every time we crash, every time we fall apart, we can stop and realize that this is an opportunity to be tender and fully embodied with this disturbance, with the most vulnerable parts of our humanity. As we do this, we discover exactly where we stand in need of healing. We feel our wounded humanity being redeemed.

Paul writes, "What a terrible predicament I am in. Who will free me from my slavery to this deadly lower nature? Thank God it has been done by Jesus Christ, the Lord. He has set me free."[8] God uses time and mortality to create beings who can withstand Eternity. The Love, the Light, the sheer energy of Eternity is so immense, it takes time to get used to it. We have to get used to the intensity of true joy as well as the intensity of our disturbances. The energy centers show us precisely where we collapse. What feel like the most awful aspects of mortal life are actually Grace Absolute in disguise. The energy centers are like spiritual growth plates. They're right where our soul is yearning for further expansion.

What's more, when we learn to stay present to our own disturbance, we learn to stay present to all disturbance. In the end, it doesn't matter if it feels like "my" disturbance or "your" disturbance. Disturbance is simply disturbance. It is a form of contracted Love, hidden in the shadows yet still seeking the Light.

We are Love's means. Christ didn't simply carry out the at-one-ment once and for all, he showed us how to at-one each moment of our lives through great acts of Love. When we are *at-one* with disturbance—the pain and vulnerability of our human-divinity—we redeem one another in Holy Presence. Bringing a greater measure of Love, a higher intensity of Light to disturbance, to the inclination towards sin, we heal the human family as Christ's true body. ✸

This essay is an adapted excerpt from Thomas McConkie's forthcoming book, At-One-Ment: Embodying the Fullness of Human-Divinity, *published by Faith Matters.*

1. I highly recommend Bruce Tift's masterpiece, *Already Free: Buddhism Meets Psychotherapy on the Path to Liberation,* for a full treatment of this topic. Bruce Tift, *Already Free: Buddhism Meets Psychotherapy on the Path to Liberation* (Boulder, CO: Sounds True, 2015), 26.
2. Laozi, *Tao Te Ching* (New York: HarperCollins, 1988), ch. 9.
3. Matthew 4:3 NLT.
4. Matthew 4:4 NLT.
5. Matthew 4:7 NLT.
6. Matthew 4:10 NLT.
7. Mark 1:14–15, trans. Lynn Bauman.
8. Romans 7:24–25.

"AGAINST THESE THINGS"

Crossing the Great Deep with Rebecca Jensen

EMMA BELNAP

"And behold, I prepare you against these things; for ye cannot cross this great deep save I prepare you against the waves of the sea, and the winds which have gone forth, and the floods which shall come."
—Ether 2:25

IN REBECCA SORGE JENSEN'S STRIKing painting *Against These Things,* the viewer is given a sense of how helpless the Jaredites were on their journey to the promised land. The woman in the barge is facing immense odds. "The waves of the sea, and the winds which have gone forth, and the floods which shall come" (Ether 2:25) are here exemplified through the exaggerated size of the fish and the barge. She has no hope to make it across the ocean without the guidance of the Lord. This helplessness is further exemplified by the woman's body language; she lies in the fetal position, almost as if she were a child in the womb. Her eyes are closed and she appears to be praying, begging the Lord to help them with this seemingly impossible voyage.

This image also stands out because it tells a part of the Jaredite story not discussed in the scriptural account. Moroni glosses over the difficulty of their journey in his abridgment of their records. The crossing of the sea only receives

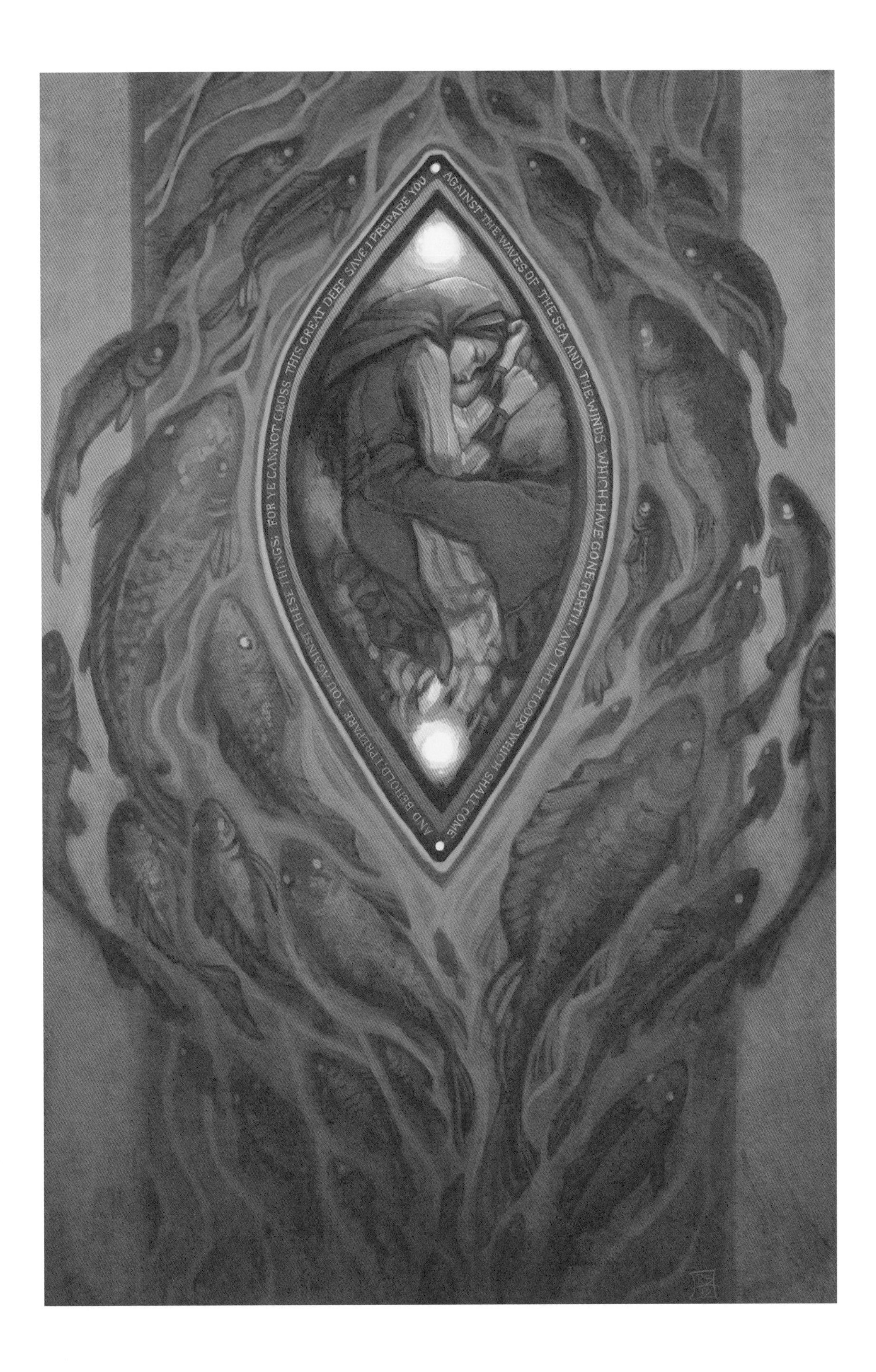
AND BEHOLD, I PREPARE YOU AGAINST THESE THINGS; FOR YE CANNOT CROSS THIS GREAT DEEP SAVE I PREPARE YOU AGAINST THE WAVES OF THE SEA AND THE WINDS WHICH HAVE GONE FORTH AND THE FLOODS WHICH SHALL COME

nine verses in Ether 6, all of which highlight the Jaredites' gratitude for the blessings of the Lord, rather than the hardships they experienced. Sometimes I see this reticence to discuss hardships in our modern-day church culture too. We may gloss over our difficult experiences so as not to seem pessimistic or ungrateful. But while gratitude for our blessings is important, so is talking about the hardships that make us truly grateful for those mercies.

I've learned through my own experience the gratitude we can experience in times of adversity. I was a missionary in upstate New York when COVID hit in March 2020. I will never forget the morning my companions and I woke to a text from our mission president telling us that we were in quarantine for the next two weeks. I was suddenly confined to my apartment, only allowed outside for an hour and a half every day. Instead of knocking on doors and street contacting, I spent my days calling phone number after phone number. Our isolation gradually extended to a month, then two, then indefinitely. With few people picking up the phone and even fewer showing kindness when they did, I began to feel like I was no longer fulfilling my purpose as a missionary. I started to plead with the Lord to let me go home but, after weeks of asking, it became apparent that the divine intervention I was so desperate for was not coming.

I imagine this is how the Jaredites also felt on their journey. Traveling in airtight barges with little light inside, submerged for hours and days at a time, and being completely unable to help themselves would be unimaginably challenging. I am sure the Jaredites woke every morning with a prayer that this would be the day they would reach land, only to be disappointed when the sun set and their deliverance had once again not come. Yet, they did not abandon hope. They continued to trust in the Lord and turn to Him, even and especially when His plan was not their plan. This is a painting about faith: faith that the Lord would carry them across the turbulent water to land, faith that He had a plan for them, the faith that, as they relied on Him, He would take them where He needed them to go and turn them into who He needed them to be.

Rebecca Jensen

As I gaze at the painting, I feel this Jaredite young woman's story has become my own. I, like her, was secluded in a small space, not knowing if or when my deliverance would come. I felt battered by the metaphorical waves, winds, and floods of my journey. Even in this moment of desperation, though, the artist makes it clear that the Lord has not forsaken this young woman. Two of the glowing stones He touched rest at her head and feet, reminding her that she is not alone and that His light is with her in her silent struggles. Although the time I spent serving from my apartment on my mission was one of the hardest things I have experienced, I can look back now and know that I too was not forsaken. The Lord's light was with me, even when I didn't recognize it there. ✱

This essay is part of an essay series about Brother of Jared artwork curated by Jenny Champoux, Book of Mormon Art Catalog Director, available on the Wayfare website. With more than 2,500 images, and new pieces added constantly, the Book of Mormon Art Catalog is the largest database of Book of Mormon visual art and is a resource for scholars, artists, teachers, and members of the Church. Learn more at bookofmormonartcatalog.org.

OUR LADY OF SEEDLINGS IN THE OLD-GROWTH

DAYNA PATTERSON

Mother trees [. . .] nurture their young,
the ones growing in the understory.
—Suzanne Simard
You might even say they are nursing their babies.
—Peter Wohlleben

shade-shackled we glum in the valley of your shadow
marcescent stems hunger-spun to shrivel & droop we
    knot & burl
slub & warp in this thick dark above us {we want to believe}
your zillion green hands lace a lightscape where our
    thoughts can't quite leaf Mother {are you there} in a
    dress of moss we press root tips
our listening parts outward to perceive your
    language its crackling
hertz music us through fungus: mycorrhizae hyphae
    mycelium probe our reaching roots penetrate root hairs
    invaginate our cells
make a meetinghouse of rhizosphere speak
chemical to our open pores pheromone to stomata
    we believe
{we want to believe} you're preparing us for theosis ascent
where you grow we grow girthy and bark-thick
are we baby gods or the scapegrace of darkness
    decay-bound

lash us with your branches {are you near} score us
with arborglyphs
{can we bear} on our birchskin aleph & zed scar & seal
yes we're all foodwish imperative gift-poor
yes we clear cut yesterdays but crave tomorrow assure us
there's more than humus dust wormshit & earth-shush
Mother find us with your filaments tender tendrils chapel
us your green reach

YGGDRASILL,

Oluf Olufsen Bagge

ABUNDANCE AND ANTINATALISM

Embracing Risk, Encountering Wonder

LIZZIE HEISELT

I COULDN'T HELP BUT HEAR TWO teenagers talking behind me as I stood swaying on a packed crosstown bus. "Do you think you'll have kids?" one of them asked. My ears perked up and I could almost feel their eyes on me—the woman with a child on her back, another clinging to her leg, two more chatting in a nearby seat.

They discussed the limitations that come with having children, the trade-offs they expected. I heard the words "tied down"; I heard "bad for the environment." But also, I heard them say that they would make good parents. I heard in their conversation shadows of the universal push and pull that any important decision brings. The sacrifices, the benefits; the joy, the suffering; the paths that feel familiar, the ones that are full of mystery.

And there I was, on the bus, practically dripping with children. Feeling the abundance of it every day—the busyness, yes, but the fullness and fulfillment, too. My hands are loaded with all the best things, and while there is some juggling involved, like any proper circus it is often accompanied by laughter and delight. (And collapsing with relief behind closed doors when the juggling has been accomplished and everything is safely in its place.)

I chose to have many children because that has always been my heart's desire. But for others, the choice to have children becomes ever more fraught and freighted. A few generations ago it was hardly a choice at all. For most of our grandparents and great-grandparents, children either came, or they didn't. Within only a few decades, medical advancements changed what was once a function of biology and opportunity into a decision of morality, ethics, wealth, education, faith, fear, and any number of personal experiences and judgments centering on the loaded question: *Why have children at all?*

There's a word for the proposition that we shouldn't have children: antinatalism.

Antinatalism argues against having children from the moral position that doing so increases suffering in the world and that all suffering, any suffering, is bad. It could be that the children themselves will suffer without ever having given consent to be born. It could be that children will cause suffering as they consume limited resources. In antinatalist thinking, no joy or pleasure that we experience in life can compensate for the inevitable suffering.[1]

Antinatalism may seem like an extreme view held by a few morose individuals until we

Brooklyn Swenson

Brooklyn Swenson

ask ourselves: To what degree has our society accepted the premises of antinatalism? How much does our culture discourage childhood—or parenthood? There seems to be an invisible tide pulling us individually and as a whole away from the desire to have children.

We can feel this pull on society at large in our collective anxiety about environmental instability, or as governments and economies attend endlessly to capitalist values that place a premium on a person's economic productivity. We feel this pull individually in more personal decisions—like should I delay family life for the socially approved pursuit of professional, political, or educational ambitions? Can I financially afford a child? What would I have to give up? Depending on how a person answers these questions, she may be precluded from having a child at all as the biological clock ticks ever forward.

Other modern values, like a focus on unfettered autonomy above all—and the perception of children as a burden—may promote antinatalist attitudes. Take for example that strain of feminism that sees family life in general as a form of female bondage.

But more poignant are those who turn away from family life because they grew up in families full of trauma, feeling like they were at best a burden and were at worst resented and abused. This happens on a very personal level, but also on a macro scale as some people may feel the entire modern Western culture has perpetrated such colonialist atrocities on the world that it should not be continued. Such experiences and beliefs generate a deep sense of inadequacy and unworthiness.

If only these value judgments were limited to the personal decisions of the individual. But as a mother of more than a few children in one of the most dense urban environments in the world, I can testify that judgment about the propriety of having children abounds—as can any parent who has existed with children in places not made specifically for them. There, where children's presence may compete with or distract from the societal values of productivity and wealth, ease and convenience, parents and children are often treated with disgust and derision, impatience and intolerance.

For further evidence, read the comments section of any personal essay by a mother who expresses any hint of the challenges of raising children.[2] "Should have thought of that before you had kids!" "Stop whining, you brought this on yourself," and "I'm never having kids," are not uncommon sentiments. Lacking in these responses is any sense of understanding that mothers have hard yet essential jobs with bad days, or that society compounds their burdens with the impulse to blame and shame.

It isn't just anonymous internet lurkers who opine on the number of children women shouldn't have. French President Emmanuel Macron commented at the 2018 Gates Foundation Goalkeepers conference that a great way to decrease the birth rate is to educate women because, "what woman, being educated, would have seven, eight, or nine children."

Implicit in this kind of rhetoric is the idea that women with many children lack education and intelligence, and surely those who are better educated will not choose the kind of difficulty that parenthood offers.[3]

Monsieur Macron and the antinatalists may be right in one way: parenthood is truly hard. Unquestionably, it is intense, backbreaking, soul-stretching work. Raising kids is a complex endeavor with countless invisible, unknowable moving parts that take years or even decades to develop. Supporting that kind of black box work is risky and (yes) scary. People can suffer a loss of possibility when they have children. A loss of freedom. A loss of identity. It is easy to feel like a stranger to yourself when, instead of finally taking the time to read Anthony Doerr's *Cloud Cuckoo Land,* you offer up a repeat performance of Mo Willems's masterpiece *Nanette's Baguette.*

But instead of investing in a healthy, hopeful future by easing the burden of childrearing, our society seems to have chosen to accumulate wealth. Perhaps this impulse is driven by the feeling of scarcity: that our world is not up to the task of raising humans, that the earth isn't big enough to support us, that we, as individuals, will never have the time and the energy it takes to do the job right (and not sacrifice ourselves in the process).

Perhaps these pressures against perpetuating the human race are the starkest evidence of a sick society—and the result is that children are devalued, marginalized, oppressed. The space they take up is too much. The noise they make is in conflict with more important voices.

The more a society orients itself according to antinatalist arguments, the more difficult it is to parent. And here we see how antinatalism accelerates itself: The more we act, individually or collectively, as though children increase suffering, the more they actually do. It's a great snake eating its tail, until finally there is nothing left. No suffering, but no life.

But this is where the lie of antinatalism reveals itself. Because while it is undoubtedly true that if people choose to have children, they will suffer and their children will suffer, fear and anxiety are not the drivers of full, fulfilling lives. Avoiding risk may be safe, but it is also small. Accepting, even embracing, the black box of child-rearing—and here I include anyone who is lovingly committed to the well-being of a child, for one does not need to be a parent to cherish children and relish the beauty of life—is a literal gift. Raising children blasts us with information, experiences, and perspectives that are challenging to find if we are not bumping up against new and developing people. Taking the risk leads to untold rewards.

But how can we find the courage to take that risk? Perhaps we, as a society, need to rethink our values and how we are trying to live them. Let's look at the fear and the scarcity, the suffering and the anxiety and try to understand why we are shrinking from it. What does it mean? What *can* it mean?

If suffering begins at birth, perhaps a closer look at that process can be instructive—but focusing on the moment of birth alone, with its blood and tears and cries of pain obscures the magic of the entire process. A successful delivery unfolds not as a mother resists the painful process of childbirth, but as she allows the pain to work the miracle of that first breath. Birth signifies not suffering, but transcendence over that suffering, and beyond that, the intense connection to humanity—to the tiny new human, to the partners in the birthing process who witnessed the strength and struggle it took to endure the suffering, and indeed to the whole human race as a new mother contemplates the astonishing fact that every single individual of the eight billion that people the earth was born from a mother's womb.

And even further on and deeper in, the sense of purpose, meaning, and responsibility that replaces the aches and pains of pregnancy (a grace, by the way, that continues as a baby grows, as evidenced by the practice of wistfully scrolling through photos of children who, though peacefully sleeping now, were forcefully playing all the wrong notes throughout the day). Deeper still, we find that suffering in another sense—simply *allowing* the pain—delivers love. Love, humility, and the choice—available to anyone, parent or not—to prioritize the needs of someone in need.

It is a great paradox: While children do in fact increase suffering, they also bring with them the way to transform and be transformed by that suffering. Love, a sense of purpose, opportunities to learn and grow—all these can flourish in a family. Behind us lies scarcity, fear, and suffering. Before us still lies scarcity, fear, and suffering, but now we have the means to overcome them: all the unimagined potential of a new life, the constant change of each day, and the love we hold for our child.

Of course, beyond childbirth lie other types of suffering, encased in the process of parenthood. There are expectations for ourselves and

> **Then somewhere, somehow, I forgot to count. I didn't remember how much sleep I got or how much I was missing. Whatever it was, it would just have to be enough.**

our children. There are comparisons with peers or celebrities, the bright and shiny social media versions of others' lives that glare at our own unkempt and lived-in families. There are disappointments when those expectations are unmet, the status markers unachieved. These, too, we must allow.

Allowing, accepting, and even embracing the risks and uncertainties inherent in raising children requires us to look beyond what can be seen or known. It is a leap—of faith, maybe, or of hope for the future. Perhaps it is an expression of trust in ourselves to rise to unknown challenges. Or a recognition of the gift of existence, of the beauty of the world, and of the expansion that comes from sharing it with others and seeing their wonder reflected back.

In taking the leap, or stepping into the black box, we find that if we are to decrease the suffering, it is not the children that we want to let go of. It is those expectations, those limiting beliefs about what happiness is, those unattainable mirages that distract and detract from *what is really happening* that must go. We can free ourselves from those feelings of not being enough, or not having enough, or missing out on whatever it is the world has to offer by sitting with what we do have. Then we see and know that our lives are richer and fuller with children than without and are willing to suffer the derision and disdain society sometimes offers because we value them so highly.

In fact, family life is ideally suited to help us transition from a world of suffering and scarcity and competition to abundance. Because children are ever-changing and ever-growing, we are constantly adapting, learning, and letting go—of limiting beliefs, of "easy" paths to happiness, of the illusion of control. Shedding those ideas is transformational.

My own journey on this path included a realization early on when I had three young children and a lot of insecurities about my role as a mother. My life was full of people and places and activities that I loved, and yet at night I would struggle to sleep, thinking about my friends whose marriage was rocky, and the talents I wished I was improving, and the minutes of sleep that were ticking away as I lay restless and awake. *Only five hours and forty-five minutes tonight,* I would think. *Tomorrow is going to be hard.*

The next day, unsurprisingly, would be hard. How was I to deal with tantrums and manage food for three little people or even leave the apartment for some fresh air on less than six hours of sleep?

Then somewhere, somehow, I forgot to count. I didn't remember how much sleep I got or how much I was missing. Whatever it was, it would just have to be enough. And, surprisingly, it was. Whatever I had was enough. With my focus off the things I lacked, it was easier to see what I had.

What I had were three small teachers helping me identify and reorder my priorities, guiding me through the tasks of helping them become more independent, giving me opportunities to go places I'd never been and try things I never would have before. At every turn were moments of wonder and awe. My empty cup was suddenly running over.

That is where and how our perspectives can change. There is nothing about raising a family that is not a community experience, where all time and paths and belongings are jointly held. A hundred times a day raising children has us facing our expectations and letting go of them, finding new, unexpected ways. It has us humbling ourselves in tasks as small as putting a toddler's shoes on her feet and as large as advising a teenager on how to approach the rest of his life.

These are moments, not of scarcity, but of abundance. Even a moment as difficult and public as a tantrum in the aisle of a grocery store can be an exercise in empathy, humility, and repair as we acknowledge our mistakes and try to do better.

Again, and again, and again, we are being birthed anew with new perspectives and experiences and emotions. With each of those moments come opportunities to learn and become something more than we once were.

Part of that abundance that we feel comes through welcoming the difficulty and the risk inherent in parenthood. The range of emotions on any given day, as previously mentioned, can be surprising—shocking, even—but it can also be instructive. The great scope of experiences allowed in a life in which there are *more lives* lived in intimate proximity also allows for more understanding, wisdom, and empathy, for a broader range of colors and tones, for shades of meaning and nuance we couldn't otherwise see.

In very real and practical experiences we are allowed to see that while we may wish for worldly accolades and material goods, joy can be found simply in helping a child learn to read, or in being the hero that found the baby's lost pacifier, or getting to sit quietly with a child who is scared of the dark until she relaxes into sleep. Seeing, and sitting with, the suffering of someone else, walking with them through it, can help us see our own suffering differently—not as a meaningless slog, but as important information about who we are and what we are capable of.

Despite its aims of reducing suffering in the world, antinatalist attitudes have increased it. Our society can approach suffering in much healthier ways—ways that do not put children, like those teenagers on the bus, in a position to wonder (subconsciously or not) if they are burdens on their parents and the world. Children who grow in an abundant environment, where their needs are opportunities and their voices are gifts—both in their homes and in society—are empowered to be our teachers. From their perspective they can show us things we cannot see. Unburdened by adult cares, they can blaze trails for us to follow. Parents and caregivers, properly supported, can raise children to meet their potential—not to live, stunted, by a life in shadow and scarcity, but to thrive and flourish. Society as a whole has more eyes and ears and hearts and hands to approach the suffering we find and carry us through to the other side.

Brooklyn Swenson

I want to tell those teens on the bus that, perhaps, we have it wrong, or backward, or upside down. If every day is growth, and time can stretch and contract, then maybe there is more of it than we have been led to believe. And there is more to life than we can see and feel. People may be a scourge, but they are also the salve to our suffering. It's possible that your children will lead you through the problems you face. That in raising them, loving them, connecting with them, and sharing your lives with each other, you will become more than who you are, and more than enough. And maybe you can have kids and travel too—to places that don't exist on any map. ✸

1. Though we have our own modern version of antinatalism, arguments against having children have existed for thousands of years. Some early Christian sects discouraged procreation for similar reasons: more births meant more deaths, more pain. More recently, the Shakers promoted celibacy because they viewed sex as the root of all evil.

2. One such example is Elizabeth Skoski, "The Perpetual Rage of Motherhood," *The Cut,* January 11, 2022.

3. Many women around the world who are both educated and mothers to a large brood sent him postcards, politely showing him that the two aims of education and family are not mutually exclusive.

THE SIN OF FEAR

TIM CHAVES

FOR A TWO-WEEK STRETCH LAST summer, Aubrey and our thirteen-year-old daughter were in Costa Rica on a trip with our daughter's science teacher. This was a highly anticipated journey, and they'd gamely taken along an AirTag so I could follow their adventures from afar and make sure that they stayed reasonably close to the predetermined path.

While the first stretch of their absence had passed swimmingly and I'd received an occasional "we have service!" text, or a picture, those little notes stopped suddenly a few days in. I checked in on the AirTag and got the response any Apple user with a bit of anxiety wants to avoid: "No Location Found." I worried a little and tucked it away.

Those of us that remained at home spent that evening out and about together, having fun as we said goodbye to our eleven-year-old son for a few days; he was leaving the next morning on our ward's summer Trek. The youth were heading to Martin's Cove for a twenty-mile hike through the desert, with a near-record heat wave predicted in the area they'd be traveling.

He was excited, but as Trek had gotten closer and I contemplated him actually going, he started to seem, suddenly, smaller and younger. At church, he looked a foot shorter than the other boys passing the sacrament. He was barely old enough to go and had never been away for an extended period on his own before.

After the kids went to bed the night before he was going to leave, I got stuck in my head. I ruminated on the potential disasters that might have happened in the jungles of Costa Rica or that could happen in the Wyoming desert, as half of my family slipped so many miles out of my grasp. My heart beat fast and my stomach clenched tight. I scribbled a semicoherent note in my journal:

> *My anxiety, as I write this, is sky high. Aubrey is in Costa Rica with [thirteen-year-old daughter]. I can't get a signal on her AirTag. [Eleven-year-old son] is leaving for Trek tomorrow. We just had a wonderful evening—we played football, he danced around with his sisters, doing his signature "airplane" move. More wonderful than we've had in a while. The joy was foreboding. Then, the sunset. A beautiful sunset. A peaceful sign, perhaps of the worst to come? A comfort in advance of a devastating tragedy?*

I tried to reassure myself that everything would probably be just fine, but my worries felt like a full-body warning, like "the Spirit" was telling me to shut it all down, to pull back into our cocoon of safety. I seriously considered keeping my son home. What if I ignored this feeling, in the name of conquering my anxiety—and then something really did happen?

As irrational and off-base as my thoughts seem now when I simply read them off the page, it seems that I'm not alone in the occasional disproportionate worry—particularly among young people, anxiety is at or near all-time highs in the United States and elsewhere.[1] And we Latter-day Saints often take it a step further, giving ourselves a theological justification for our distress: the questionable doctrine of the *spiritual warning*.

Though we're very comfortable referring to the Holy Ghost as a comforter, it seems that in practical terms, we just as often describe the Spirit as a "warner." Some of my most vivid memories of stories told over the pulpit are those in which the Holy Ghost told someone that something really bad was going to happen, usually followed by a miraculous escape.

I don't want to cast doubt on the idea that the Spirit can warn. But I think I took the wrong message from these stories. What I took away was that the Spirit warns us through fear—in direct contrast to what we read in 2 Timothy 1:7:

For God hath not given us the spirit of fear;
but of power, and of love, and of a sound mind.

We can acknowledge the reality of spiritual warnings—but from a Spirit that would do so through power, through love, through a sound mind—not through fear. Not through the stomach-churning, sweaty-palmed anxiety that keeps us awake at night.

Looking back, of all of the pending disaster "warnings" I've thought I received, never—not once—has one come to pass. And I've received a lot. In the meantime, it's caused a whole lot of unproductive anguish, a lot of missed sleep and even missed experiences.

I think that's a sin. Not in the sense that I've broken a particular law, or that I need to feel guilty, or beat myself up, or take a series of steps to regain God's favor. But in the sense that, certainly, a loving God must mourn to see us deprive ourselves of experiences that would stretch us, or bring us joy, or move us to tears. After all, the

Brian T. Kershisnik

Greek word most commonly translated as sin in the New Testament is *hamartia* (*ἁμαρτία*): literally, *missing the mark*.

And so it seems to me that as easily as "sin" can be a trespass, it can be cosmic missing-out, a step in the wrong direction, away from our goal and our potential to live in eternal love and adventure. And by this metric, fear may become every bit as sinful as anything else in our usual list. Perhaps this is why Richard Rohr has advocated for fear to be added, along with deceit, to the list of the seven deadly sins.[2]

But perhaps to an even greater extent than with other sins—fighting off the sin of fear is easier said than done. My body—my natural man—has gone through an evolutionary process that places a couple things as top priorities: procreation and the survival of my offspring. Accordingly, I have a hyperactive danger detector pumping me full of adrenaline and cortisol at the slightest hint of bodily harm to me or my loved ones. In small and moderated doses, or in the face of real, present danger, these can be good, of course! As a therapist friend told me, no emotions are bad in and of themselves—especially when they remain in their intended, helpful domains; our built-in danger *detectors* should probably keep us away from cliff sides on gusty days or from weaving through traffic on the freeway at high speeds.

And at the same time, I have to face what's true for me and was truer for me that evening before Trek than it ever had been: my body was urging me into the *sin* of fear—a reactionary state where I'd refuse to allow any of us to do anything that could possibly hurt us.

In this sense, my "natural man" truly can be an enemy to God: by living, all too often, in the sin of fear. But my body is also my vehicle to get to life's richest experiences. Without my body, I could never have the relationality that leads to the fear of losing it; without my body, I can't arrive at the adventures and misadventures that stretch and grow me. It's clear that to repent from the sin of fear isn't to retreat from the body. So what might it look like?

And here, ancient wisdom and modern science beautifully align. The corresponding virtue to fear, of course, is courage—what might be modestly

Brian T. Kershisnik

defined as an intentional facing of that which we fear *in spite* of the fear it causes. Nelson Mandela said that he "learned that courage was not the absence of fear, but the triumph over it." And this is exactly what modern therapeutic techniques call for in the face of anxiety.

In the 1950s, a new form of behavioral therapy called "systematic desensitization" was developed by psychiatrist Joseph Wolpe. In time, systematic desensitization evolved into what's called *exposure therapy*, which is widely used today to treat clinical anxiety disorders.

The idea behind exposure therapy is simple: when something triggers our anxiety, we often begin avoiding the thing that triggers it to avoid the anxiety itself (for example, keeping one's son home from Trek). But this intuitive reaction gives more power to the thing we fear and can increase the anxiety the next time around. Exposure therapy very gradually exposes sufferers to their anxieties (a fear of spiders, for example, might call for a gradual increase in exposure to the idea of spiders—it could start with something as simple as a picture). As anxiety falls, the level of exposure increases, bringing anxiety up again while remaining manageable, until the person suffering the anxiety is able to fully face the thing they feared and successfully manage the corresponding anxiety.

While exposure therapy is used in clinical settings for debilitating anxiety and related disorders like OCD, its basic principles can also be used to great effect in our everyday lives. We don't need to be in a therapist's office to practice them: when our anxiety rises, when we're afraid—what courage and proven therapeutic practice both call for is noticing our reactive retreat from fear, engaging it, gaining some "observational distance," and maybe even moving further into it at a measured and even pace.

As with everything, this idea can be taken too far—it's possible to begin to fear our fear. What I'm hoping is that we can healthily engage and overcome the *sin* of fear: the kind of fear that stunts the spiritual growth we would gain through experience. The call to courage (root word cor, the Latin for *heart*) is not a call to charge into battle, replacing one amped-up emotion with another; it can be as simple as getting out of our amygdalas and into our hearts: vulnerably sharing our burden with a friend, sitting in the quietness of contemplation, or finding, as Peter Enns has said, a "deep trust" in God and moving forward in uncertainty.[3]

For me, last summer, that meant letting Aubrey and my daughter "be lost" in Costa Rica and sending my son to Trek. I took him to the departing vans early the next morning, and off he went. When my thoughts of Costa Rica turned anxious, I didn't start calling backup numbers or trying to get in touch through other members of the group. I sat with that fear. And it turns out, that day was OK. And so was the next one.

A week later—as I'm sure you guessed—everybody got back just fine, happy and healthy with lots of stories to tell. There were frog sightings and river splashings and jellyfish encounters and hot sauce discoveries. There were new experiences. There was learning and growth and joy.

When we find ourselves fearful and responding to that fear by covering up, or missing out, or holding ourselves or others back from that experience—it might be nothing more than our "natural man."

I believe in spiritual promptings—even the kind that can prevent bad things from happening. But I no longer believe in the kind of prompting that makes us afraid. While I'd never attempt to proclaim what God can or can't do, the scriptures suggest we can believe in a Spirit that moves us to act, that inspires us to greater compassion, that makes our thoughts clear and lucid and productive. *For God hath not given us the spirit of fear; but of power, and of love, and of a sound mind.*

Maybe the reason God doesn't give us the spirit of fear is because God can't encourage us to sin. It seems God moves only forward—urging us to stretch and expand and grow through experience. When we find ourselves fearful and responding to that fear by covering up, or missing out, or holding ourselves or others back from that experience—it might be nothing more than our "natural man." Often, it's our body doing its best to protect us—and we can be grateful for that. But we're capable of much more; and when we repent from the sin of fear, we can move joyfully into the wild and wonderful adventures that God has in store for us. ✱

1. Renee D. Goodwin et al., "Trends in Anxiety among Adults in the United States, 2008–2018: Rapid Increases among Young Adults," *Journal of Psychiatric Research* 130 (November 2020): 441–46.
2. Richard Rohr and Andreas Ebert, *The Enneagram: A Christian Perspective* (New York: Crossroad Publishing, 2001), 32.
3. Peter Enns, *The Sin of Certainty: Why God Desires Our Trust More Than Our "Correct" Beliefs* (San Francisco: HarperOne, 2016), 120.

ALMA BLOCH, NÉE TREPKA

MARK D.
BENNION

After Carl Bloch's Christ in Gethsemane II

We don't need tradition to say
you are the tone and texture,
the whorl and oil in his paintings—

everywhere in the amber rays,
color of the eyes, arm gestures,
even in the shadows straining

toward Messiah. You were ballet
in his brushstrokes, the figure-
angel to pull us into the pain

of how God alone can pray,
how you held Him like a river—
His sweat purging before hanging

for us all on the longest day.
You steadied more than an hour
every time you posed, waiting

like the only one knowing the way
to strengthen Him, to comfort
after betrayal, during forsaking.

You, the soul of the house, stayed
amid the wounds, bonds, and failure,
even as he knelt there shaking,

painting the coil of blood that could pay.
Such embrace for husband and Savior—
a frame of infinite breaking.

THE BODY OF CHRIST & HUMAN EQUALITY

An Ancient Ideal

TERRYL GIVENS

"History has been invaded by God in Christ in such a way that nothing can stay as it was. All terms of human community and conduct have been altered at the deepest levels."
–David Bentley Hart[1]

DAVID BENTLEY HART'S DESCRIPTION of the impact of the Christian message was borne out visibly and conspicuously in early Christian communities. One historian described the "social diversity" in these congregations, accompanied by an "ideal of human equality." The Christians, he noted, taught that in Christ "all were equal, and the distinctions of rank and degree were irrelevant. In church meetings, educated people sat as equals among other men's slaves and petty artisans."[2] The new faith emerged in the context of cultural structures organized around brutal inequalities: freedmen and slaves, rich and poor, men and women. Christianity could not—initially—challenge the social status quo in the larger society. However, the gospel could and in its best moments did remove such limitations and boundaries within the circle of the Christian community.

Many scholars have confirmed that in these early congregations, "members of different social strata became extremely close to one another, supporting each other."[3] While freedom from broader political oppression may have been of limited scope, equality within the Christian community was not.

THE CHRISTIAN FAMILY

We modern minds may have a hard time feeling the shock of that astonishing idea intrinsic to such fellowship—namely, that God walks among us as a minister and mentor and fellow traveler. He breaks bread with His companions, weeps over the death of a friend, dines with sinners, and washes the feet of His apostles.

Following this model, some of the first Christians successfully turned ad hoc communities into a society governed by love. A historian of early Christianity confirms the world-defying novelty "of a group joined by Spiritual power into an extended family."[4] Morwenna Ludlow uses the same language, writing that the "Christians described themselves as a kind of extended family or household."[5] This is not just nostalgic fantasy.

Fra Angelico

Early Christians were in fact ridiculed "because we call each other brother and sister." Indeed, as these early Christians insisted to a skeptical world, "We are your brothers and sisters as well." The feature marking these early believers was their practice of lovingkindness—as one writer observed, "'Only look,' they say, 'how they love one another.'"[6]

The words of one contemptuous critic actually confirm the success with which Christians at times moved the marginalized to the center of concern. "Well, what do we have in the end? An impressive god indeed: one who desires nothing more than to adopt sinners as his children; one who takes to himself the creatures who stand condemned by another, the poor wretches who are (as they say of themselves), naught but dung."[7] The satirist Lucian similarly mocked the Christians for their gullibility and solidarity with their fellow sufferers. "They show incredible speed whenever" one of their number is the target of public sanction.[8]

BONDS BEYOND BLOOD

Until the arrival of Christianity, most forms of community—even religious communities—were ethnic or kinship based. "Christianity now allowed religion to be conceived as an entity independent of the ethnic-cultural components that were normally (and inevitably) attached."[9] The sociologist Joseph Henrich confirms that Christianity's transformation of Western culture was cataclysmic, signaling the demise of various forms of tribal loyalty to kin and clan in deference to "voluntary associations" with "groups of strangers." In this way, Christianity inculcated and motivated a version of love that transformed the world.[10]

This was not an incidental side effect, but a deliberate strategy. Any bonds strong enough to transcend tribal and familial loyalties had to be more than theoretical. Wayne Meeks argues that Paul's letters reveal universal hybridization as a conscious effort at community building—with each church "by intention" becoming "ethnically and socially mixed. It was Paul's strategy. Each of Paul's revolutionary cell groups was deliberately developed to be a microcosm of the global reality that Paul and other early leaders believed was coming."[11] In the letters of Paul that shaped early Christian society, Wilhelm Wrade notes, "his zeal for community . . . always takes first place; the question he always asks is, 'what builds it up?'"[12]

COMPASSION FOR ALL

Christian love surpassed anything the ancient world had seen. Rodney Stark notes how through recurrent plagues, as citizens fled infected areas, Christians remained behind to nurse and minister to the sick at the cost of their lives. Around 260 AD, at the height of yet another epidemic, the Christian Dionysius recorded,

> Christians showed unbounded love and loyalty, never sparing themselves and thinking only of one another. Heedless of danger, they took charge of the sick, attending to their every need and ministering to them in Christ, and with them departed this life serenely happy; for they were infected by others with the disease, drawing on themselves the sickness of their neighbors and cheerfully accepting their pains. Many, in nursing and curing others, transferred their death to themselves and died in their stead.[13]

A century later, the fourth-century monk Rufinus described how Christians in Egypt treated arriving visitors:

> As we drew near to that place and they realized that foreign brethren were arriving, they poured out of their cells like a swarm of bees and ran to meet us with delight and alacrity, many of them carrying containers of water and of bread. . . . When they had welcomed us, first of all they led us with psalms into the church and washed our feet and one by one they dried them with the linen cloth they were girded with, as if to wash away the fatigue of the journey. . . . What can I say that would do justice to their humanity, their courtesy, and their

> love? Nowhere have I seen love flourish so greatly, nowhere with such quick compassion, such eager hospitality.[14]

SKEPTICISM AND CHALLENGES

In trying to decipher the appeal of early Christianity, the cynic Friedrich Nietzsche could only marvel at the gullibility of the teeming throngs of converts who had found this "better way." Power and dominion were the source of the only real happiness, he insisted. The rich, the well born, the noble—these possessed the genuine article, until clever priests convinced them that some phantom joy was only found in pity, humility, selflessness, and fellow feeling.[15] Yet even that great skeptic could not really explain how the noble, the powerful, the rich—how they too were persuaded to willingly forsake their privilege and aspire instead to humility, to selflessness, to compassion.

Christianity quenched a thirst that had never found perfect resolution: as Martin Buber diagnosed the essential human condition, "The

Fra Angelico

longing for relation is primary."[16] Beneath the world of transactional relationships based on commerce, power dynamics, and self-interest, Christianity exposed the deeper roots of our being: fragmented individuals finding fulness only in a thriving web of relationships. The template for a society of perfect love and deep unity had been drawn: "Here there is no Gentile or Jew, circumcised or free" (Col. 3:11).

Nor, said Paul, "is there male and female" (Gal. 3:28). "The Magna Carta of Humanity," one scholar called this Pauline pronouncement. "There is nothing like it in all of antiquity."[17] A second-century witness wrote "if one or other of them have bondmen and bondwomen or children, through love towards them they persuade them to become Christians, and when they have done so, they call them brethren without distinction."[18] Justin Martyr wrote how "we who hated and destroyed one another, and on account of their different manners would not live with men of a different tribe, now, since the coming of Christ, live familiarly with them."[19]

Even leaders, of course, are encouraged to act as servants of all, like the angels who call themselves humankind's "fellowservants" (Rev. 22:9). And even Christ, God embodied, washed the feet of His disciples and said, "I do not call you servants . . . but I have called you friends" (John 15:15).

Certainly, the revolution never found its perfect form. Paul beseeched Philemon to treat Onesimus as "no longer a slave but more than a slave, a beloved brother" (Phil 1:16); but he did not repudiate the institution of slavery. Just as Paul maintained that male and female were no different "in Christ," but went on to make men "the head." Still, the deeper threat to social hierarchies like slave/master and patron/client was real, and opponents of the Christian revolution were not slow in recognizing the transformations afoot, however incomplete. Revisiting those witnesses to the transformative impact of the gospel revealed in Christ is important for two reasons. It is a testament to the ways in which we have fallen short of an original vision. But it can inspire us with the confidence that we, too, might yet be

Fra Angelico

able to astonish our contemporaries by a more conspicuous, godly love that sees the image of Christ in everyone. ✸

1. David Bentley Hart, *The New Testament: A Translation* (New Haven: Yale University Press, 2017), xxiii–xxiv.
2. Robin Lane Fox, *Pagans and Christians* (New York: Knopf, 1987), 337.
3. Lampe quoted in Michael J. Kruger, *Christianity at the Crossroads: How the Second Century Shaped the Future of the Church* (Westmont, IL: InterVarsity Press, 2018), 27.
4. Elaine Pagels, *Beyond Belief: The Secret Gospel of Thomas* (New York: Random House, 2003), 6.
5. Morwenna Ludlow, *The Early Church: The I. B. Tauris History of the Christian Church* (New York: Bloomsbury Academic, 2009), 742.
6. Tertullian, Apology 39.7, in Philip Schaff, ed., *Ante-Nicene Fathers Vol. III* (Grand Rapids, MI: Christian Classics Ethereal Library, 1885), 68.
7. Celsus, *On the True Doctrine,* trans. and ed. R. Joseph Hoffmann (New York: Oxford University Press, 1987), 102.
8. Lucian, *The Passing of Peregrinus,* in *Lucian Vol. 5,* trans. A. M. Harmon (Cambridge, MA: Harvard University Press, 1936), 13–15.
9. Michael J. Kruger, *Christianity at the Crossroads: How the Second Century Shaped the Future of the Church* (Westmont, IL: InterVarsity Press, 2018), 5.
10. Joseph Henrich, *The WEIRDest People in the World: How the West Became Psychologically Peculiar and Particularly Prosperous* (New York: Farrar, Straus and Giroux, 2020).
11. Meeks, the First Urban Christians, cited in Steve Chalke, *The Lost Message of Paul* (N.p.: SPCK, 2019), 268.
12. W[ilhelm] Wrede, *Paul,* trans. Edward Lummis (London: Philip Green, 1907), 60.
13. Quoted in Rodney Stark, *The Rise of Christianity* (New York: HarperCollins, 1996), 82.
14. Diane Butler Bass, *A People's History of Christianity* (New York: HarperCollins, 1989), 64.
15. Friedrich Nietzsche makes this argument in his *Genealogy of Morals* (1887).
16. Martin Buber, *I and Thou,* trans. Walter Kaufmann (New York: Touchstone, 1996), 78.
17. John J. Collins, *What Are Biblical Values: What the Bible Says on Key Ethical Issues* (New Haven: Yale University Press, 2019), 137.
18. Aristides, "The Apology of Aristides," in Philip Schaff, ed., *Ante-Nicene Fathers Vol. IX* (Grand Rapids, MI: Christian Classics Ethereal Library, 1885), 514.
19. Cited in Ludlow, *Early Church,* 35.

James Rees

MY SEARCH FOR EXPANSIVE SPIRITUALITY

JON OGDEN

ONE SUNDAY MORNING WHEN I WAS a teenager, a member of the stake high council rattled my world when he told our congregation that his favorite book was *Meditations* by Marcus Aurelius.

He didn't hedge. He just said it, with conviction.

I didn't know you could do that.

After the meeting I tracked him down and asked if he'd let me borrow his copy of the book, which he happily agreed to do.

When I returned home and started reading *Meditations,* I didn't comprehend most of what I read. But I sensed the book's quiet power. Here was an emperor of Rome—possibly the most powerful human alive at the time—writing notes to himself full of humility, grace, and wisdom.

Paige Crosland Anderson

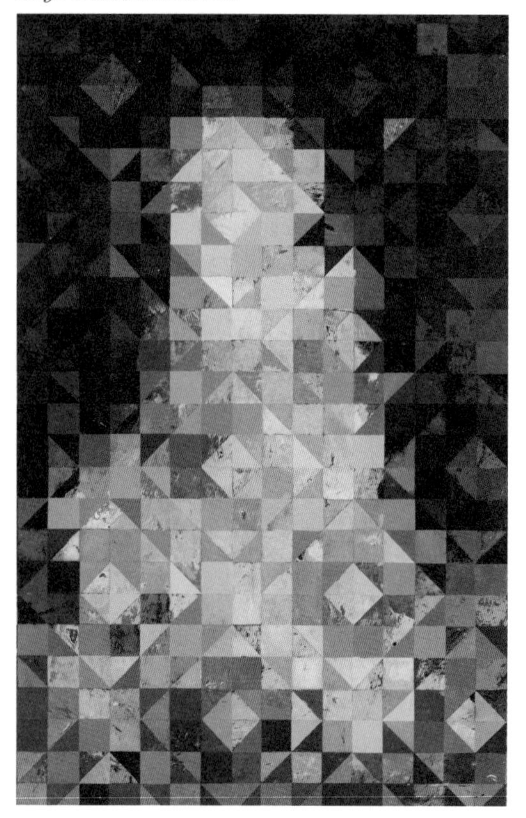

"Very little is needed to make a happy life," Aurelius wrote.

"Remember that neither the future nor the past pains thee, but only the present."

"Nothing is required of us than to accomplish well the task at hand."

The more I read, the more I simultaneously felt exhilarated and confused. Here were words that stirred the same spiritual feelings within me that I felt while reading LDS scripture. And yet *Meditations* lacked the gold-leafed edges and thin, near-transparent paper I'd come to associate with sacred texts.

What did that mean?

I wasn't sure, but I wanted more of the feelings that *Meditations* stirred in me.

Not long after, I discovered a book of conversations between a Christian reverend and a Hindu devotee that helped me confidently cross a threshold toward expansive spirituality. In the book, the Hindu devotee claimed that the New Testament phrase "*all scripture* is given by inspiration of God"[1] indicates that Christians should be open to a spiritually expansive worldview—one that includes the scripture of Hinduism among other traditions.

The reverend said that he initially disagreed with such a view but that he had recently discovered a passage from a book that made him think twice.

Which book?

The Book of Mormon.

"I went through my reference library and found a wonderful statement in The Book of Mormon," the reverend said, "which, mind you, is a book that I generally have no connection with and rarely ever read."

Then he showed the Hindu devotee a passage in 2 Nephi 29:

> *"Know ye not that there are more nations than one? Know ye not that I, the Lord your God . . . bring forth my word unto the children of*

> *men, yea, even upon all the nations of the earth? Wherefore murmur ye, because that ye shall receive more of my word? . . . Wherefore, because that ye have a Bible ye need not suppose that it contains all my words; neither need ye suppose that I have not caused more to be written."*

"This is wonderful," the Hindu responded.

"I really like it quite a bit," the reverend said, "although it definitely substantiates your point of view."[2]

There I was, reading LDS scripture through the lens of someone who wasn't LDS and realizing that yes, *this* was my tradition.

The Latter-day Saint call for an expansive approach to spirituality goes well beyond the Book of Mormon. Joseph Smith claimed that "one of the grand fundamental principles of Mormonism is to receive truth, let it come from whence it may."[3] The Doctrine and Covenants urges the Saints to "seek ye out of the best books words of wisdom."[4] The thirteenth article of faith says to seek "anything virtuous, lovely, or of good report or praiseworthy." Brigham Young said that whether the truth surfaces "with the Universalists, or the Church of Rome, or the Methodists, the Church of England, the Presbyterians, the Baptists, the Quakers, the Shakers, or any other of the various and numerous different sects," we should gather it.[5] And Orson Whitney said, "God is using more than one people for the accomplishment of his great and marvelous work. The Latter-day Saints cannot do it all. It is too vast, too arduous, for any one people."[6]

In some sense, this expansive approach to spirituality is the work of ongoing restoration. After all, the restoration isn't a lifeless process, like bringing a classic car back to its original condition. That kind of project might be a fine hobby, but, as Patrick Mason wrote in his book *Restoration*, "We weren't put on earth to watch reruns, no matter how good those old episodes were."[7]

Restoration is the work of digging deep to tap into the living source that's always already here and then living from that place: here. It's the work of planting seeds in soil, allowing the nutrients inside and outside ourselves to do the rest. "The farmer sleeps at night and is up and around during the day," Jesus said, "Yet the seeds keep sprouting and growing, and he doesn't understand how. It is the ground that makes the seeds sprout and grow into plants that produce grain."[8] This ground of being—the living source itself—breaks us open for growth. In time, it also brings death to our old selves, which pass away like seeds newly sprouted.

"If we embrace wisdom from anywhere," the thinking might go, "won't some people leave the fold?" The answer is that they might. Anything is possible.

As Jesus said, "Unless a grain of wheat falls into the earth and dies, it remains just a single grain, but if it dies it bears much fruit."[9] Death gives way to life in an ever-present restoration.

And so I continue to dig and plant, searching for words and practices that sprout something in me. I'm struck to stillness reading Taoist questions such as, "Do you have the patience to wait till your mud settles and the water is clear?" and "Can you remain unmoving till the right action arises by itself?"[10] I'm called to care for life when I read the Buddha say, "The wise live without injuring nature, as the bee drinks nectar without harming the flower."[11] And I feel hope when I hear the repetitive conviction of Julian of Norwich, who wrote, "All shall be well, and all shall be well, and all manner of thing shall be well."[12] Mystics and meditators from all traditions offer these fruits and so much more—brothers and sisters who've experienced the same eternal living source I yearn to live aligned with.

Some Latter-day Saints might worry about what will happen if members embrace this expansive approach to spirituality. "If we embrace wisdom from anywhere," the thinking might go, "won't some people leave the fold?" The answer is that they might. Anything is possible. But consider the spiritual hunger of Joseph Smith—a hunger that led him to explore the Apocrypha, Hebrew and Latin languages, myriad translations of scripture, and more. The founder of the LDS faith had a deep hunger for expansive spirituality, and it was from this hunger that revelation poured through him, the way it does through us all. Hunger feeds revelation.

So I ask: What if we don't embrace wisdom wherever it's found? What if we *aren't* expansive in our spirituality and instead are content to simply maintain it? What's the risk?

One risk is that we won't be ready for the inevitable exposure that upcoming generations will have to these texts. Two hundred years ago, these texts were available to only a subset of scholars. Today, by contrast, the words of wise women and men around the world (past and present) are instantly accessible to read or listen to via our phones. What happens when the next generation encounters these words, as many inevitably will? Will they be troubled by the fact that such texts are full of wisdom, as I was when I first encountered the words of Marcus Aurelius? Or will they celebrate, knowing such wisdom is part of one great whole?

We also risk getting stuck in the zero-sum debate that rises from a paradigm of either/or, in/out, and pure/impure. Chances are that we all know what it feels like for someone to engage us in such a way—to not see the nuance in our position and instead flatten us to being "the bad guy." People of one sect do it to people of another, believers do it to nonbelievers, and nonbelievers do it to believers. Embracing an expansive spirituality allows us to be more resilient to such attacks because we play by a different set of rules. We sidestep the premise that we are 100 percent right and another group is 100 percent wrong. We realize that we can find wisdom even from those we disagree with and in doing so turn "enemies" to friends, as Jesus urged people to do.

Finally, and perhaps most importantly, we risk stunting our individual and collective growth — like trees stuck in planters too small for their roots. Such trees never reach their full height, and when we limit our sources of growth, we risk the same result. We need firm soil, true, especially early in life when we're sensing into identity and community, and in this way, a planter is a solid place to start. But if our spiritual life grows stale, we suffer. And, as part of the body of Christ, when we suffer, the whole community suffers. And so we must faithfully follow that which nurtures genuine life in us, for the kingdom of God contains people who are alive.

In one of the most famous passages of an ancient Hindu text, a boy is sent to school for twenty years to study the scriptures of his tradition. He returns full of knowledge but also full of unfounded confidence, certain he's discovered all the insight that the world could possibly offer him.

The boy's father, sensing his son's confidence and knowing it to be misplaced, decides to teach him a lesson.

"Go and get the seed of a banyan tree," he tells his son.

So the son does.

"Now break it open and tell me what you see," the father says.

"I see nothing," the son says.

"Exactly," the father responds. "And yet from this invisible essence, a tiny seed grows into an enormous banyan tree."

Then the father tells his son that he, too, is this invisible essence. "You are that," he says.[13]

Eventually, as the father continues to present his son with a series of similar analogies, the son returns to a state of humility, realizing that even though he had studied the scriptures of his own tradition for twenty years, he still didn't know all the mysteries of life and should instead remain open for new growth.

It's a story rich with insights, one of which is that we should never convince ourselves that we've "made it." The confidence we gain from studying the wisdom of our own tradition (or the wisdom of any tradition, for that matter) lies not in our possession of knowledge, but in the *source* of that knowledge.

"My work is not yet finished," reads 2 Nephi 29:9,11, "For I command all men, both in the east and in the west, and in the north, and in the south, and in the islands of the sea, that they shall write the words which I speak unto them."

As we remain open to this divine reality—this invisible essence spoken of in the Hindu story

Paige Crosland Anderson

of a father and son—we can't help but grow. What will such growth look like? How does it work? Like the sower in the parable of Jesus, we can't know. And yet the more we remain open, allowing the divine to work through us all, the more we'll grow toward a Zion more beautiful than we can imagine.

"Enlarge the place of your tent," Isaiah writes, "And let them stretch out the curtains of your dwellings; Do not spare."[14] ✸

1. 2 Timothy 3:16, KJV.
2. Alvin V. P. Hart and Satyaraja Dasa Adhikari, *Krsna Consciousness and Christianity: East-West Dialogues* (Bengal, India: International Society for Krishna Consciousness, 1989), 8.
3. Joseph Smith, in History, 1838–1856 [Manuscript History of the Church], volume E-1, 1666, josephsmithpapers.org.
4. Doctrine and Covenants 88:118.
5. "Remarks," *Deseret News,* October 26, 1859, [1].
6. Orson F. Whitney, in *Ninety-Eighth Annual Conference of the Church of Jesus Christ of Latter-day Saints* (Salt Lake City: The Church of Jesus Christ of Latter-day Saints, 1928), 59.
7. Patrick Q. Mason, *Restoration: God's Call to the 21st-Century World* (Meridian, ID: Faith Matters, 2020), 34
8. Mark 4:27–28, Contemporary English Version of the Bible.
9. John 12:24, New Revised Standard Version, Updated Edition.
10. Lao Tzu, *The Tao Te Ching,* trans. Stephen Mitchell (New York: HarperPerennial, 2006).
11. Buddha, *The Dhammapada,* trans. Eknath Easwaran, Easwaran's Classics of Indian Spirituality Book 3 (Tomales, CA: Nilgiri Press, 2007).
12. Julian of Norwich, *Revelations of Divine Love,* trans. Grace Harriet Warrack.
13. Paraphrase of the Chandogya Upanishad.
14. Isaiah 54:2, NKJV.

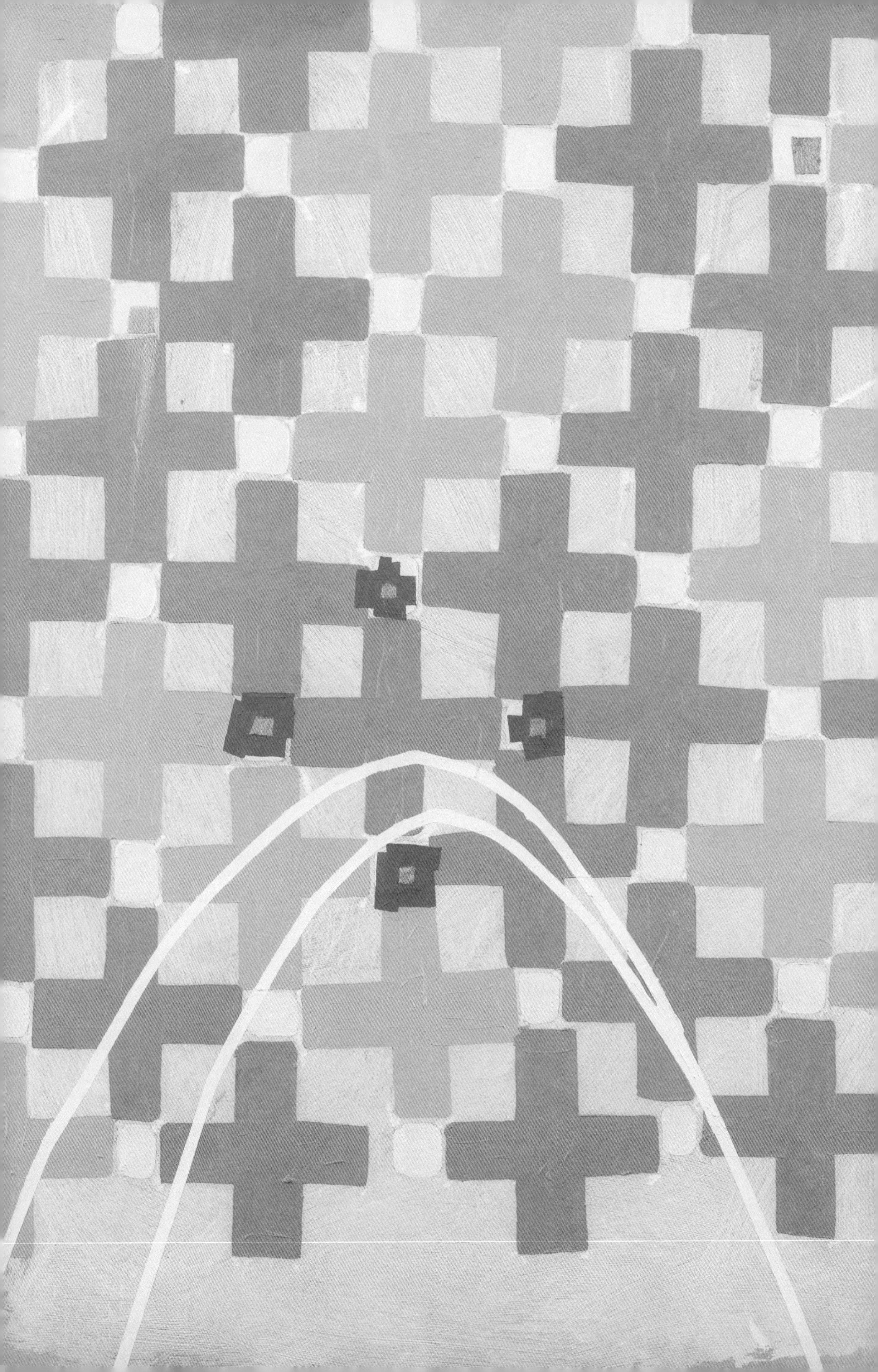

A TAPESTRY OF LOVE

Forgiveness and the Task of Reweaving

TESIA TSAI

THERE'S A JOKE AMONG ASIAN Americans that to disappoint your parents, you simply need to exist. In Confucian ideology, children are the literal extension of their parents' flesh—meaning that your every mistake reflects directly on them.

And there are many ways to make a mistake.

I was that rare, shining child my parents bragged about at dinner parties, the one they told my siblings to emulate—and the one who breathed a mental sigh of relief each time my parents said, "We're lucky you've always been so obedient and easy." As the oldest daughter of Taiwanese immigrants, I'd learned early on not to wrinkle the perfect tapestry of my parents' pride. I worked hard in school, spent time with the "right" friends, attended church, and followed all the rules without complaint.

But I had a temper. And sometimes that temper revealed the frayed threads of my filial piety—especially with my mother.

As a teenager, I occasionally fractured my golden image and fell into tiffs with my mother over small things. She would nag me about something, I would shoot back snarky comments, and we'd simmer for a day or two before returning to normal, as if the argument had never happened at all.

I knew my mother was a difficult woman to love; she was critical of her children's academics, weight, dress, and recreational activities. She would often remind my siblings and me that she had raised and fed us, and the least we could do in return was offer her our exact obedience. Our bodies and existence belonged to her, simply because we had come from her womb.

This idea was a thread I sometimes picked at but never yanked—because I wasn't merely a daughter of Chinese immigrants. I was also a daughter of Christian converts, and to be Christlike meant to avoid contention. My father once told me, "I was attracted to the Church because its teachings are similar to Confucian ideology. The only concept missing from Confucianism is Jesus Christ."

My parents love God, so much so that they uprooted our entire family and moved us from California to Utah, where most of the population shared our faith. They love the church they nurtured us in, and I learned to love it too. And in some ways, that love allowed me to look past my parents' imperfections and respect them, despite their high expectations. It also allowed me to shut down arguments with my mother to prevent irreparable harm.

Daniel Callis

Daniel Callis

For a long time, I thought that would be enough.

When I was twenty-seven, my mother broke my heart. I had stopped squabbling with her in my early twenties, having established a peaceful relationship built on held tongues (me) and happy obliviousness (her).

But one December afternoon, we stumbled back into past patterns. I was wrapping Christmas presents on the living room floor while she ranted about one of my cousins, who had different standards of dress.

"Her clothes are too immodest," my mother said. "Is she looking for trouble?"

"Of course not," I said, attempting to defend my cousin. "She just likes to dress that way. It's none of our business."

"Girls shouldn't dress like that," my mother insisted. "She's basically asking for men to assault her."

I tensed at her accusation, staring hard at the creases I was pressing into the wrapping paper. My mother was a fierce woman, worthy of her tiger zodiac, but she often lent that fierceness to painfully outdated beliefs. Usually, I ignored her comments to keep the peace. But she had hit a particular nerve that riled my own ferocity.

"A woman's dress is not an invitation for men to do anything," I said tightly. "It is a man's responsibility to respect women, whatever they're wearing."

"Maybe," my mother replied, "but women have a responsibility too."

I looked up then, my voice hard. "Are you saying it's a girl's fault if she is raped?"

"Yes, if she's dumb enough."

"Then I must be dumb."

The words came out before I could stop them, before I could consider the consequences of such a simple response. But I had spent twenty-seven years maintaining my golden image—and I had spent twenty-one of those years swallowing a secret I knew would unravel everything.

"What do you mean?" my mother said. The room suddenly felt so quiet.

I paused long enough to remember that at six years old, I left the house with a man my mother trusted, who took my siblings and me to Chuck E.

Cheese and brought us to the park when we were bored. I remembered that my brother and sister were sick that day, so they couldn't go to the public library to play on the computers as planned. But I went, just me and the man. I remembered him driving me up into the California hills, parking in a secluded grove off the main road, and touching me in ways I did not understand. I remembered him buying my silence with a box of chicken nuggets from McDonald's. I remembered returning home, my tears having already dried, and seeing my mother. We were going to a church activity at the beach that afternoon, and I remember her telling me, "Don't let any of the men hold or touch you in a strange way," thirty minutes too late.

For twenty-one years, I held my tongue in the hopes that my parents would remain happy and oblivious forever—or at least until we were all in heaven, too exalted to fret over earthly matters.

But that day, I felt angry enough to confess.

I looked back down at my Christmas wrapping and said, "It happened to me."

My mother immediately began asking questions.

"When?"

"A long time ago, back when we lived in California."

"Who was it?"

"It doesn't matter."

Even in my anger, I wished to protect my mother from potential guilt.

"Why didn't you tell me?"

"It doesn't matter."

And then she asked the question I had been fearing for twenty-one years: "Why did you let that happen?"

I always knew my mother's thinking was narrow and unbending, limited by sexist assumptions and prone to victim blaming. But I convinced myself that as long as I told her nothing, and as long as she never asked that question aloud, I could pretend that she would respond differently—with love and sympathy and protectiveness.

But she asked *that* question. And in it, I heard her accusation: *It's your fault.*

In church, I learned that a mother's love for her child is the closest thing to God's love for us.

My mother had hit a particular nerve that riled my own ferocity.

I thought that even my mother, whose culture practiced conditional love, would love me unconditionally where it mattered. But in that moment, I felt betrayed by the person who was supposed to love me most.

I did not speak to my mother for two weeks. It hurt to be in the same room as her, to look at her, let alone talk to her. I continued to punish her with my absence until one day, my brother gently but firmly reminded me, "Forgiveness isn't for the offender. It's for you."

I thought of the Savior and how he'd asked the Father to forgive his murderers as he hung from the cross. Those words, "Father, forgive them," did not change his enemies' hearts. The men and women who'd condemned him did not even hear his agonized whisper. But Christ's plea for forgiveness could clear *his* heart as he prepared to be perfected. It might even have brought him peace in his final moments of mortality.

I wanted that peace. And I was so tired of being in pain. So, I buried my anger and moved on. I spoke when spoken to and even found the ability to smile at my mother again. As time passed, I patched over the tapestry that was our relationship, concealing the knots and tears underneath with colorful new silk.

Still, my mother had affirmed my long-held suspicion that she was an incorrigible woman who cared more about her traditions and opinions than her daughter's needs. I accepted it, and stopped expecting anything else.

Two years later, I had a mental breakdown, stemming from a general dissatisfaction with my life. I was pouring myself into other people's cups and forgetting to fill mine, because that was how I'd been raised as a good Chinese, Christian daughter: dedicate your life to others while forgoing your own needs.

I poured and poured and poured until I turned one day and found depression holding my empty cup. And suddenly, everything else in my life felt empty too—my relationships, my service in church, my job, my hobbies, my passions. Fortunately, through talking to my church leader, therapist, and closest friends, I gradually pulled myself out of the emptiness and started to refill my cup.

A few weeks after, I sat at my parents' dining table with my mother, confessing my recent struggle with depression.

"I'm working on it," I said.

"But why are you depressed?" she asked. "Young people these days are always crying depression."

I grimaced at the dismissal in her tone. But I responded honestly. "I'm not saying I'm suicidal. I'm just saying that sometimes I feel really, really burned out and exhausted and gray."

"But why?"

In the past, I would've shrugged and given a vague answer, too tired to explain myself to a woman who seemed to want to contradict my every feeling. But my therapist had been teaching me about communicating boundaries and needs, and I felt brave enough to try.

"You really want to know why?" I knit my fingers together as I looked at my mother. "It's because of you. Because you taught me to be this way. You and Baba always tell me to be a good example, and you always brag about me with your friends."

"We brag because we're proud of you."

"I know, and I understand that," I said, meaning it. "But it puts pressure on me, and it reinforces this idea that I have to be perfect, that I have to be responsible for other people all the time. I've been taught that if I have a problem, I have to swallow it and focus on getting other things done. And it makes me feel exhausted."

My mother paused for a moment, then said, "You sound like your aunt."

She was referring to her sister, also the firstborn in her family. I didn't disagree with my mother's assessment. My aunt and I both had a temper, a similarity I'd always noted in passing.

"Maybe it's because we're both the oldest," I said.

"Maybe," my mother agreed.

She looked at me, expression unusually calm and gentle. In my mind, my mother has always been the sharp-edged matriarch, her tongue existing only to spew gossip, dogma, or criticism. But at that moment, she looked thirty years younger, her dark eyes clear and compassionate.

"I understand," she said. "I won't do that anymore, put pressure on you. Just focus on yourself, and stop giving everything to other people."

A disbelieving laugh tripped over my lips. "Really?"

"Yes," she said. "I'm sorry I put that kind of responsibility on you before."

I'm sorry.

My mother never said sorry—at least not without the words being dragged through her teeth. But there they were, so unexpected and casual and soft.

I recognized empathy in my mother's response. For the first time, I felt that she was hearing me, listening to me, and humbling herself toward change. My mother had always been like a mountain, rigid and immovable. But that day, I noticed the trees on the mountain slopes shifting in the breeze.

"OK," I said. "Thank you."

In church, it is often said that repentance is change. But forgiveness is change as well. As I studied my mother that afternoon, I did not think she was suddenly a different person. Our relationship did not suddenly resurrect into something perfect. But I felt thin, gold threads of forgiveness weave through our tapestry, undulating over and under past hurts, offenses, and confusion. For once, I wasn't ignoring the knots but allowing love—mine, my mother's, and the Savior's—to untangle and mend. I didn't know what the tapestry's image would look like in the end, but I had hope that it would reflect true peace and healing.

A few minutes later, I stood at the sink, rinsing out dishes, while my mother complained about my sister—still very much the mother I knew.

"She never listens to me," she said. "You should talk to her about—"

"Hold on," I interrupted. "What are you asking me right now?"

My mother paused, stared at me, then laughed.

"You're right," she said. "Never mind. Never mind." ✱

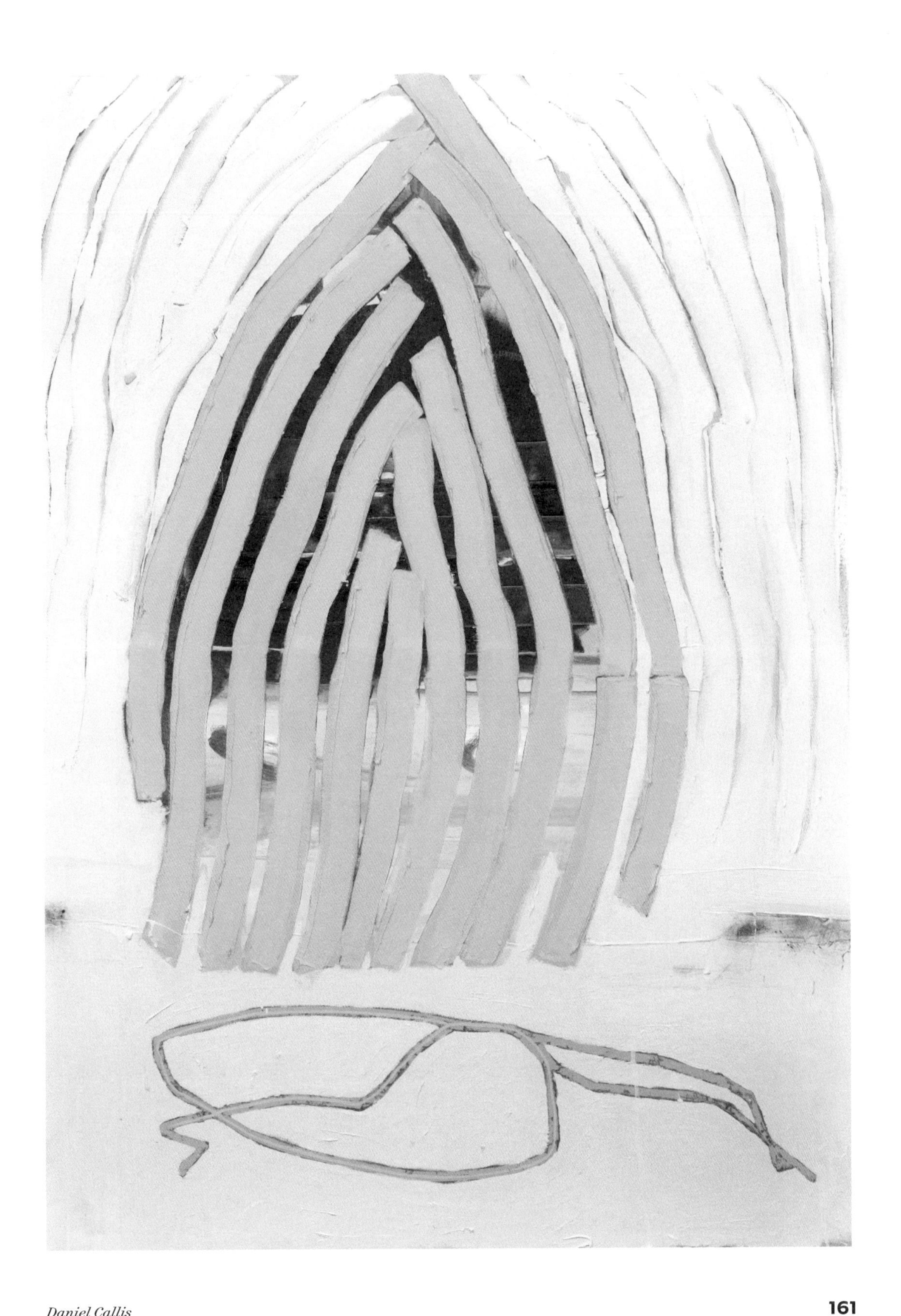

A PEBBLE

JIM RICHARDS

It is difficult for us, Maker, to write sonnets
to you today as they did before. Yous
don't ring as reverently as thees and thous,
which have echoed from the belltowers
for centuries but now sound as wrong
as cows mooing from the steeple. Rhymes
likewise embarrass us like a cellphone's song
going off mid-eulogy, so that we have to hide
the music with silent mode. What sounds
can we make today to reach your ears
that don't strike us as awkward, like a lover's
pebble tossed against glass? I can see you
in there—a light, a shadow—come to the window.

THE GIFTS OF DIVINE MARRIAGE

JENNIFER FINLAYSON-FIFE

ONE IMPORTANT CHARACTERISTIC OF a divine marriage is that the union creates greater wisdom and capacity than the aggregate of each individual's abilities. This synergy happens as a couple celebrates and amplifies the unique strengths of each partner. In a collaborative partnership, neither spouse is threatened by the capacity and individuality of the other, nor makes their own way-of-being superior to the other. A couple's ability to value and benefit from individual strengths is dependent upon each partner's willingness to let their gifts and wisdom emerge, not hiding who they are—as well as the ability to limit their ego sufficiently to amplify the gifts and aspirations of their spouse. When each partner is an equal and valued contributor, couples enjoy the happiest marriage and a marriage emulating our Heavenly Parents.

Perhaps because of its functionality, personality differences are a primary feature in romantic attraction and desire: we are compelled, in part, because the one we love embodies what we do not yet understand or haven't yet developed in ourselves. The mystery and wonder in our beloved's way-of-being compels and bewitches us. The inherent gift in our attraction to difference is the immediate access it gives us to a wider spectrum of capacities and perspectives. Partnering allows us to access greater intelligence and ability than we alone possess. And if we embrace this, we can then live better, parent better, provide better, and respond more adeptly to the demands inherent to life. Our ability to give what is necessary is maximized when two unique perspectives and skill sets are developed and applied. This collaborative process makes the couple stronger than either could be individually.

As valuable as this reality is, most of us resist and even resent our spouse's divergent tendencies when they bump up against our own. While transfixed by a spouse's spontaneity at first, we can come to resent their lack of organization when a task needs to be completed. Or while compelled initially by a spouse's joviality, we may later begrudge their extroversion when it conflicts with our preference for solitude. Yet, to resent the very differences that we initially desired is weak and unloving of us. It is a way of resisting the responsibility to value our spouse's strengths, and it is a way of resisting the growth that their differences invite us toward. As long as we convince ourselves that we are victims of the invalidation inherent to our spouse's differences, we don't have to address our own limited ability to value, support, and make room for a person who doesn't necessarily reinforce us.

In the face of invalidating differences, many of us demand that our way of thinking and living prevail. We may even attempt to convince a spouse that capitulating to us is the definition of love—"If you love me, do what makes me comfortable!" Others instinctively avoid conflict by yielding to a disgruntled spouse to "keep the (false) peace," but diminish their own gifts and wisdom in the process. And hiding who you are will always weaken the intimacy and honesty of your marriage. While these are very human responses—to demand or yield in the face of marital differences—these reactions come from our lesser selves and, if indulged, limit the capacity and freedom in a marriage. If we hope to create a marriage of equals, and a marriage in the image of our Heavenly Parents, we must offer our strengths and honest perspectives to the marriage, while supporting the same in our spouse.

Understanding and integrating a spouse's varying point of view can be uncomfortable, and supporting a spouse's unique gifts and endeavors can stretch us, but making room for our spouse's differences and strengths will expand our ability to truly love. To love another is to let them prosper, even if their strengths don't necessarily reinforce us. To love another is to support them in the development of their gifts, even though this may mean sacrificing our time and at times our own interests. While sacrifice for

Ben Crowder

the benefit of the other is inherent to a thriving marriage, marriage researchers consistently find that this is what the happiest couples do: Happy couples value their spouse's happiness on par with their own, they encourage their spouse in their endeavors and struggles, and they are committed to their individual and mutual growth. While this kind of sacrifice can take courage, it blesses the couple with a deep sense of belonging to one another while also belonging to their own endeavors and dreams.

Divine marriages are built by allowing what is best and honest in each spouse to flourish, so those strengths can also inform and bless the marriage. If we truly celebrate the strengths in each other, we will grow into wiser, better people who thrive together in having learned how to love. ✸

Excerpt taken from In the Image of Our Heavenly Parents: A Couples' Guide to Creating a More Divine Marriage, *edited by Bethany Brady Spalding and McArthur Krishna.*

HYMNS COME FROM SOMEWHERE

A Musical Origin Story

ANDREW MAXFIELD

I STARTED READING WORDS IN about 1984 and music in about 1986, which is to say that by the time I was old enough to crack open any hymnal in sacrament meeting, it was the 1985 Green Book that I was opening. I didn't think of it as the *new* book, which it was. I thought of it as the *only* book. I assumed that whatever was in there had probably been in there forever—a little like when my family moved into a new neighborhood in 1987, seven-year-old me assumed that everyone there had always lived there.

Granted, some of the contents of the Green Book were indeed quite old. For example, the text for "O Savior, Thou Who Wearest a Crown" began in the medieval Latin poetic text *Salve mundi salutare* (though it was altered substantially, not just translated, for our hymnal), and the music made its way from Hans Leo Hassler (1564–1612) through J. S. Bach (1685–1750) through various and now effectively anonymous arrangers into the chorale harmonization we Latter-day singers know.

Meanwhile, it turned out that some of the Green Book Top 40 are only about as old as I am and written by people I know, meaning that these musical lauds weren't *eternal* like God, *timeless* like chant or carols, or even *just plain old* like so many of the Victorian nuggets we've collected. For instance, I realized that the music for "Press Forward, Saints" (with the magical, "modally borrowed" chord that sets "Al-LE-LU-ia" apart from the rest of the text) was composed by my very own, beloved and loving, elementary school choir teacher, Vanja Y. Watkins (1938–). Similarly, I discovered that the music for "Lord, I Would Follow Thee" was composed by K. Newell Dayley (1939–), for whom I worked as a teaching assistant when I was an undergraduate music student at BYU.

The fact that these texts and tunes came from *somewhere,* that they were created by *actual people* nearly as ordinary as I am, took a long while to sink into my creative awareness. Over time I came to appreciate and admire the poets, lyricists, tunesmiths, and composers who expressed their *personal* devotion and spirituality through their consecrated creative work. The 2018 announcement that the Church would update the great Green Book itself moved hundreds, maybe thousands, of Church members to

Gaudenzio Ferrari

funnel their personal devotions and feelings into text and music, and it caused me to wonder why I hadn't done the same.

Despite having written quite a bit of music, including a fair amount of commissioned liturgical music for other denominations, I hadn't ever really used my craft to serve my own tradition, and certainly not to express my personal devotional sentiments. Perhaps I felt that, despite our theological attachment to an open scriptural canon, our culture had come to accept something like a (tightly) closed musical canon—after all, if it wasn't in the Green Book, our congregations essentially didn't sing it. Simultaneously, the pragmatic professional composer in me did the math: few LDS congregations spend much money on music, and in the digital era, what used to be the tiny "Mormon music" market had become even tinier, even less viable. I can't think of a "professional" argument for writing LDS hymns.

The Church's deadline for hymn submissions came and passed, and my skepticism and reservations had hamstrung my own participation.

Finally, I found myself on a flight to the London Festival of Contemporary Church Music, where I would network with music directors and vocal ensembles who perform my music. I wondered: *What kept me from using my creative skills in service of my own tribe, when I was willing to fly so far away to make music for other tribes?* Something shifted as the plane bumped through the air, and I remembered "Sister" Watkins, who had recruited my sister, brother, and myself from our elementary school choir to sing on the Church's early 1990s recordings of the *Children's Songbook.* She had communicated something like "pure religion" through her ebullient eyes and radiant smile as we rehearsed and recorded hundreds of songs, some of which she had written.

I assume—that is, I hope—the roar of jet engines covered my spontaneous humming and vocalizing as I scratched out three verses of text, reflecting my desire to grow as a disciple, and a melody that struck me as artful but plain, not quite Appalachian but intuitive and singable (with a little Renaissance-era compositional trick at a key moment). Later I worked out a four-voice harmonization that pleased me and, to my ear, supported the feeling of the text, taking a page from Sister Watkins's own playbook in employing a distinctive "modally borrowed" chord in the final phrase.

Ultimately, all hymns, no matter how old or venerable, come from somewhere, and unless they were sonic transcriptions of the "music of the spheres," they came from somewhere inside *someone.* And this one comes from *me* out of a growing desire to connect my faith to my craft, sparked by a memory of a loving mentor who pressed forward in doing the same. ✸

PURE RELIGION

ANDREW
MAXFIELD

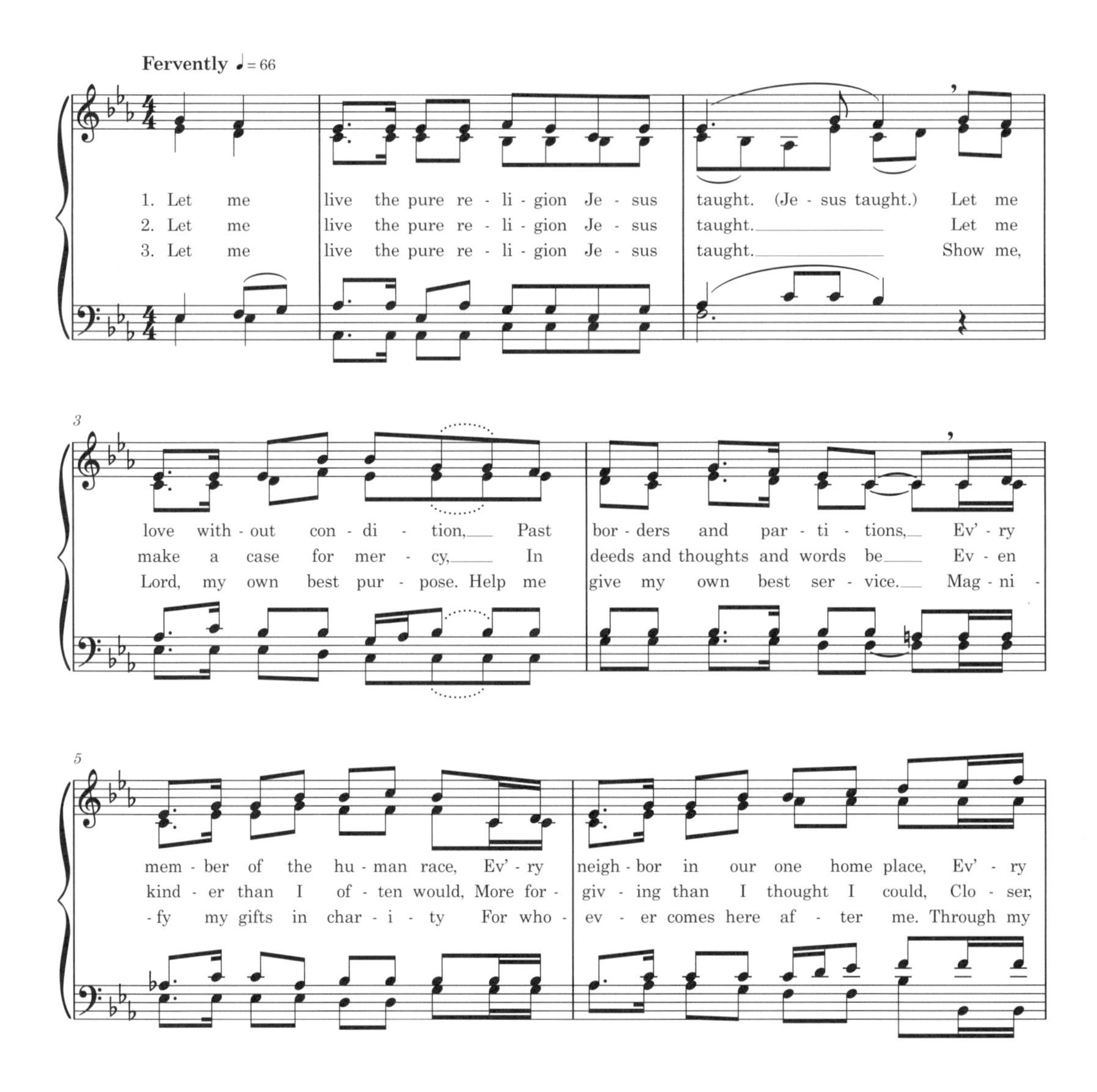

Words & Music
Andrew Maxfield
(See James 1:27)

AWAKENING TO GRIEF IN MONTREAL

How Love Enters the World

CANDICE WENDT

IN SPRING 2019, I REGULARLY LAY sleepless in my apartment in Côte-des-Neiges with silent tears streaming down my face. A few weeks before, while picking up my first-grade son from his school in downtown Montreal, he told me that a second-grade boy from his school had been hit and killed by a car on a dark road the evening before.

The next day on the school grounds, I pondered how someone else's child had been playing there in my field of vision just two days before but would now unexpectedly never return. I forgot to hand my son's backpack over to him and started making my way home. When I returned, I found the secretary looking downcast. "I completely understand. We're all having a bad day here," she said. My mind was darkened with a sense of mourning for weeks. I realized that if my own child died, all kinds of small things would intensify the devastation, from jackets left on coat hooks, to drawings on the wall, or bedding retaining my child's scent.

My husband informed me that a school portrait of the deceased boy had been posted with a message encouraging students' families to donate to his funeral fund. I asked him to donate, but I could not bear to look at the photograph myself. His death already felt deeply personal to me. Having never had this kind of response to a death before, at first I didn't understand what was happening. Why did this disrupt my daily life? How could I feel intense love for a family and child I didn't know personally?

I couldn't see it then, but my grief would lead me into closer communion with God and challenge me to expand my vision of God's nature, love, and plan for Their children. I would learn that charity paired with spiritual longing holds great creative and revelatory power. My cries would be answered with revelation that my pain, longing for a better world, and love for others were answers from God in their own right and echoed in divine intimations across generations.

In the fall of 1964, my grandmother, Etheleen, woke one morning and went through her morning routine in her small brick home in Syracuse, Utah.

Bruce Herman

She prepared lunches for her three schoolchildren: my father Bryan, ten years old; Paula, nine years old; and Gayle, six years old. First-grader Gayle asked her mom to style her hair in pigtails, which she did as they looked at one another in the bathroom mirror. She hugged Gayle and sent the children out to catch the school bus.

That school lunch was the last meal Gayle ever ate, that hug was the last one they'd ever share. The next time Etheleen saw Gayle, she was

I tried to gaze into this space without shutting my eyes. What do people experience when they lose their children?

lying on the street after being hit by a speeding driver. She died on impact right in front of their home. Gayle had been with her older siblings but ran out ahead in excitement to see her mom. Bryan and Paula ran into the house and pleaded with God for Gayle to live, while an ambulance came and took her away.

I picture my family during the first nights after the death. My dad sitting in his bedroom grappling with the new reality that his little sister was never coming home again, regretting that he did not happen to be holding her hand that afternoon. In the next room, Paula thinks she hears Gayle's spirit pressing the keys of the piano. Across the hall, Etheleen lies in the master bedroom. After finally drifting off, she wakes, the stupor of sleep wears off, she remembers the scenes of Gayle's death, starts weeping, and can't fall asleep again, many times over.

Etheleen was tenderhearted. When she parted ways with a loved one, there were tears and hugs. The sudden loss of her six-year-old was harrowing. Normally full of zest for life, she descended into severe depression that lasted several years. For the rest of her life, she resisted talking about Gayle's death with my dad. Avoiding her trauma prevented her from reassuring him about the events surrounding the accident and of her continued love for him. The fallout of my aunt's death hurt me and others in ways beyond the scope of this story, but my personal awareness of how much suffering one child's death can cause certainly increased my sense of grief and wonder as I pondered the death of my son's schoolmate. The suffering and schisms caused by one child's death can make lasting, damaging ripples in a family.

In my apartment in Montreal, I realized that I wasn't only mourning with a family in my community but also with my own family. The depths of grief opened before me. The wood floorboards of my bedroom split open into a deep tenebrous chasm, the seemingly bottomless sadness of children's deaths. For the first time in my life, I tried to gaze into this space without shutting my eyes. What do people experience when they lose their children? As Grandma's traumatic wound flared up within me, I could not bear the thought that any child should die an untimely death, and the thought that any parent should endure a lifetime of mourning and grief caused me to tremble and despair in the face of human suffering.

I did not connect with the sadness of Gayle's death growing up, even though my grandparents' house was full of reminders of her absence. Gayle's last school portrait hung in a room decorated for a young girl kept as if it were waiting for her return. Grandma shared the story of her death at bedtime, which always ended with my grandparents raising Gayle during the millennium. Hope in temple blessings was their way of moving forward to live content lives.

Grandma taught me not to wear black to funerals. She showed me photos of her mother's funeral, where she wore a brightly colored floral dress. We took pride in our confidence in the physical resurrection and reunion of families taught in the restored gospel. I now believe Grandma preferred sharing about death this way precisely because the devastation was unspeakable. She wept at length when she mentioned her mother or my grandpa after they passed. The

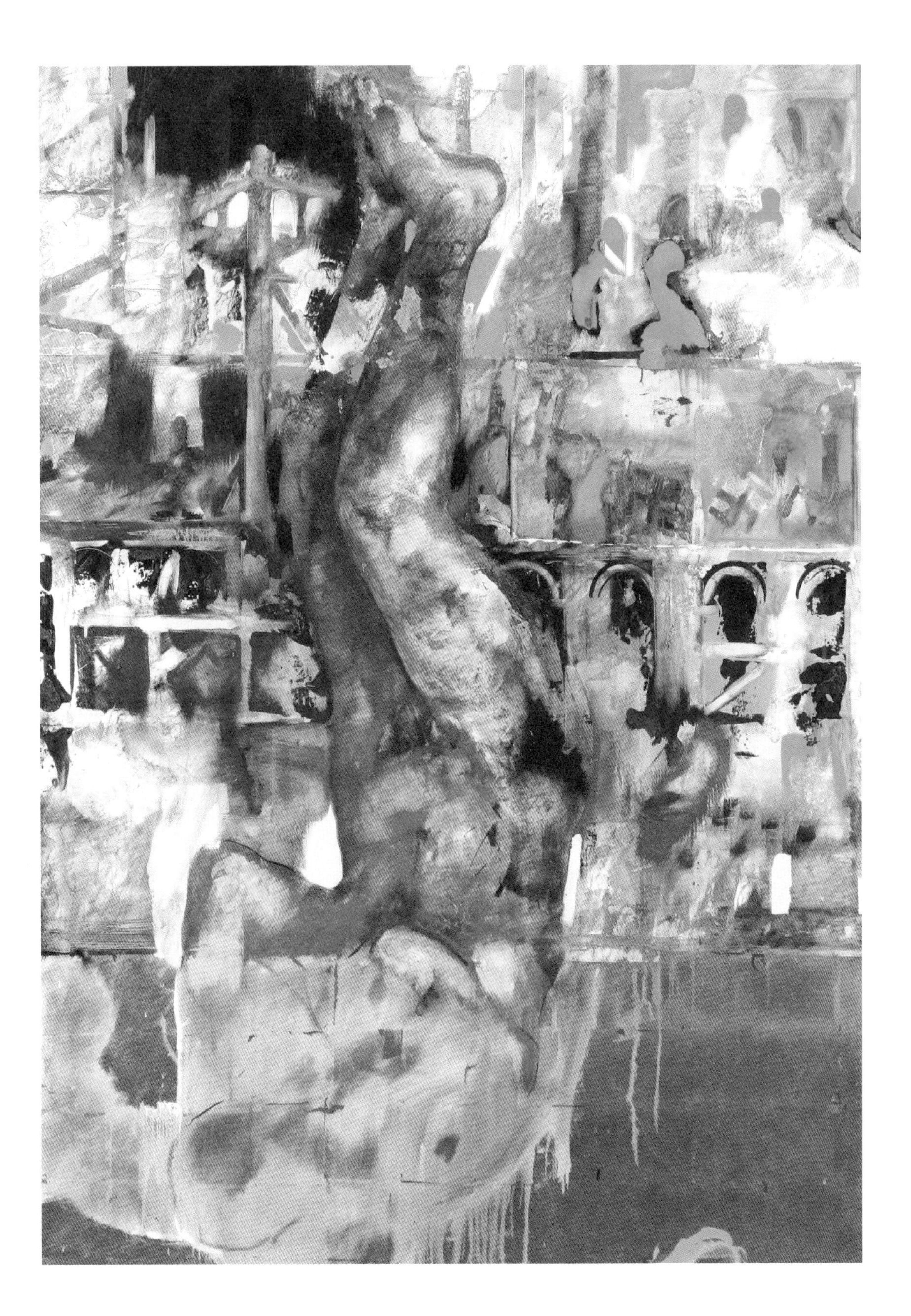

grief was in plain sight, but I resisted acknowledging that losing someone might be horribly sad even when faith is intact.

A few years before my move to Quebec, I found an album in Grandma's basement with worksheets Gayle completed just before her death. The handwriting and crayon marks had grown very faint. Behind them was a letter to my dad that Grandma never delivered. She apologized to him for being cold, angry, and withdrawn after the accident. I wondered what had kept her from following through with this urge to reconcile with her young son. Grandma's visits and enthusiastic love were central to me as a child. How could grief lead someone who loved me so much to hurt me and our family? Was my own current sense of mourning something I needed to go through to understand and accept my Grandma's mental illness and actions?

I chose to move to Montreal feeling inspired that this would bring greater spiritual light and growth into my life, but my faith seemed to be disintegrating in this new place. In my international urban ward, I was mostly cut off from people who shared my lifelong faith experience and roots in the Intermountain West. I felt more at home with secular people at work and often had the impression they were happier than I. Church responsibilities weighed heavily on top of my hectic life as an immigrant mom entering a bilingual workforce and helping young children navigate school in French, a language none of us had learned before.

I also needed to find belonging in a society with robust critical sensibilities toward Christian traditions. The Québécois people made a mass exodus from the Catholic faith in the '60s and '70s, sacrificing their faith to build a society more conducive to women's and families' well-being. While not all is peaceful and resolved in the province's relationship with faith (as Bill 21, a policy that prohibits wearing religious symbols and apparel for many jobs, attests), the aspects of the Quiet Revolution that empowered women stunned me. I witnessed remarkable benefits in my own life and neighborhood. Quebec's history validated my pain and anger about misogyny and undue pressures I had faced as a Latter-day Saint woman, and it provided a comparative reference point that challenged many things I'd been taught about God's will and vision for me and my own needs and desires.

As I excavated fractures in my faith, my foundation became shaky. I no longer felt sure about what happens after death. Human life seemed to teeter on the edge of a precipice overlooking a dark abyss. I asked myself: *Where can I find God in the midst of children's deaths here and now, rather than at some long distant day? Do They ask too much of us in sending us to a world where our children can so easily be torn from us? What are They doing to support grieving families who have lost faith and hope because of the blindspots and missteps of their faith traditions?*

Walking into Cirque du Soleil's headquarters (where I taught English), and later outside the gates of McGill campus, I overheard a couple of conversations mocking my faith tradition as something naive and quintessentially absurd. My French tutor told me Québécois individuals often perceive Latter-day Saints as an ultra-religious dogmatic cult. Was my past joy in God's love and eternal life based on a far-fetched sham? My safety rope of certainty having snapped, if I found God again, it could only be with a new appreciation for God's power to offer humans hope and healing in our precarious and tragic situations.

My dark thoughts kept returning for months, partly because I couldn't avoid exposure to events that added to the grief. Art and artifacts in Montreal led me to descend to a deeper level of questioning. I visited an exhibit by Indigenous artist Kent Monkman featuring his painting *The Scream,* which depicts children being forcibly torn from their families by church and Canadian officials to attend residential schools where they suffered abuse, neglect, and often death. I also visited the Montreal Holocaust Museum two blocks from my apartment, where I witnessed histories and photos of children about to be taken to concentration camps, enter gas chambers, or be euthanized.

I looked on the suffering of these children and families and cast my head down with my hands over my eyes. The weight of their indignation and grief were beyond what I could bear. I didn't want these deaths to be the history recorded in my own neighborhood. Why so much trauma in the lives of young souls? How did God expect me to have the strength to mourn with these thousands in my state of intensified love and grief?

I had internalized narratives about God assigning suffering to humans in order to purify us and correct our missteps. Deep down, I was afraid my anguish was punishment for damaged religious trust and growing moral independence. I felt abandoned by God, and I worried that victims and their families might feel stuck in similar states of despair and abandonment.

At Gayle's funeral, a church leader had said it was God's will she die because there were more important things for her to do in the spirit world. Yet what could be more important than finishing first grade? How could God inflict intergenerational trauma on my family? From my own communion with God, I knew no answers to such questions but could only believe God knows and loves humans, weeps with us, and encourages and heals us.

I told God I could only bear my increasing love and grief with Their accompaniment. God whispered the quietest messages, so soft I could easily have denied or ignored them, slowly over time. Once They gently gestured to my own heart, as if saying, "This love that's in you, this grief that's in you, this is Our grief. This is Our love. It is through you that Our love enters the world. The compassion you seek is already within you. Your heart is the answer to your prayers and pleadings." My longing drew me into greater closeness with God; my cries of sorrow were echoed in Their sacred answers. I've come to believe that my and others' compassion and grief are a central part of God's great work of wiping away all tears and creating a new earth in which there will be no more death or despair.

In an effort to faithfully reimagine my thoughts about death, I wrote a letter heavenward asking what God does to support and comfort children who die. Then I wrote a detailed response using the dreams of family members, scripture, past experiences with prayer, and my own imagination. This was a way to ground myself in faith that God is actively accompanying human souls now rather than waiting for some future time. This kind of creative activity resonates with the answer God gave me: love, sorrow, and longing provide a sacred space within which I could seek, imagine, and discover answers to my questions. It is a space in which I've come to believe that God's love for us is more pure and unfailing, and more compassionate and full of care, wisdom, understanding, and resilience than I had been taught to believe or ever imagined before.

I envisioned children being immediately embraced and cared for by Heavenly Parents and ancestors standing ready and prepared. I imagined beloved communities welcoming them. I imagined wounds being tended to and tears being wiped away. I saw friendship and belonging, music, study, and learning. I pictured children I've grieved over tapping God on the shoulder and adding a little note of their own as a postscript:

"Thank you for remembering us and loving us and having faith in our future. Don't despair. Our suffering is over. We're already beginning to enjoy eternal life in the presence of our Heavenly Parents. We see their loving faces looking upon us continually.

"Soon we will be reunited with our parents, siblings, and friends, and God will finish healing their hearts and wiping away all the tears from their eyes. There will be a new heaven and a new earth. The things that Jesus prayed for us will be fulfilled

Bruce Herman

in us—blessings so great they are beyond what human words can express. There will be special recompense to make up for all that has been suffered or missed because of our early deaths. The Savior feels our experiences and needs keenly and will not rest until all is fulfilled and restored.

"Always trust that like us, you are known and loved, and your sadness is fully understood. Our Heavenly Parents weep with you. If you have another bad day, remember that their love and comfort will always be there. With love from all the children you care about who are now in God's presence."

Remembering the inspiration and the tears of joy that flowed while writing my letter from God has been one of the things that has helped me the most to exit states of despair.

* * *

One night, an image of my great-grandfather walking through his garden flashed in my mind. Belvin Gerald lost his mom to cancer when he was twelve and spent his life caring for his blind father and siblings. He supported them with subsistence farming and factory laborer wages. Like his daughter Etheleen, Belvin was tenderhearted. He is still remembered in his community in rural South Carolina for kindness. As his image flashed in my mind, I felt he was speaking to me, saying, "Candice, I know you and I love you." I felt immersed in warm acceptance. Grandpa used to hide jars of coins in family members' closets, and feeling his love was like finding a message he'd hidden just for me. He passed two years before I was born, and I marveled that there he was—alive, well, and even speaking—in my mind and heart, even though we never met in life. I pondered the power of love to survive decades beyond death.

I hope that my love will spread to others' lives like Grandpa's has. I felt this most keenly recently while sitting in sacrament meeting when my now eleven-year-old son hugged me after the prayer. I unexpectedly thought of Irina Sedler, who rescued Jewish children during the Holocaust. It was the great love of her father, who was very generous with his hugs and who served the poor and marginalized as a physician, that energized her audacious missions that prevented thousands of deaths. As I looked into my son's face, I felt a surge of confidence that my love, and the love of all the people around me, will lead to unforeseen miracles and relief for many generations to come. ✸

ALL OF IT

LAURA STOTT

It has no name, this flower, this bird, this mountain we pray to,
the trail to the summit
where we'll hang a flag.
No name. The cats
will leave tracks, the ghost ones,
dogs too. Wolf or leopard. A friend, Tibetan,
takes us to a lake, iced over.
There we hang our flags on an auspicious day.
Burn the incense he takes out of a bag with his large hands.
He offers some to me and tells me what to call it.
But we don't speak the same language.
Kanchenjunga. Say it again.
I kneel because this is how I've been taught to pray.
I pray for the whole world. I do this again in another life.

In my backyard, twelve years later, a full moon,
winter solstice, we make a little fire.
I've kept the same plant he burned
and gave me
all this time.
When we hang the flags, I want to have more faith in the wind
to send the words to God, to the hearts of politicians,
to the hearts of human hands, to the ocean, to the center
of the earth. Here, this breath,
a bird that dives and dives and dives.

THREE PARADOXES OF THE CHURCH OF JESUS CHRIST OF LATTER-DAY SAINTS

A Unique and Misunderstood Faith

NOAH FELDMAN

THERE ARE THREE PARADOXES that to my mind characterize the external view of The Church of Jesus Christ of Latter-day Saints in the United States today, and actually through the church's history.

PARADOX ONE: OPPRESSED & SUCCESSFUL

In the history of the United States, there has never been a religious denomination oppressed formally, legally, and institutionally like the LDS church. Federal statutes were passed in the early history of the church effectively outlawing belonging to the church.

The founder and prophet of the church, Joseph Smith, was assassinated with some degree of governmental participation. Lynching, as we know from the history of lynching in the South, was not purely an act of individuals acting outside the law, although we sometimes depict it this way. The communities that practiced lynching thought of lynching as an extension of the political community. It was a murderous form of what is sometimes called "politics out of doors." So in that sense, when a community engaged in lynching, the whole community was taking moral responsibility for the evil act that they were performing. And that I think extends demonstrably to the assassination of Joseph Smith. This was, then, a feature of the oppression that drove the early LDS church to seek a location where it could effectively control a state government—in the first instance, in order to make sure there was no prohibition on plural or celestial marriage. And by that effort, the church ended up in the Intermountain West.

Getting state status was extraordinarily difficult, long, and complex, but in the end, with tremendous compromise, the church was able to effectively create a state—unique in US history—in which the church and its membership has remained the dominant political part of the community.

Consider the beehive, which is both a symbol of the church and a symbol of the state of Utah itself. We don't have an endorsement doctrine for the establishment clause anymore. But if we had the endorsement doctrine, you would ask, is the beehive an endorsement? And it would be an archetypal endorsement, you would imagine. A symbol of the church is the symbol of the state.

From that base in Utah, members of the LDS church and the church itself have become

> **The same church that was oppressed in the United States has turned out to be extraordinarily and uniquely successful in so many ways.**

nationally and globally powerful and successful. Church members are wildly overrepresented, especially in a wide range of elite circles—not only educational, but business and politics and so forth. And that disproportionate effect of the church's power remains true today.

And so that is a paradox: The same church that was so profoundly, uniquely oppressed in the United States has turned out to be extraordinarily and uniquely successful in so many ways. The oppression occurred openly in a country that claimed religious liberty as one of its core values from the beginning and yet never applied that to the LDS church. To be blunt about it, the US treated the LDS church as an exception in the other direction—subject to greater oppression. Yet the church not only prospered, but preserved Utah as, to a great degree, an LDS-dominated political entity. That is a paradox, and it is extraordinary.

PARADOX TWO: OPEN & PRIVATE

Now to the second paradox: The LDS church is uniquely open and simultaneously uniquely private. It is uniquely open in that there's no other organized denomination in the United States or in the history of the United States that makes a comparable effort to draw in people to the beliefs of and the communal participation in its church. Nobody else has anything like as organized a system of missions, not only domestically, but globally. And to do that, an extraordinarily high percentage of members of the church go out and actively, openly seek to draw other human beings into the church, as well as provide support for existing LDS communities. Nobody else does that. It's unique in its openness.

And simultaneously, the church is unique in the privacy (to use a term that I suppose I'm trying to choose for neutrality reasons) with respect to core temple practices, which remain ritually separate from the view of outsiders and even of an LDS person who doesn't have a temple recommend. But the teachings behind those rituals and the content of those rituals remain to a large extent protected from the public eye in a manner that is reminiscent of the ancient history of what are called mystery religions.

The category of mystery religion includes, by the way, many denominations of Christianity, including the Eastern Orthodox tradition, where to this day the moment of communion takes place behind a screen or a curtain—unlike in a Catholic church, where the moment of the consecration of the host occurs in public view. A historian of religion would likely say that, in the case of the Eastern Orthodox churches, the practice descends from ancient Greek practices like the Eleusinian mysteries, which is where the technical term *mystery religion* comes from. And saying nothing about the historical relationship between that and the LDS church, which is a very rich and complex topic in its own right, I would just observe that there is a similarity there and that the similarity is not any great outlier with respect to global Christianity.

But the mystery religion component is a great outlier with respect to contemporary US practice, since there aren't very many Eastern Orthodox people in the United States. And it's a remarkable paradoxical outlier when it's compared to the church's outreach.

This paradox—unparalleled openness coupled with highly unusual privacy or secrecy—deserves deep investigation. To me, it's utterly fascinating from the standpoint of the history and the sociology of religion.

But it's an ongoing challenge for the LDS church in terms of how it is perceived, because at once the LDS church is perceived as deeply committed to outreach, which of course it is. And at the same time, the LDS church obscures by divine design much of the content of its core ritual and indeed of belief. And that's something that is remarkable and paradoxical.

Zoë Petersen

PARADOX THREE: MAINSTREAM & MARGINALIZED

Zoë Petersen

That leads to the third paradox. The LDS church, I would say, is uniquely a modern American institution, both modern and mainstream American. And simultaneously and paradoxically, the LDS church is uniquely "other" in its commitment to an alternative scripture. The unique scripture functions to make it at the opposite extreme of contemporary, mainstream American life and religion—both from the standpoint of the most literally believing evangelical Christians and also from the standpoint of secular, agnostic or atheist, or "none" Americans.

So let's just explore for a moment the two sides of that paradox. Mormonism isn't the only denomination to have its birthplace in North America's soil, but it's the only one to have a scripture that fully integrates, accounts for, and makes central the Americas in the cosmic story of divine salvation and revelation.

The LDS church is therefore the only religious denomination to have fully grown up in the American context, to have fully both transformed that context and (I think) been transformed by it. That's the first part of the distinctively American aspect of the church. And it's also distinctively modern because the church's evolutionary practices and pathways, including the reality of ongoing revelation, have enabled the church to become deeply mainstream American over its history—even though the early history of the church involved a set of church teachings that were in many respects disjunct from mainstream American society of the 1830s, '40s, and '50s. So the gradual mainstreaming of the church has come to lead to a result where, from the outsider's perspective, Mormons seem archetypally like modern Americans.

That's really noteworthy, especially when juxtaposed with the other side of the paradox. The other side of the paradox is that, in a country that remains overwhelmingly Christian and overwhelmingly Protestant, the LDS church is both a Christian church and simultaneously a church that is fundamentally, and I think irreducibly, committed to a new testament of the Christ that differs from that of other Christian denominations, and that renders the church "other" in a fairly fundamental way. The insistence on that truth as literal reality therefore differentiates church teaching from what I would call mainline American Protestantism, which already 120 years ago had reached a point of what you might call spiritualized metaphorization that still persists among many, though by no means all, American Christians, according to which one need not have a literal belief in, say, the passion and the resurrection, but could metaphorize and spiritualize those beliefs in order to reconcile those beliefs with modernity.

Now, 120 years ago, Protestant *fundamentalism* came into existence as a movement using the word fundamentalism precisely to oppose that metaphorized spiritualization. So there is simultaneous to the LDS church, a little bit later in historical time, but overlapping for much of its history, American evangelical fundamentalism that also remains deeply committed to the literal truth claims of scripture. So in that sense, the LDS church's literal truth claims are not

such an outlier. But what's outlying is that the LDS church's commitment includes and extends beyond the substantive beliefs held by American evangelical fundamentalists, and in that sense leaves the church at odds with those folks.

So what you see there in the second half of the paradox is that the LDS church is to a certain degree cabined on two sides. It's cabined on one side by the metaphorization or full secularism of mainline Protestants and of people who've moved away from mainline Protestantism. And it's cabined on the other side by evangelical believers who share a commitment to the literal truth of scripture, but the Venn diagram of what counts as scripture is a little bit smaller, and meaningfully so.

So when you take that and compare it with the uniquely American mainstream nature of the church, you get this third paradox: the LDS church is uniquely modern and mainstream American, but also in some sense uniquely "other" to mainstream American Protestant practice and tradition from both sides.

These paradoxes are so powerful that I think they are what characterize most non-LDS Americans' views of the church. And what I mean by that is, most non-LDS Americans don't have any idea what to think about the church. They really don't. At a human individual level, they admire LDS folks. They admire the people they know from work, they admire the people they know from school. There is even a trend of idealizing social media representations of the LDS community. It's got its own complexity, but that goes to a certain phenomenon of mainstreaming as well.

In the long run, it will have attitudinal effects in the polls. I think those will probably be overwhelmingly positive, but because they're social media images, they're not real (since that is the nature of social media), and they won't resolve the paradoxes or contradictions. But when those same Americans who think very warmly of LDS people and are admiring of LDS people think about the content of what it means to be an LDS believer, their combination of ignorance, which is not entirely their fault, and uncertainty about the ways in which the LDS church is an outlier to American life leaves them in a position of uncertainty. I think that uncertainty is a product of these three paradoxes. ✸

Madonna & Child

MEGAN KNOBLOCH GEILMAN

MR. JONES & MR. NISBET

TIMOTHY FARRANT

FOR YEARS I HAD ASSUMED THAT my relationship with libraries and antiquarian bookshops was quite separate from my human relationships—my loving ties with family, close friends, work colleagues, and neighbors. After all, the time I'd spent surrounded by books in my office required me to suspend all human conversations, and the time I'd spent in conversation with others necessarily took me away from my books. I cannot offer an exact date for when the penny dropped, and when I realized these worlds were actually not-so-very-distinct, but I am convinced that two significant, and yet quite different, friendships played an important role in this. Both friendships sprang up in the very same town in Somerset, England.

One friend was initially a friend of my parents who later took a deep interest in the progress of my studies and would comment enthusiastically on a Sunday School class I taught when I was a doctoral student at the University of Oxford. For the purposes of this essay, I shall call him Mr. Jones. The other was an antiquarian bookseller I befriended before I commenced undergraduate studies at the University of Bristol. His name, Mr. Nisbet, was no secret to his friends and customers. As very different as Mr. Nisbet was from Mr. Jones, both affected me in profound ways.

I was always struck by the generosity Mr. Jones displayed in his interactions with others in his community. He taught early-morning seminary at his local congregation and encouraged young people to lift their sights, expand their minds, and broaden their horizons. He worked at his town's YMCA and developed positive ecumenical relations during a particular religious moment characterized by skepticism (in terms of how other Christian traditions viewed his personal faith). He was remarkably athletic in his day and taught many young athletes the importance of sportsmanship, personal discipline, and strong work ethic. And, after observing my own academic development and attending the Sunday School classes I taught for a brief period, he demonstrated a wonderful openness to new thought and ideas.

Each time he attended one of my lessons, Mr. Jones would find me afterwards and catch me by the arm to tell me with great emotion what had been opened to his mental view before imparting his unique perspective of the world to me. Before I left the levels and shires of England to embark on my current position at the Maxwell Institute

Giuseppe Arcimboldo

at BYU, I visited with Mr. Jones. Now weakened by the ruthless effects of Parkinson's disease, and having only enough energy for me to sit with him a while, he expressed his unparalleled excitement for the next part of my own life's journey. To his faith-affirming openness and generosity, I responded with the human hug of friendship. And as we bore each other's fears and excitement together, in the very same space, we parted ways—but not in spirit.

Mr. Nisbet lived through the same decades of the twentieth century into the twenty-first, only a couple of miles from Mr. Jones. I'm not certain they ever met. But at a similar time to my developing friendship with Mr. Jones, Mr. Nisbet allowed me to accompany him on part of his life's journey as he read, bound, and sold books. He was a renowned and respected bookseller in Somerset—and our relationship worked rather well. He sold books, and I bought them. Beyond this, however, Mr. Nisbet was also a wonderful man who was integral to the life of his local community. Not only were the towering bibliographic walls in his eccentric bookshop to be treated as old friends but he, by his very nature, was also a good friend and neighbor to those who lived in relative proximity to him. I spent many afternoons chatting to him as he sorted books, smoked cigars and pipes, and assisted his customers. I remember him allowing one customer to pay for items in installments. I remember him providing book-sorting work to another man who had suffered a series of mental health challenges. I remember him assisting an elderly neighbor with the sale of her house, to ensure she wasn't taken advantage of. Over the course of a few years, our friendship grew. When I moved away from Somerset, the news of his declining health—and later death—reached me. Although his bookshop has long since been lost to the death we call UK property development, and his body has gone the way of the earth, his voice of kindness still rings out in my ears.

Although his bookshop has long since been lost his voice of kindness still rings out in my ears.

Mr. Nisbet inspired my fondness for books, and Mr. Jones reinforced my pastoral sensibilities. For the longest time, I always thought these two things, "books" and "humanity," were entirely disconnected. At least in my mind, people's relationships with their personal book collections can sometimes be defined by bibliometrics. The act of endlessly counting and sorting reading materials, and considering progress made wading through massive repositories of knowledge in the hermitical library, can almost be considered as an exclusive mark of honor or intellectual achievement—one that sets one human apart from all others in their literary greatness. But even if we were to dwell on the extreme end of the bibliographic spectrum, would it be true to assert that the most bibliometric, even misanthropic, reader is alone in their reading? My instinct had been to say that they are—but my own experience of reading, and the encounters I have had both within and beyond the realms of the text, teaches me otherwise.

The perceived tension between book collecting and human interaction can be loosened by placing my friendships with Mr. Nisbet and Mr. Jones in conversation with a short reflection written by Umberto Eco. In this reflection, Umberto defends his own sizable private library.[1] In addition to being an avid writer, Umberto Eco was a prolific reader. This, by his own admission, poured into his home life. Having guests enter his house and encounter the masses of books he had accumulated seemed to occur frequently. Inevitably, at some point, these visits would lead to the question: "What a lot of books! Have you read them all?" As Umberto indicates, there are many responses that can be offered in such a situation, and he is not short of a repertoire of retorts. Inspired by Roberto Leydi, Umberto first suggests throwing back the answer: "And more, dear sir, many more"; but goes on to settle on his favorite: "No, these are the ones I have to read by the end of the month. I keep the others in my office." Of course, Umberto's imaginative responses must be understood in the context of his dry wit and command of expression. Only in satire does one realize that he grapples with the reading of infinity! As Umberto himself remarks: "Confronted by a vast array of books, *anyone* will be seized by the anguish of learning, and will inevitably lapse into asking the question that expresses his torment and remorse." In this, Umberto turns the sheer vastness of the library on *anyone,* including himself. A similar sentiment is expressed by Terryl Givens, who, during a childhood trip to a bookshop with his father, became excited at the prospect of new knowledge and began snatching at eclectic titles to purchase. However, it wasn't long before Terryl became aware of the massive and looming reality of the shop's collections, leading him to abandon his previous hopes and return the titles to the shelves. In his words, he recounts: "I remember vividly the next moment, when I returned all the books to the shelves and went to the car, despondent and defeated by the impossibility of it all."[2]

With Umberto's comical and sobering episode in mind, and Terryl's comparable experience, I feel compelled to ask myself the following question: *why do we collect books at all?* In formulating a response to this, it is important to realise that Umberto presents an outsider human to his readership, to whom book collecting is a foreign phenomenon. This creates a tension between Umberto's bibliographical fortress and his inevitable interactions with humans from the outside world, and it suggests a chasm between "books" and "humanity." Indeed, the very presence of an actual human figure intruding into the space of his library initially provokes anxiety in Umberto. He thinks through several responses designed to deflect his own perceived relationship with books, which he then goes on to lament. And perhaps his sobering confession of being "seized by the anguish of learning" leading to "torment and remorse" is exactly that—the inability to make any real progress in the library, even the private library. Perhaps it is, as Terryl suggests, "the impossibility of it all." Or perhaps, for Umberto, it is something more than that. Perhaps Umberto is both emphasizing absurdity and profundity around the question of *why we collect,* pushing us instead to consider the very nature of the book itself and how this might ironically connect to

Andre Martins De Barros

human lives (rather than discourage human lives from entering in).

Returning briefly to Terryl's experience at the bookshop, I find it intriguing that the same feeling of hopelessness he first experienced as a child still follows him to this day. At other times, however, his book collection leads him in the direction of humanity. Indeed, his own private library—composed of books he has personally sought out, negotiated, handled, and sorted—presents to him the impossibility we greet in Umberto. In Terryl's own words: "At times the old hopelessness descends even now." But in another breath, the impossibility of making any progress through infinite volumes provides a portal to another realm of thought—one where human actors live on as if unaffected by the permanence of the grave. As Terryl goes on to explain: "At other times, I run my hand along the bookcase and retrieve a volume acquired decades ago, never opened until this moment. And I marvel anew at how fresh and alive a voice sounds, that so patiently waited in quiet neglect over the passing years." The sentiment contained here reminds me of an observation made by the Anglican theologian Elaine Graham—namely, that a phenomenon's "primary distinguishing feature" is often its soberingly "human context."[3] After all, what could be more human than our collections of books that beautifully preserve the human voice?

So *why do we collect books at all?* Well, it's obvious that we collect books to read. But maybe it's less obvious that we collect books to connect ourselves more fully to the human world rather than to retreat from it. The infinite library reminds me that books are distinctly human, created by human hands and filled with the complexity of human life and thought. Any progress one makes in the library is, by its very nature, an act of collaboration in a community that is distinctly human. Just as it would be impossible to read all of Mr. Nisbet's book collections, and downright absurd to *expect* that he or anyone had read all of the countless books in his antiquarian bookshop, so too would it be an impossible task to meet and sit with all the humans that make up the town in which his bookshop was once situated. The sheer impossibility of the task of knowing everyone in a town would never stop a human from continually encountering other humans and deepening relationships. So why should the impossible dimensions of the private library distract from the fact that reading books provides a way of connecting with human voices, both living and dead?

This realization prompted me to feel less anxious about the metrics of collecting and reading, or of memorizing and regurgitating. It helped me recognize the profundity of Umberto's reflection—that reading all of our books is not only impossible, but contrary to the basic nature of the book. So now, I am more inclined to view the library as a portal to human interaction. Reading becomes a way of connecting to human voices far removed from the reader, whether through distance or death. As for writing, well, that becomes a way of giving voice to human lives that might otherwise be lost to the same inevitable destructive forces.

The lives of Mr. Nisbet and Mr. Jones may never have crossed directly. But I hope by this point, my own reader will understand why I am convinced that Mr. Nisbet's relationship with his books was a distinctly human affair—pushing him further into the human world inhabited by Mr. Jones. I now recognize that the seemingly solitary hours Mr. Nisbet spent hidden away surrounded by biblio-piles not only enriched his ability to interact with the human world but was also the embodiment of it. The lives of both friends were spent continuously immersed in a sea of human voices, whether within or beyond the written word. From this, I suppose books were never quite what I once considered them to be. Ink pressed into the paper page, or scribbled across the manuscript folio, is not there to enable the reader to advance in their own literary brilliance or to excel beyond the intellectual capacity of others measured on the bibliometric scale. No. Rather, these marks we labor to decipher are mere symbols that connect us to a broader human community, enabling us to transcend the book itself and enabling the human lives therein to transcend the necessary evils of mortality.

I began by writing about the beautiful impact of two human friendships on my own life and the lives of their respective communities, before indicating the way death, sickness, and declining health tragically affected them. By virtue of writing these small, connected paragraphs—and making the connection between "books" and "humanity"—I live in the hope that the human impact of Mr. Nisbet and Mr. Jones is not merely locatable in the human spaces their radiant lives once occupied. Rather, through these few words I provide here, detailing something of their own human stories, my intent is that the written word fulfills its most noble purpose. In the face of death and sickness's inevitability, the written word transcends the hospital and grave, and through it human life lives on. ✸

1. Umberto Eco, "How to Justify a Private Library," in *How to Travel with a Salmon & Other Essays,* trans. William Weaver (New York: Harcourt Brace & Company, 1990), 115–17. It is worth mentioning that, at least in Europe, Umberto Eco is practically a household name. His award-winning novel *The Name of the Rose* has sold over fifty million copies, ranking amongst the best-selling novels of all time. And the sheer thought of more than fifty million books makes his reflection all the more relevant.

2. Terryl Givens, *Let's Talk About Faith and Intellect* (Salt Lake City: Deseret Book, 2022), 108–10.

3. Elaine Graham, "The Human Face of God: Notes on a Journey through Practical Theology," *Practical Theology* 13, nos. 1–2 (2020): 32–45.

MEMOIR AS SACRED WITNESS

RACHEL RUECKERT

AT ITS HEART, MEMOIR AS A GENRE IS when someone honestly and generously grapples with the truest truths of their lives with all the strength they can muster. I found this quality on every page of Matthew Wickman's *Life to the Whole Being: The Spiritual Memoir of a Literature Professor*,[1] a triumph of a book rendered with love, rigor, and nuance. And it is unmistakably, beautifully, a memoir.

Wickman recounts his journey through vivid snapshots: the moment he decided to serve a mission, the day he bought Nietzsche at a local bookstore, painful moments of faith transition, the academic conference where he bravely decided to talk about spirituality, the moment when he first met his wife, the sound of his daughters' footsteps, and windswept scenes from Scotland where he reckoned with one of the most difficult personal and professional decisions of his life. Through these portraits, we see the interconnectedness of his spiritual and literary paths told with humor, self-deprecation, and dimension. As he puts it, "I took up the serious study of literature because it seemed like a continuation of my spiritual odyssey" (5). Literature, in turn, taught him "to read [life] a little more deeply, appreciate it a little more fully" (7).

As a student of literature—including as a former student of Wickman—I appreciate the way he closes the distance between academia and

Denise Gasser

Denise Gasser

spirituality. A decade ago, I didn't have the language to articulate that seeming divide, but I do remember listening to professors like Wickman speak with a passion, excitement, and enthusiasm that made me think, "This person is brilliant. They could teach anywhere. Why here (Brigham Young University)? What does shuffling into sacrament meeting feel like to them? With such an active mind, what are the contours of their deepest held beliefs? And how did they arrive there?"

In examining that perceived divide, Wickman discusses the similar language used to describe experiences with the Holy Ghost and literature, how both "inform each other" and are "practically born from the same impulse" (66). Spiritual sensitivity, like literature, "stimulates the mind and stirs the heart, fostering greater empathy and thus increasing our capacity to feel and perceive" (24). Literature, in turn, he sees as "a natural vehicle of spiritual experience" (32).

Wickman describes some of the ways God speaks with him in fresh, curious ways: in fragments, in wondrously strange or subtle or kinetic ways, with gentle irony, with patience and poignancy, through "beguiling and enchanting and breathtaking" impressions (76), with rigor and defamiliarization, in silences and gaps, and with "divine shadow" (81).

This resonates with me, as a lifelong student of words who has felt at home with books but

> things to happen—a God who took vitality and promise and twisted it into complexity, into (something like) literature, into (something like) elegy. I did not wish to live in a novel like Woolf's. . . . [I was] not so much praying as gazing in God's direction, incredulous. (132)

Wickman does not flinch away from the hardest parts of the human condition, learning of "God's abiding presence in my sorrow, of his silence alongside my mourning, almost a form of solidarity" (134–35). He is unafraid of questions and familiar with the existential.

Wickman also illuminates how spiritual journeys, like memoirs, come in an infinite array of shapes. He writes, "we as a religious culture could probably be a little more diverse, more discerning, in how we discuss spiritual experience" (22). *Life to the Whole Being* makes space for exactly that. It resists didactic, flat, binary portraiture and does instead what true memoir does best: describes experience without rejecting what Wickman calls "the awkwardness of religion," something he thinks is a crucial element, rather than a reason to dismiss it (53). Wickman identifies as a pilgrim and a seeker. "Rightness is loud and has all the answers," he says, where "truth speaks quietly, a virtual whisper across the wind and waves" (116). Wickman honors God as a poet, someone who has "always managed to convert the emptiness" of his own experience into something meaningful (70).

After reading this book, I am left with a renewed reverence for memoir. In a culture that often emphasizes what "we" believe, there is, paradoxically, a humble yet astonishing *power* found in the limits of the lone "I." To me, writing a memoir feels like a sacred process, and reading it feels like witnessing—another spiritual act. What if we all told the truest truth of our own lives with such candor and courage? Though solitary soul-work in its inception, Wickman shows that the act of genuine truth-sharing can elevate us all. ✸

sometimes not as at home within the spiritual frameworks I grew up with. But this book is not only for people interested in literature, but for those who crave a new language to describe and understand spirituality—language that feels expansive and more inclusive.

For me, chapter 8 is the tour de force. Here, Wickman weaves together scenes of the early death of his brother and, much later, the death of a friend, with a reflection about Mr. Ramsey from Virginia's Woolf's *To the Lighthouse*. He writes,

> I felt myself falling. I did not doubt that God existed, but I now knew I did not understand a God who permitted such

1. Neal A. Maxwell Institute for Religious Scholarship, 2022.

A LOST SHEEP

Mortality and the Broken Body of Christ

MELISSA INOUYE

AT FIRST, THE HALLUCINATIONS were entertaining. I looked up at the wall of my hospital room and saw children's handwriting scrolling down the flat surfaces, like a screensaver. It was never print. Always handwriting, and always the slightly uneven scrawl of children. When I shut my eyes, another colorful spectacle presented itself: big cheap polyester blankets, red and yellow, slowly descending, shedding bits of fluff. Even the grimy grout between the tiles in the bathroom had suddenly become full of entertaining messages: "SLUG BAZAAR," "JESUS PEEPS," "WHISKEY TRY IT."

I was in Bethesda, Maryland, at the National Institute of Health. A team of smiling doctors had just injected 108 billion lymphocytes into me. The cells came in a squarish IV bag that reminded me of packages of Taiwanese drinkable yogurt. These lymphocytes had been painstakingly genetically engineered to fight my cancerous tumors, then multiplied until there were around ten times more of them than existed in a normal human body. I had just had a cheery ceremony to celebrate the birth of "Melissa 2.0"—new immune system, new birthday. Everything was going great.

Along with the lymphocytes, I received four doses of IL2 (aldesleukin), a chemical that generally helps immune cells grow and boosts immune response but which also does some horrible things to the body. As I've been told, when under IL2, people's kidney function tanks, causing hallucinations. In extreme situations, people's airways can collapse. I had been warned about the hallucinations and the other potential acute reactions, but I was sure I would be fine. I could deal with some trippy visions. Besides the very minor detail of cancer, I was young, healthy, and strong.

On Friday, the first day after receiving my therapy and the first doses of IL2, I felt mostly fine, though I started to get tired. On Saturday, slightly weird hallucinations started.

The hot water kettle on the window sill sat just behind a chair where a coat was draped. It looked, from my bed, like a head above a body, as if one of my cousins or aunties was sitting there. I kept trying to ignore this because it was weirding me out, but eventually I just embraced it. "Hi, Auntie," I would say, waving from my bed at the silent sentinel in the corner.

On another occasion, I was sure that my son was sitting in the room, just on the other side of the IV pole. I knew he was there. He was observing everything that happened in the room and

Alyce Bailey

watching Netflix with me. Hours later, I checked the space. No son. Sometimes people appeared in the room, like the blonde lady wearing a red top and black pants crouching at the right side of the bed, who disappeared when I took a second look.

I recorded these initial observations in my journal with steadily disintegrating penmanship. And then, my notes abruptly stopped.

Over the next few days, I lost track of time. I lost track of where I was. I lost my grip on what was real. I lost my ability to walk or hold things in my hands.

I lost myself.

I have little memory or record of those missing days. I do remember once telling the team of NIH doctors how glad I was to be at "Huntsman" (a cancer center in Utah, not where I actually was).

I remember a sort of constant chittering sound in the back of my mind, like a robotic insect, as the visual hallucinations became corrupted (bits of broken script now scrolling down the walls and across the countertops instead of whole words or phrases) and everything sort of disintegrated into general sensory disruption.

I remember restless nights obsessing about things that weren't real, like how there was an evil plot on the internet to create the opposite of glamour shots, taking everyone's photos and corrupting them a little to make them wrong, but how there were people going around finding these corrupted photos and fixing them, always finding them and fixing them, always . . . I remember waking up from nightmares with a pounding heart, having had to escape mortal danger by bludgeoning an attacker to death, over and over again . . .

I spent my nights and days in other worlds, preoccupied with the troubles and anxieties of those other worlds, which had no connection to actual reality, the life I'd lived, the person I'd always thought I was. Only as the chemicals began to slowly leave my system, and my kidneys began to recover, did I begin to notice that I was still in the same hospital room, even the same hospital bed, as I had been in about two weeks ago.

But I was not the same person who had cheerfully presided over my own second birthday party. I was broken. I was mentally shaken and physically shaking. I had trouble walking and standing. I could not hold anything for more than five seconds before my hands would twitch and drop it.

Before IL2, I had been writing to the family email list daily with long, chatty updates. After going silent for several days, I finally tried to text my husband. I am grateful that these texts have been preserved as a sort of primary source, though I must say, the first time I had the mental and physical ability to re-read this text chain, I burst into tears because it was so painful. Since then it has become funnier to me. I have added clarifications in small brackets to make it more clear what I was trying to say:

> they they will give me a flood [BLOOD] transfusion because current me is still too psichy [?] and
>
> scary and ubacle [UNABLE] to use her phone
>
> I thought I was at bjntman [HUNTSMAN] rather than at nih
>
> Oh bother I really jane [HAVE] turned into a dragon
>
> :_._where is the stupid asterisk, I want to say *asterterik
>
> Shoot I mean ? *aseerq *asterisk I rrl-rthinnk that's right
>
> but I keep hitting myself on my fa face with my phone
>
> oh buddy i am so sad and confugysed
>
> is there a move [MOVIE] irirle [TITLE] aboiutr that

I have to give my hallucinogenic self some credit for two attempted literary references—one to *Voyage of the Dawn Treader* and another to the 90s film *Dazed and Confused*—but Joseph found the messages alarming. He called my cousin

Alyce Bailey

Mika, who jumped on a plane. The next day she appeared in my hospital room and started taking care of me.

When I saw Mika, I knew who she was. I had heard she was coming and was glad of it. But I couldn't smile, and I couldn't offer words of welcome. That part of me just wasn't working either. Mika circumvented my lack of communication by rubbing my feet, which for many people in my family, myself included, elicits a sort of (blissful) Pavlovian reaction.

Over the next few days, Mika helped bring me back to myself, like a guide leading a soul back out of the underworld. She ordered food and coaxed me to eat. She updated me on family news. She took me on (very short) walks, holding onto a loop on the "gait belt" around my waist like a dog walker holding a leash. She kept a detailed record in my journal of the things I said and did. ("Now I'm like Joseph Smith. I have scribes keeping my journal for me!" she recorded me exclaiming the second day after her arrival.) She talked on my behalf to my husband, the Relief Society president, the members of the family, because I didn't have the energy to make plans, be social, or otherwise have adult conversations.

Some things I found especially overwhelming. One was the suffering in the world. I know that this is a standard Buddhist tenet, a staple of moral philosophy, the most basic of basic truths, but I found it overpowering. I knew that as far as suffering in the context of the history of humankind goes, my days- or weeks-long struggles with back pain, drugs, mental confusion, physical disability, and so on were fairly small potatoes. All around me, and all around the world, in my own family, in my circles of friends and friends-of-friends, there was loss, trauma, difficulty, and despair. Because of my recent experience below-the-line, and still under the influence of some pretty powerful drugs, the weariness in the world felt like too much.

"Everything is so sad," I wept in a phone call with my husband. "I'm just so sad."

As I slowly regained my strength, mobility, and hand-eye coordination, I noticed I was also regaining religiosity, for lack of a better word. Once again I felt to read the scriptures. Once again I felt to pray. Each time, prayer amounted to singing Psalm 126, "Shir Hama'alot." I had heard this beautiful psalm sung in Hebrew by Jewish friends after Shabbat and Passover dinners, and one of my pass-time-in-the-hospital projects before IL2 had been to learn the tune and lyrics. Over the course of thousands of years of history, Jewish believers certainly had many opportunities to lean into the lines: "Restore our fortunes, O God, as the streams revive the desert; those who sow in tears shall reap in joy."

If you only live in a beautiful, prosperous world in which the beautiful and righteous prosper, then people who spent the day curled up in pain are not for you, and you are not for them.

Still, I was deeply troubled about the emptiness I had felt and to some extent continued to feel. Where had God been in my darkest of dark places? Why was "religion coming back to me," like a rebooting superego, only several days after my ordeal, only when I was once again becoming rational and self-sufficient? Was that what religion was? God is for the sane, the coherent, the well-dressed, those who discuss theology and type accurately on smartphones? But not for the lowest of the low, the saddest of the sad, those stinking and vomiting and trapped in the grip of their own dark preoccupations?

The hospital chaplain, Ellen, was a kind and wonderful person. She had helped officiate at my boisterous "cell ceremonies" in the earlier part of my hospital stay, bidding farewell to my old immune cells and welcoming the new. She had made little fluttery flags with plastic knives and strips of printed paper that read "Go Go Melissa 2.0!" that were taped to the wall of my hospital room. Several times, awaking from confused dreams, I would see those flags and try to wrap my head around the fact that I was yet in that room. She knew I was a Latter-day Saint, and we had had pleasant, stimulating conversations about interfaith ministry and theodicy.

Now she was coming to see me on the other side of something huge. We hadn't known each other long, but I felt as if she would find me a different person. When last I saw her, I had been wearing my own normal-person clothes; now I was half-naked in hospital scrubs. The person she last conversed with was Melissa Inouye: historian, author, faith-promoting-essay writer, professional religious-y person. That person now felt light-years away—in this moment, completely inaccessible.

We sat quietly.

"I didn't know who I was," I told Ellen.

"I didn't feel God," I said. "I was in such a deep, dark, place. But God wasn't there."

My eyes filled with tears.

"I felt alone," I said.

Ellen was silent for a while. Then she told me a story she had heard about a sheep who went missing. After years the shepherds finally found him hiding in a cave, fleece overgrown and matted, barely able to see.

"Maybe you were a lost sheep," she said. "You were in a place where you couldn't see or feel God, though God never stopped being aware of you."

On Sunday, five days after Mika's arrival, the doctors declared that I would be ready to go home on Tuesday. I had graduated from my walker and my gait belt. I was eating three small meals a day. I had regained much of my hand-eye coordination. I was still really tired.

On Sunday afternoon, when my brother Abraham came to the hospital to pick up Mika for her afternoon flight, he wore Sunday clothes and brought the sacrament. He knelt at the side of my hospital table and blessed the bread, then the water.

I found these blessings incredibly moving. I wept. At the time, however, I couldn't really explain why.

Surely part of it was the familiarity of a comforting ritual, a return of some of the structure of my normally highly structured life, a recollection of my family and community.

But now that I have had time to process, I think what I was feeling was also a gift from the Spirit. It was the Spirit of Christ waving for my attention, beckoning toward a new understanding of what it means to be broken.

At the Last Supper, Jesus presented his disciples with broken bread, to represent his broken body.

So often we talk about Christ as the lamb without blemish, giving us images of a nice, clean, fuzzy white lamb. But these photo ops occur at a moment in time before the lamb is slaughtered, gutted, and butchered. In the course of the sadistic, gruesome process of crucifixion that drove the breath from Jesus's lungs and overcame his great heart, Jesus's body also manifested infirmities inherent to physical mortality—dirt-encrusted, sticky blood, stale and stinking sweat, tense and trembling muscles. For at least a small moment, his mind was also beset with a piercing question shared by so many who suffer in loneliness: "My God, my God, why hast thou forsaken me?"

Perhaps some might think that it is impertinent to so directly describe a shaking, stinking body if that body is the sacred body of Christ, or to dwell on perhaps the most difficult moment in Jesus's life, when he felt forsaken and utterly alone, when his usual assurance about his relationship with God was broken. At this moment he was, in some ways, "the least like himself" in the sense of the Son of God who saw the bigger picture and wielded power over the elements and over death itself. Yet in this moment he was, in other ways, "the most like himself" in the sense of becoming the Savior who gained healing power through his own mortal experience.

He who called himself the Good Shepherd also knew what it was like to be a Lost Sheep.

Perhaps this sounds blasphemous to some. But this is where the prophet Alma's discourse on Christ in Alma 7:11–12 leads us: "he shall go forth, suffering pains and afflictions and temptations of every kind . . . he will take upon him the pains and the sicknesses of his people. . . . and he will take upon him their infirmities, that his bowels may be filled with mercy, according to . . . their infirmities."

Christ shrank from none of the bitter indignities of mortality, in order to be someone who is not insulated from our difficult lived reality. If you only live in a beautiful, prosperous world in which the beautiful and righteous prosper, then people who spent the day curled up in pain are not for you, and you are not for them. But through his hard-won experience of mortal griefs and sorrows, Jesus sees us, knows us, is with us. He was the lowest of the low, the saddest and most "confugysed" of us all.

Since the beginning of the human experience, humans have been trying to make sense of pain. But sometimes there is no sense. Sometimes, rich as they are, cultural practices, religious rites, and thoughtful theologies simply fall short of the realities of lived experience.

So, at least for now, I am unable to conclude with a coherent declaration that ties everything up with a bow. I have nothing systematic to offer our theologies. Only this am I able to say:

I know how it feels to be lost and broken.

And so does Jesus. ✱

Alyce Bailey

TRANSCENDENCE & TRANSFORMATION

An Interview with Charles Stang

Charles Stang is the Director of the Center for the Study of World Religions (CSWR) and Professor of Early Christian Thought at Harvard Divinity School. Wayfare Editor Zachary Davis sat down with Charles to discuss his life as a scholar of religion and learn more about his research initiative, Transcendence and Transformation.

How did you begin to study religion the way that you do? What was it that pulled you into this path?

As an adolescent, I became gripped by certain kinds of existential questions that I first hoped would be addressed by my church community. I was raised in the United Church of Christ in suburban Minneapolis, and I found my upbringing in the church pretty wanting. I wasn't so much repelled as I was just bored. I don't remember listening to a single sermon.

So when these existential questions began to arise in me—What are we humans? What are we doing here? Are we meant to be in relationship to the divine? Are we ourselves divine?—I turned to Christianity, but I didn't find that the church community I was a part of was particularly interested in fielding those questions.

College was a real turning point for me because although I had what I would now label as religious or spiritual questions, I first turned to literature and philosophy to get traction on them. The study of literature repelled me immediately. I thought I would love it, and I found out that whatever went under the banner of literary criticism in the university bore little relationship to the questions I wanted addressed. But I did find that place in philosophy, especially at the margins of academic philosophy, in ancient Greek philosophy and in modern continental philosophy. The main current of philosophy in this country is what's called "analytic" philosophy, and that tradition seemed to have little interest in the sorts of questions I was interested in.

When it came time to leave college and think about what might come next, two things happened. First, I think I got tired of my late adolescent atheism, which was a sort of brief phase in my life. I was honestly a kind of half-hearted atheist even then. And I sort of gave up on that—I just stopped pretending that I was an atheist. And I thought, I can be a theist without being Christian.

When I returned to religion, it was first and foremost by believing in God, or maybe it's better

Alonsa Guevara

Alonsa Guevara

to say the sacred; I wasn't sure that the divine that was pulling me was a person, God the Father, God the Son, or even God the Spirit. But I decided that I had unfairly shed my Christian identity and thought that I needed not just to study Christianity but to step back into it and inhabit it.

And at the same time, I realized philosophy was not a place I could ask and answer the kinds of questions I was interested in. The study of religion was actually much more capacious. It included a lot of philosophers that academic philosophy had largely discarded. At one point certain philosophers who in many ways were hostile to religion became for me incredibly powerful sources of religiosity. Ironically, Nietzsche in particular was a huge catalyst for my return to religion, to Christianity. I think in some ways his book *The Anti-Christ,* which he wrote late in life, catalyzed my own interest in learning about early Christianity.

What was it about Nietzsche's writing? Was it the seriousness with which he took these questions?
Yes, nobody takes questions as seriously as Nietzsche—but also with a fantastic sense of humor! But what really gripped me with Nietzsche was this idea that we can become so much more than we are. That was like a siren call that just went straight into the center of me, and I think it was what I was always hoping Christianity would be about.

And in some way, of course, Christianity *is* about that. But the version of Christianity I encountered in a suburban Midwestern upper-middle-class white church seemed not at all to foreground that project of self-transformation and self-transcendence. I heard it in Nietzsche and I fell hard for him, and that question has been an absolute mainstay of my adult life, personal and professional, academic and existential. What is the human? What can we become in relationship to what we're calling the divine? And I spent a large portion of my adult life trying to explore that within the bounds of the church, and have stepped out of the bounds of the church more recently, both personally and professionally.

Why did you feel you needed to step away from your Christian community?

I've been in the Episcopal Church for about twenty years. My frustration with contemporary Christians, at least of the flavor I encountered, is that I don't think they really believe in God.

I don't think they believe in the transcendent, the transformative. I think contemporary Christianity is overwhelmingly about do-gooding with a kind of biblical veneer or mandate. And I think the call to do good, the radical call to love your enemy that Jesus demands, is a hugely transcendent and transformative call, but I don't really see that radical call foregrounded.

I see my experience with Christianity as a lot of people who sort of roll their eyes at the explicitly religious, who are there largely to instill morality in their children and to feel a kind of call to do good in the world. And I don't know that we need Christianity or any other religion to do good in the world. Quite apart from that, I needed something else from religion than that.

Many Latter-day Saints are leaving their own congregations today—perhaps for similar reasons, that they perceive their spiritual lives to have stagnated and for one reason or another aren't finding nourishment in an institutional setting. But I fear a lot of the people leaving don't really have a serious plan for continued spiritual growth, and I fear that the alternative to "stale" American middle-class Christianity is stale, middle-class secular nothingness. Same spiritual stagnation, just more lonely. How are you trying to awaken from a spiritual slumber and shake yourself into a different trajectory, and is the path that you have been on something that any seeker could pursue?

> **Emerson tried to activate a relationship to the world in which we humans are not the sole agents of consciousness walking in an inert landscape, but in fact, we are crowded with other persons, nonhuman persons, and that this world is alive, vibrantly so, with consciousness.**

Great question. I do recognize myself as a seeker. I'm proud to be a seeker. One thing that has kept me in Christianity has been recognizing that whatever frustrations I may have with the contemporary church, this is a tradition with amazing resources, sages to be studied and followed, and so I have tried to find my sages and follow them, and you don't really need that many sages in your life. You just need a handful. Some of mine are Christians and some aren't. So one thing for the disaffected is to go back to your tradition and look for the sources of living water—they're always there. And that may be within the LDS tradition itself, or it may be part of the longer Christian arc from which the LDS church emerges.

A second lineage I love and attach myself to is the New England Transcendentalists. An initiative that we're following here at the Center for the Study of World Religions is called Transcendence and Transformation, and is quite obviously an attempt to connect ourselves to that ancestry. I think about those disaffected Christians (and Emerson was certainly a disaffected Christian) and what they did. He found sages within and outside the Christian Church, and he activated what he called a new animism.

And I find that category very suggestive and appealing. Emerson tried to activate a relationship to the world in which we humans are not the sole agents of consciousness walking in an inert landscape, but in fact, we are crowded with other persons, nonhuman persons, and that this world is alive, vibrantly so, with consciousness. And he found that belief reflected in some of the sources that he and others were excavating from the "Western tradition." And I think he found it in this landscape, and I've worked really hard to step into this landscape and let it introduce itself quite literally and speak. And as I've learned to listen, I have met all kinds of non-human persons out and around these parts.

I'm a great admirer of St. Francis of Assisi, who expressed great love for the natural world. He wrote a hymn called *Canticle of the Creatures* where he addressed even celestial bodies in familiar terms, thanking God for Brother Sun and Sister Moon. This way of seeing ourselves in concert and communion with the created world is both a radically new way of living in the world and also the most ancient. How has your own experience in the world changed as you've tried to pay attention to the more-than-human world?

I'll answer with a story. About six years ago we got a dog named Xena, with remarkable powers of communication and perception. I can't tell you how uncanny it is, what she knows about us. She's a vizsla, and vizslas, especially when they're young, need to be off leash outside every day. And so my wife and I, sometimes together, sometimes apart, were outside with our dog every day in the woods through all seasons. And that was a bit of a baptism into the animate world.

This practice of regularly immersing myself in nature was more transformative than I expected. And then, I started reading in what's sometimes called neo-animism. These are folks who are trying to revive the category, which was a term of derision largely for indigenous traditions around the world in the late nineteenth century.

In anthropology, animist traditions were framed as sort of primitive forms of religion. And on this view, the evolution of religion tended towards monotheism of course, Christian monotheism being the perfection of that evolutionary scheme. But this reading in the literature of neo-animism has given me new vocabulary that is

Alonsa Guevara

also feeding into my practice, and my practice is enriching the reading.

I also began to get into the very vibrant world of the anthropology of the Amazon. Eduardo Cohen's book *How Forests Think* was my gateway drug into that world that continues to bend my mind.

And you mentioned St. Francis, who I regard as a bit of a lone voice. There are few prominent Christian animists in the tradition, which is unfortunate. But I've also derived great benefit from going back to the world I know better, which is the ancient Mediterranean world, and looking at other kinds of polytheistic, animist worldviews, and trying to inhabit those as well.

If someone's thinking, OK, I'm bored with my current church and I want to grow spiritually, but I also know that I'm really shaped and transformed in communities of mutual love and commitment. How do you approach that recognition of the social dimension of spiritual life?

It's a fantastic question, and I think it's one that haunts the seeker of spirituality. I take inspiration from what I'll call communities of discernment or fellowships of spirituality that have stepped out of the ready-made community of church, but recognize that they need to form other fellowships, other communities. I think the Transcendentalists recognized this. They weren't just a collection of individuals, they were a deeply entangled community of thinkers and practitioners.

Traditional Christianity will scorn seeker spirituality for being individualistic. The terms change, but the basic charge is the same: cafeteria spirituality, just picking and choosing what you do and don't like. I think that's unfair; it's a caricature. It's speaking some truth, but the fact is a lot of traditional Christianity, at least modern American Protestant Christianity, is also individualized cafeteria spirituality.

I would advise people to not be afraid to be a "selfish" seeker, and to search out other seekers and form cells of spiritual community. I think there is good reason to think a cellular model is what we need, one that has the agility necessary to meet contemporary spiritual longings.

You've led an initiative called Transformation and Transcendence. What are the major currents that you and your researchers have been examining, and what are you personally most energized about?

Well, it was an initiative in some way meant as a provocation. I feel like the study of religion, not unlike contemporary Christianity, has lost sight of a certain North Star, which I could just call the sacred. It doesn't really believe in the sacred. It doesn't seek to encounter the sacred. It doesn't seek to transcend or transform. I sound hopelessly out of fashion. I feel as if the study of religion has tried to fit in with the humanities by becoming a kind of secular enterprise of critique.

I think it will lose if it competes on that field. I think the study of religion needs to understand that there is something unique in this enterprise and that people are drawn to it because they sense that we humans are more than the humanities are telling us that we are. So it was a provocation that tried to give shape to that impulse around these two poles of transcendence and transformation. We've had reading groups on the divine feminine, on plant consciousness, on Henry Corbin, who is a twentieth-century philosopher of religion and scholar of Islam, who I think holds great treasures for the study of religion and for philosophy and spirituality more generally.

We've also had speaker series exploring psychedelics and the future of religion (which is an ambivalent scene for me). There's a lot of noise, and I've been working hard to try to find the signal amidst the noise in the contemporary conversation around psychedelics and religion.

I'm particularly fascinated by your explorations of plant consciousness. What about that conversation is generative for you?

Recent work in the humanities in the social sciences has generated new interest in the age-old question of the relationship between matter and spirit and its relevance for the environmental crisis we now face.

"Vibrant materialists," such as the political theorist Jane Bennet, have asked us to revise our view of matter as an inert object we manipulate and invite us to think instead of the vibrancy of nonhuman and allegedly inanimate things, that is, their agency and creativity.

This promises to cultivate a different ecological sensibility and different sorts of political interventions in the environmental crisis. Some environmentalists have revived interests in spirits. Actually, interest in spirits has never died down, but scholars are taking it seriously again.

And they're taking these phenomena seriously if not literally as occasions to widen our notion of agency. Perhaps humans are just one expression of a more widely distributed agency, an agency spread across the full spectrum of this alleged antinomy between matter and spirit.

The decentering of the human is sometimes called the nonhuman turn or the more-than-human turn. Could it be that by shifting our focus away from the human, to the more-than-human, we actually summon an ecological imagination that better safeguards humans, precisely by displacing them from the center of all our inquiry?

One person I've learned a great deal from is Robin Wall Kimmerer. She is trained as a scientist and wrote an influential book on moss, but

I feel like the humanities is living in a bit of a flatland, and I believe in more than two dimensions, many more.

is also an Indigenous practitioner and has tried to bring those two worlds together in her book *Braiding Sweetgrass.* She says that science is an incredibly sophisticated language of objects. That is to say, it presumes a subject/object dichotomy and treats its objects of inquiry as just that, objects. And therefore, that applies a certain lens to the material world.

What you will find in the work of scientists like Robin Wall Kimmerer, Monica Gagliano, and Suzanne Simard is a questioning of that very frame and lens. And that's at the heart of neo-animist ontologies and epistemologies as well. That is to say, a suspicion that what we are dealing with here is not humans encountering a world of inert objects or even other living beings that maybe have some remarkable capacities, but that these plants, animals, and maybe even those things we label inanimate are persons, subjects like us, and yet importantly different.

And that changes the nature of the inquiry, it changes the nature of the experiments that are afforded, and it changes the nature of the results. So I'll just say that things like objectivity and iterability become very complicated if what you're dealing with is something that is interacting with you as a person.

I think what's really exciting is that research is pressing on these really fundamental questions about what ways of knowing science can claim, and what is revealed and concealed by those ways of knowing.

In a recent essay called "The Dream of the Sphere," you called for a post-critical study of religion. What was your goal with this essay?
The title of that piece is a reference or an allusion to a late nineteenth-century novel called *Flatland.* It's a world of two-dimensional beings in which one square has a dream of a sphere and tries to tell all the other squares what a three-dimensional object might be and how it might interact with their two-dimensional world. And it's a great shock to the two-dimensional world.

The square is persecuted and eventually put in prison, and all talk of spheres is outlawed. So I use that as a provocative analogy to where we find ourselves in the humanities today. I feel like the humanities is living in a bit of a flatland, and I believe in more than two dimensions, many more.

What we're calling the sacred exists in dimensions beyond the two. Once we acknowledge that, we can begin to think critically about how the sacred interacts with the dimensions we are accustomed to perceiving. And our perception can be expanded as well, but the sacred will always exceed the capacities of our even expanded perception.

The *Flatland* essay was an attempt to surface traditions and practices that recognize this and work with this many-dimensioned reality. And the fact is, what we'll just call the modern Western secular flatland is convinced that we know what is real, and that conviction is a huge exception in the history of humanity, and in fact, it's the exception in the global present.

We are actually a tiny minority suffering from this view that we are convinced is the truth, and we scorn and ridicule anyone else around the globe who has a different ontology and a different epistemology, and we look down on traditions from the past that have different ontologies and different epistemologies without recognizing that we are just this very thin crust on the human enterprise.

I don't think this thin crust is serving us particularly well. I think this view is deeply tied to the predicament, spiritual and environmental, political, and psychological, that we find ourselves in. So, here at the Center for the Study of World Religions, we're at the periphery of the university quite literally trying to use this fulcrum to bend the conversation towards transcendence and transformation, to help others recognize, encounter, and experience the sacred. ✱

WRITERS

MEGAN ARMKNECHT is a writer, historian, and PhD candidate in history at Princeton University.

MICHAEL AUSTIN is the Academic Vice President and Provost at the University of Evansville. He is the author of eight books, including *Re-reading Job: Understanding the Ancient World's Greatest Poem* and *Vardis Fisher: A Mormon Novelist.*

EMMA BELNAP is a senior at Brigham Young University, where she is studying art history and curatorial studies. She is a research assistant for the Book of Mormon Art Catalog.

MARK D. BENNION is a poet and English professor. He is the author of *Psalm & Selah, Forsythia,* and *Beneath the Falls.* He and his wife, Kristine, are learning how to parent two married children, two teenagers, and one tween. They welcome your advice.

SAM BROWN is a physician scientist who also wonders about bigger questions. He's parenting three children at the cusp of adulthood and writes books from time to time.

ADRIENNE CARDON is a poet, graphic designer, and author of *And Still, Birth: Death and New Life in a Pandemic.*

TIM CHAVES is a podcast host and board member at Faith Matters and a tech entrepreneur.

ANNABELLE CLAWSON is an academic editor, feminist historian, and freelance writer, and a graduate from the University of Cambridge and Brigham Young University.

ZACHARY DAVIS is the Executive Director of Faith Matters and the Editor of *Wayfare.*

JAMES DEWEY is a poet whose work has appeared in *Irreantum, Inscape, Perspectives,* and *Reformed Journal.*

TIMOTHY FARRANT is a Postdoctoral Fellow at the Maxwell Institute, having previously worked in chaplaincy and higher education in the UK. He grew up in the South West of England and studied at Bristol, York, and Oxford.

NOAH FELDMAN is Felix Frankfurter Professor of Law at Harvard University.

JENNIFER FINLAYSON-FIFE is a licensed therapist who specializes in working with LDS couples on sexuality and relationship issues.

TERRYL GIVENS is Senior Research Fellow at the Maxwell Institute and author and coauthor of many books, including *Wrestling the Angel* and *The God Who Weeps.*

GABRIEL GONZÁLEZ NÚÑEZ is a translation professor at The University of Texas Rio Grande Valley, the author of eleven children's books, a book of poetry, and a short story collection, all of them in Spanish. He translated his *Estampas del Libro de Mormón* into English as *Book of Mormon Sketches.*

GEORGE B. HANDLEY is Professor of Interdisciplinary Humanities and Comparative Literature at Brigham Young University and author most recently of *The Hope of Nature, If Truth Were a Child,* and the novel *American Fork.*

LIZZIE HEISELT is a writer, runner, and bridge crosser living in Brooklyn, NY, with her husband, Micah, and their six kids. She has an MA in journalism from NYU, but she still can't play video games.

MELISSA INOUYE is a historian specializing in modern Chinese history, Christianity in China, women and religion, and the history of global Christianity.

RACHAEL JOHNSON is a postdoctoral fellow at the Maxwell Institute with research interests in theologies of embodiment and materialism, inspired mostly by the joyful messiness of raising three littles.

ANDREW MAXFIELD is a composer based in Provo, UT, whose "rhythmically vital ... superbly judged ... [and] tender" works (Fanfare Magazine) have been performed by The Gesualdo Six, The Choir of Royal Holloway, Salt Lake Symphony, Utah Opera, and others.

THOMAS MCCONKIE is a meditation teacher and founder of Lower Lights School of Wisdom.

JON OGDEN is a cofounder at UpliftKids.org, which helps families explore spirituality together.

NATHAN B. OMAN is the Rollins Professor at William & Mary Law School, where he teaches classes on contracts and legal theory. He lives with his family in James City County, Virginia.

DAYNA PATTERSON is the author of *O Lady, Speak Again*, *If Mother Braids a Waterfall* and *Titania in Yellow*. She's the founding editor (now emerita) of *Psaltery & Lyre* and a co-editor of *Dove Song: Heavenly Mother in Mormon Poetry*.

STEVEN L. PECK is an Associate Professor of Biology at Brigham Young University and the author of *A Short Stay in Hell* and *Heike's Void*.

ELIZABETH PINBOROUGH is a poet and artist from Salt Lake City. She is coeditor of *Young Ravens Literary Review* and loves exploring the brain in her art.

ISAAC JAMES RICHARDS is an award-winning poet, essayist, and scholar of rhetoric currently doing graduate work at Brigham Young University.

JIM RICHARDS is a poet whose work has appeared in *Poetry Northwest*, *Copper Nickel*, *Hotel Amerika*, *Sugar House Review*, *Prairie Schooner*, *Dialogue*, *Literature and Belief*, *Irreantum*, and *BYU Studies*. He teaches literature and creative writing at Brigham Young University–Idaho.

RACHEL RUECKERT is the award-winning author of *East Winds* and the Editor in Chief of *Exponent II*.

JEREMIAH SCANLAN is a fiction writer and birdwatcher, currently studying law.

CHARLES STANG is Professor of Early Christian Thought and Director of the Center for the Study of World Religions at Harvard Divinity School.

LAURA STOTT is the author of two collections of poetry, *Blue Nude Migration* and *In the Museum of Coming and Going*.

TESIA TSAI is a writer and teacher living in Provo, Utah. She received an MFA in creative writing at Brigham Young University.

CANDICE WENDT is a writer who supports students of all backgrounds and belief systems in their spiritual lives at McGill University's Office of Religious and Spiritual Life.

DARLENE YOUNG has published two poetry collections (*Here*, and *Homespun and Angel Feathers*, both from BCC Press). She lives in South Jordan, Utah and teaches writing at Brigham Young University.

ARTISTS

ARTISTS CONTINUED

Whitney Johnson